# *MORE* STUDIES IN
# ETHNOMETHODOLOGY

SUNY series in the Philosophy of the Social Sciences

Lenore Langsdorf, editors

# *MORE* STUDIES IN ETHNOMETHODOLOGY

KENNETH LIBERMAN

STATE UNIVERSITY OF NEW YORK PRESS

Published by
STATE UNIVERSITY OF NEW YORK PRESS, ALBANY

© 2013 State University of New York

All rights reserved

Printed in the United States of America

No part of this book may be used or reproduced in any manner whatsoever without written permission. No part of this book may be stored in a retrieval system or transmitted in any form or by any means including electronic, electrostatic, magnetic tape, mechanical, photocopying, recording, or otherwise without the prior permission in writing of the publisher.

For information, contact
State University of New York Press, Albany, NY
www.sunypress.edu

Production, Laurie Searl
Marketing, Anne M. Valentine

**Library of Congress Cataloging-in-Publication Data**

Liberman, Kenneth, 1948–
  More studies in ethnomethodology / Kenneth Liberman.
    p. cm. — (SUNY series in the philosophy of the social sciences)
  Includes bibliographical references and index.
  ISBN 978-1-4384-4619-6 (hardcover : alk. paper)
  ISBN 978-1-4384-4618-9 (pbk. : alk. paper)
  1. Ethnomethodology.  2. Phenomenology.  I. Title.

HM481.L53 2013
305.8001—dc23                                                    2012017397

10 9 8 7 6 5 4 3 2 1

# CONTENTS

ACKNOWLEDGMENT     vii

FOREWORD     ix
by Harold Garfinkel

INTRODUCTION     1

CHAPTER ONE
The Local Orderliness of Crossing Kincaid     11

CHAPTER TWO
Following Sketched Maps     45

CHAPTER THREE
The Reflexivity of Rules in Games     83

CHAPTER FOUR
Communicating Meanings     135

CHAPTER FIVE
Some Local Strategies for Surviving Intercultural Conversations     153

CHAPTER SIX
"There is a Gap" in the Tibetological Literature     179

CHAPTER SEVEN
Choreographing the Orderliness of Tibetan Philosophical Debates     187

CHAPTER EIGHT
The Phenomenology of Coffee Tasting: Lessons in
Practical Objectivity     215

CONCLUSION
Respecifying Husserl's Phenomenology as
Situated Worldly Inquiries     267

NOTES 283

BIBLIOGRAPHY 291

INDEX 297

# ACKNOWLEDGMENT

There is not a worthy idea in this book that did not have its seed in the vision of Harold Garfinkel, who was my teacher for forty years. Much the same can be said about the branches, leaves, flowers, and fruit of these studies and reflections. The majority of topics are borrowed directly, including most of the research projects designed to teach ethnomethodology to students. In particular, games-with-rules, pedestrian crossings, using way-finding sketch maps, and analyzing conversations all originated in one or another of Garfinkel's seminars at UCLA during the 1960s, 1970s, and 1980s, and were part of the pedagogy of Garfinkel's teaching. Over the course of my own thirty-year teaching career, I have managed only to extend some ideas. The research assignments associated with these topics proved tried-and-true in teaching my students ethnomethodology, and here I have collected some of our best discoveries. They are revisitations of seminal matters Professor Garfinkel first discovered decades ago.

Harold Garfinkel and Kenneth Liberman

# FOREWORD

In 2005 I had the occasion to reread a set of notes that Kenneth Liberman had prepared during a two-term seminar at UCLA that he attended in 1979–80. When he was my student, Liberman had developed a special ability to write down quickly nearly every word I spoke while keeping a strong hold of its significance as he did so. At the conclusion of one course, he gifted me a complete set of these notes, which ran to more than 60 single-spaced typewritten pages.

When rereading those notes nearly three decades later, I was struck by how well they captured the freshness of many ideas central to ethnomethodology. During one of Ken's visits in 2006, I asked him to consider rewriting the notes with an eye to turning them into a book on ethnomethodology. Ken replied that he would reread the notes himself, as part of his preparation for his own lectures on ethnomethodology during the 2006–7 academic year at the University of Oregon, and then let me know what he thought of the merits of the idea.

By mid-2007, Ken also became convinced that the notes would serve well as part of a textbook on ethnomethodology. He suggested that certain aspects would require additional discussion, in line with developments in ethnomethodology since 1980, and he was eager to add some of the successful pedagogical tools he has developed himself during the course of his own 25 years of teaching ethnomethodology. Since Ken has been teaching ethnomethodology in two courses at the undergraduate level—a course for sophomores and juniors (Interaction and Social Order) and a course for seniors (Ethnomethodology)—as well as one course on social phenomenology at the graduate level, he has developed his own illustrations, expositions, and exercises for directing students to competence in ethnomethodology.

I urged Ken to take full license in expanding his notes, suggested that he be designated as author for the text, and thanked him for accepting the responsibility for seeing such a unique collaboration to publication. The resulting volume takes its place among a growing collection of publications that place in the hands of readers the skills exercised in the course of ethnomethodological investigations and analyses.

Harold Garfinkel, Los Angeles, October 21, 2008

# INTRODUCTION

These are studies from ordinary life—each topic originates with a society of people who are collaborating naturally in doing practical, everyday tasks. The thinking they do is also a public activity, and their thinking acquires its direction and vitality from that public life. The perspective of these social phenomenological investigations comes from what I like to think of as the "old school" of ethnomethodology, inquiries that retain the original radical quality of investigations into how people assemble meaning and produce local orderlinesses in their ordinary lives. The "radical" here refers to going to the root of people's mundane apprehension of their world—how they put it together, how they maintain coherent understandings, how they concert their behavior and their understanding with others, all captured *in their emergence* in the way that Edmund Husserl (1969, 153) proposed by his use of the term "radical." All of these studies bear a debt to phenomenology, but at the same time they amend and respecify social phenomenology's program in ways that I hope will prove fertile.

Nearly all of these studies originated as classroom-based research, either in my own classes or in the undergraduate and graduate courses of my professor, Harold Garfinkel. The few topics that did not begin as collaborations with students in a classroom were nevertheless presented to students and had many of their themes worked out and settled there. For 25 years, I taught three courses in the field of ethnomethodology for the University of Oregon: a graduate seminar in social phenomenology, a course in ethnomethodology for upper division undergraduates, and a course for sophomores in social phenomenology designed to prepare undergraduates to handle the challenging work of the upper division class. Discouraged by the number of students cheating on tests at my university and by an epidemic of plagiarized papers downloaded from the Internet, I followed the lead of my own professor and required my students to undertake actual worldly studies, upon which I based my student evaluations. This had the additional advantage of affording to students the opportunity to learn phenomenological and ethnomethodological ideas not only theoretically but from their own studies of real worldly affairs. All of these studies were collaborations that took place over many years of university instruction. Almost always the students worked in teams, since that way their ideas and energies were able to augment each other. It fostered a unique pedagogy, of which this volume is a record.

As Harold Garfinkel mentions in his Foreword, these inquiries were collaborative. Even the pedagogy was collaborative, and we had to learn from each other how best to explain these matters, as well as how to explore the many technical phenomenological issues that are investigated here. I collaborated as a student with Prof. Garfinkel and as a teacher with my own students. And both sets of collaborations were fueled by a sense of wonder. My students responded well not only to the intrinsic interest of these social phenomenological topics but by the authenticity that their own real discoveries fostered in their work. In particular, the crossing Kincaid study and the study of taste descriptors of coffee unfolded as revelations to my students and myself, and I eagerly shared them with Prof. Garfinkel during my visits with him; fortunately, he was able to make important critical recommendations about these inquiries as they developed over the years. So collaboration is truly the operative word for this volume of studies.

I am especially grateful that Prof. Garfinkel retained faith in my ability to capture much of this material in a way that did not lose its ethnomethodological originality nor compromise its radical character. As soon as I realized that I would need to add the discoveries of my own teaching to those of Prof. Garfinkel, I was further gratified by his enthusiastic support of that idea. Additionally, it was kind of him to insist that I be the sole author, even though the majority of ideas in this volume were his. Despite this, during the few years that I read to him the early versions of these chapters, he would at times offer the remark, "Where's the credit?" or "Those are *my* ideas!" And at an occasional point he would scold me for not referencing his thinking. He would say to me, "Just make sure you fully credit me for these ideas!" I kept repeating my offer to make the volume a co-authorship, but he held to his view that it should be my book. By 2008 Harold was legally blind, and during my reading of some chapters I would emphasize how many references to him, not only to published work but also to classes and seminars, I had included in my citations. These references were quite appropriate since the idea of this volume began with his reading of a collection of my typed notes for a couple of his seminars.

It may be said that much of the fame and notoriety of ethnomethodology was derived from Garfinkel's intellectual allure, or what amounted to real genius. But that came at a cost. Among his students Prof. Garfinkel was known for his protean character, and even his closest students could never really be certain what kind of reception their work would receive on any first-time-through presentation. Harold would be supportive during one visit but could be highly skeptical the next time. I do not think I am alone in having felt some fear each time I visited him at his home and each time I picked up the phone to dial his number. But along with this fear was always tremendous respect and admiration for his integrity and what it kept demanding from me. As another of his students, Doug Macbeth, observed, Garfinkel was always about being persistent about an inquiry, a tenacity regarding following up the "more" that any good phenomenological study can offer. He was brilliant and utterly devoted to his sense of rigor,[1] and insistent that I also work with my themes in a rigorous way. There was never such a thing as a "free pass" for courtesy's sake, and I learned as much from that as from anything else. It was not uncommon for Prof. Garfinkel to remark, during or following a long presentation, "That's b.s.," or "You're making that up!" This caused one to carefully monitor one's own practices and really base one's analyses on tangible things that one has clearly identified. Why would anyone want to compromise about rigor like that? For me, a career in academia by itself would not have been worth sacrificing what other career paths might have offered. That kind of rigor is something that was really worth doing; besides, the studies were too compelling to leave behind.

There is one set of studies that are not included in this volume, and that is the inquiries into formatted queues that derive from his 1979–80 classes and seminars. What is most unique about those inquiries is that during several terms of instruction Prof. Garfinkel kept undermining his own finding about queues, offering himself the very same skeptical assessment that he offers his students. As soon as he would catch himself routinizing his own insights, he would pull back from his inquiry and reform it from the ground up, again and again. As he once stated, "I feel like I'm at the edge of something really nice, but it's a pain in the ass. I just can't make it—it just turns into words at the very moment it should turn into worldly *things*." If it wasn't real, he would abandon it without looking back, so strong was his fidelity to his own standards. This sort of continuously reconstituted study is difficult to present, so I decided that I could not do it justice. Besides, his study of formatted queues has already been written up,[2] so I felt the need for me to present this material was not pressing.

As Harold's congestive heart failure worsened, my presentations of the material in the chapters of this book took place in what were merely short bursts. Since they raised some enthusiasm in his spirit, I persisted with them, but after 10 or 15 minutes, he would feel the need to fall back to sleep and rest. In those last months, he rarely left his bed. I had hoped that I would be able to present this volume as a final gift to him, a collection of studies from the "ethnomethodological school of ethnomethodology." But with his death, the book has changed its character.

The week after Prof. Garfinkel passed, I spent time reading his extensive annotations to his copy of my 2002 book, for which he had written the "Foreword," which was gifted to me by his wife Arlene. For that week at least, it was as if I was participating in one last tutorial session, and I learned a great deal from what he highlighted (in four colors) and from his marginal notes. The most extensive marginal notes and most heavily highlighted section were of my account of objectivation in formal reasoning (Liberman 2004, 92–106). This is an analysis of the details of Tibetan philosophical debating that applies the theoretical findings of Edmund Husserl and Alfred Schutz to describe how a formal structure of reasoning is used by Tibetans to accomplish their organization of the local orderliness of their thinking and to foster their philosophical communication. The passage most heavily highlighted was "Logic and reason may be respecified as topics of social order," which was the main point of the book: that "the philosophy finds its way already embodied in organizational work" (also highlighted).

Further, Garfinkel highlighted in red the heuristic diagram, Objectivation → Authorization → Disengagement, which outlines the methods Tibetans use for turning their collaborative insights into objective philosophical accomplishments. The phenomenon of objectivation is developed in a related way in this volume in the chapters on games-with-rules (chapter 3) and the stabilization of the meaning of coffee's taste descriptors (chapter 8).

Another important feature of Garfinkel's highlighting was that he had marked in both red and blue highlighters nearly every reference to Schutz, including my discussion of "the mutual tuning in relationship" (Schutz 1971, 173) and how Tibetan debaters use the "formal structure of thinking" as an ethnomethod for accomplishing that tuning in and for synchronizing their utterances. That synchronization by Tibetan philosophical debaters receives further treatment in chapter 6 of this volume. What I wish to emphasize here is that even at the end of Prof. Garfinkel's life, he retained an avid interest in matters phenomenological.

For some reason a number of contemporary ethnomethodologists have been trying to rewrite the story of Garfinkel's relationship with phenomenology. Some of them have even come to ridicule theorizing itself. It is true that Garfinkel was highly distrustful of all theorized accounts. He once told a seminar (Garfinkel, 1979–80), "I'll kill you if you theorize. If anybody comes in with a theory, I'll burn it publicly." Nevertheless, he read social theory all of his life and was especially given to reading the phenomenological masters, especially Husserl and Merleau-Ponty, but also Heidegger, Schutz, Gurwitsch, and Derrida. It was only at Garfinkel's insistence that I read through the following texts that were on the required reading list for his graduate seminar in ethnomethodology[3]: *The Crisis of the European Sciences, The Field of Consciousness, Phenomenology of Perception, The Visible and the Invisible, Being and Time,* and Schutz's *Collected Papers*; and it was Garfinkel himself who stuffed a copy of Derrida's *Of Grammatology* under my arm just before I set off for the airport to return to central Australia in 1977. The only non-phenomenological text on that page-long list was Wittgenstein's *Philosophical Investigations*.

Just as Garfinkel treated Durkheim's theoretical explorations seriously, he treated Husserl's inquiries with an engaged respect. He once told me that when his own thinking and research was in the doldrums, he would reread some Merleau-Ponty, and that would be sufficient to stir up his thinking again. Garfinkel's hyper-empiricist followers are free to hold strongly to their opposition to taking phenomenological theory seriously, but they cannot seriously suggest that such a perspective was Garfinkel's position. It is all the more absurd to suggest this when one recalls that the two scholars whose personal guidance most aroused his intellectual imagination and program of research were Alfred Schutz and Aron Gurwitsch. Moreover, throughout his career Garfinkel continuously credited both Schutz and Gurwitsch for what they had provided him, and he showed them the respect that grateful students offer to their masters. Significantly, this places Garfinkel in the intellectual lineage of Husserl, since both Schutz and Gurwitsch developed their ideas under the guidance of the founder of phenomenology.

This does not mean that Garfinkel was unwilling to criticize all three of these scholars when it became necessary—no genuine mentor demands slavish adherence. Certainly, Garfinkel never did. But when it came to acknowledging his intellectual debt to them, he was always ready to do so. In the final year of his life, he listened approvingly to the text of a short address that I wrote commemorating Schutz on the occasion of the fiftieth anniversary of the publication of Schutz's *Reflections on the Problem of Relevance*,[4] so his sense of affiliation to these scholars endured throughout his life. Garfinkel did read his phenomenology idiosyncratically, once explaining to me that he felt no obligation to remain faithful to their research priorities and considered himself free to take license in exploiting for his own purposes anything the phenomenologists wrote. *But he always contemplated them.*

Garfinkel took similar license in his readings of Durkheim and Mannheim. He celebrated Durkheim's (1938, 18) criticism of the phenomenon that "Up to the present, sociology has dealt more or less exclusively with concepts and not with things," and he took very seriously Durkheim's criticism of Comte for taking ideas to be the subject matter of study, when Durkheim (1938, 27) argued, "Social phenomena are things and ought to be treated as things." Garfinkel gave to worldly *things*—which had become further informed by his study of phenomenology—an importance that perhaps exceeded Durkheim's own; indeed, it is one of the most central notions of ethnomethodology. Similarly, Garfinkel borrowed Mannheim's concept of "documentary meaning" (Mannheim 1952, 47–81) and breathed the life of the real world into it, making it the seminal notion "the documentary method of interpretation" (Garfinkel 1967, 76–79 and 100–103). Another of the most vital ideas in ethnomethodology was derived from Garfinkel's reading of Durkheim's *Elementary Forms of Religious Life*, and that is the insistence that at its origin mundane activity was congregational in nature. One finds little reference in Durkheim's most famous text to individual intelligibility, but there is a great deal of description of immanent collective action, action that Durkheim places at the origin of religious sentiments. We cannot but conclude that Garfinkel's reading of all theorists was highly original, but we cannot assert that he dismissed theorizing.

What Garfinkel dismissed was not concepts *per se* but the methodological habit of replacing all worldly activities with concepts, a fault that involves the dual mistake of forcing one's own professional concepts onto worldly phenomena and reading those affairs themselves as being more concept-centered than they really are. Michael Lynch (2004) has explained clearly that the aim of ethnomethodology is not to "apply" concepts, but to "place oneself in a position" to make discoveries from a site that we do not control. Phenomena of social order have their origin not in any general concepts but in the *sites* of people's lives. We're not invoking metaphysics.

Reducing people's lives to concepts is the very problem my students have; in fact, it is part of the standard training of undergraduate departments to teach their best students how to conceal real world affairs with general concepts extracted from professional theorizing. Before my students would write up their class studies, I would plead with them not to write in theoretical "gobble-dee-gook." I advised them to always throw away their first and last paragraphs, since these paragraphs were usually the worst offenders.[5] However, the brightest students did not know how to write in any other way; hence, I would sometimes predict that the class would be one time when weaker students could get the better grades, since they did not know how to write that way and would be forced to look more directly at the real world. When asked the standard question a professor receives from students, "Well what are you looking for," I replied, "Your task in this project is to observe the water you're swimming in, and until you have a tape recording, you cannot even begin—the transcripts are due Thursday."[6] They made out all right. I owe them everything.

And yes, Garfinkel was intolerant of pseudo-studies, studies that just detail generalities. That is when one has a favorite generality and examines some "data" in order to collect everything that demonstrates the veracity of the generality, ignoring (or never noticing) the rest. When it is done properly, social phenomenological analysis does not proceed by imagining illustrations, but by *abandoning one's truth habits and letting the local affairs carry oneself away with its own temporality*. This is truly the phenomenological way to undertake research. Studies of jazz musicians that include no jazz music, studies of jurors where no legal matters are being addressed, and studies of science whose principal investigators never enter an operating laboratory are all varieties of pseudo-studies.

On a number of occasions Garfinkel emphasized that many researchers feel obligated to replace the occasional, contingent, and context-dependent naturally occurring activities with context-free versions of the same, as if nothing was properly scientific until it was represented in a generalized, context-free version. He observed, "The programmatic aim [of professional researchers] is to make the statements and explanations context-free" (Garfinkel 1966). However, everything is context dependent, without exception. It is important to recognize that in ordinary life people attempt the very same achievement in an effort to render their affairs more organized: they replace occasional expressions with context-free expressions. A consequence of this is that it enables social analysts to assert that what professional researchers do is not very different from what ordinary people do in their everyday lives, an observation that has offended a generation of researchers. But the consequence is that *the lifeworld is lost*; and Garfinkel elucidates how that world is lost in his *ironic* description of the ways that professional researchers work:

> What we would like more than anything else in the world is to have that kind of language, that kind of theory for events that would itself be atemporal, it would be universally correct, it would stand in the fashion of indifference with respect to the actual contingencies, the conditions under which the events that we are studying were studyable. We would like for our descriptive apparatus, in short, to be excused from the conditions under which the matters that it made describable were themselves occurring. We would like, in other words, for the observer and the observer's apparatus not to be caught up in the conditions under which the matters that are under study are themselves happening and studyable.[7]

Garfinkel adds that the chief problem with this is that it is impossible to work this way while also retaining access to a lived world. My recommendation is to leave aside metaphysics for a time and persevere with careful description of the details of life as it is actually lived.

In his *Principles of Psychology*, William James made a distinction between "knowledge of" and "knowledge about." The former refers to things we have some personal or intimate acquaintance with; the latter consists of much vaguer knowledge about things that are known in the abstract or are "no longer experienced" (Schutz 1970, 141–42). Schutz adopts this distinction, and Garfinkel collected it and applied it in dividing the professional papers in ethnomethodology into ethnomethodological "studies of" phenomena and "studies about" ethnomethodology. In the initial years of ethnomethodology, many articles and book sections attempted to explain ethnomethodology without ever grasping its radical foundations and without doing any ethnomethodology; instead of grounding their descriptions in actual occasions that people lived *in vivo*, they grounded their accounts in generalities. Hence, there were many pseudo-studies that would make mention of ethnomethodology, but never really witnessed what—for the people they were studying—were "the looks of the world." Many of these studies would commence by explaining one of ethnomethodology's key terms (e.g., "indexical expressions" or "reflexivity") without doing any local studies and work down, instead of beginning from the world as it is lived for real people. Just as Mannheim (1952, 33) advised, "It is not our intention to propose a substantive definition of *Weltanschauung* based upon definite philosophical premises," when he wrote a chapter explaining *Weltanschauung* (worldview), and Gurwitsch (1964. vii) wrote in the preface to his *The Field of Consciousness*, "In writing this book, I wanted to make it a phenomenological study, not a book about phenomenology." Garfinkel repeatedly warned his students, "Don't hang on my words. You can't understand it without the words, I know, but no interrogation of the words themselves will give you their meaning: you need to go outside into the world and find for yourself what they are doing, find there what we are talking about." It is in this spirit that the present volume of studies is undertaken. If I have carried out these studies in the right way, and written their accounts well enough, then they will provide readers with a clear introduction to a great many social phenomenological and ethnomethodological themes in a manner that will be accessible to them. Since these are accounts of the mundane world, they do not need to be made mysterious in order to retain their profound character, and if I have done my work properly, the reader will be able to recognize his or her world in them.

Chapter 3, "The Reflexivity of Rules in Games," provides a detailed account of a classic ethnomethodological study that was used by Garfinkel from the 1970s forward to illustrate the phenomenon of reflexivity in ethnomethodology, and it is based upon the class projects of my students carried out over more than a decade. Chapters 1 and 6 ("The Local Orderliness of Crossing Kincaid" and "Choreography in Tibetan Philosophical Debating") provide detailed ethnomethodological accounts of organizing local orderlinesses where word-meanings play no role whatsoever. Chapters 4 and 5 ("Communicating Meanings," and "Some Local Strategies for Surviving Intercultural Conversations") are phenomenological accounts of instances of intercultural communication. (Chapter 4 also offers a synthesis of Maurice Merleau-Ponty's phenomenology with Ferdinand de Saussure's semiotics in an ethnomethodological context, combining Merleau-Ponty's insights into speech communication with Saussure's account of how a signified is related to a signifier.) Chapter 2, "Following Sketched Maps," is a detailed description of an inquiry that began as one of Garfinkel's class projects and has been used for teaching ethnomethodology on four continents; its orientation is inspired by Aron Gurwitsch, one of Garfinkel's teachers, and it borrows many insights from George Psathas' investigations of giving directions. Chapter 8, "The Phenomenology of Coffee Tasting: Lessons in Practical Objectivity" is an extensive ethnography of the practices of professional coffee tasters. It benefits from theoretical contributions to identifying objectivity offered by Edmund Husserl, Theodore Adorno, and Alfred Schutz. It also had its origin as a class project in several of my courses. Chapter 7, "'There is a Gap' in the Tibetological Literature," is a critique from the perspective of phenomenology of the Orientalism of professional Tibetological practices. The final chapter ("Conclusion: Respecifying Husserl's Phenomenology as Situated Worldly Inquiries") lays out in specific detail the relationship between Edmund Husserl and ethnomethodology.

ONE

# THE LOCAL ORDERLINESS
# OF CROSSING KINCAID

A new colleague of mine at the University of Oregon stepped out of the elevator at the eighth floor and confessed in the hallway, "It seems to be a real confusion there in front of the bookstore—I try to avoid crossing there if I can." About the same time, another colleague reported, "As a driver I find it frustrating at that intersection because so many kids just seem to walk without paying any attention." The reader can catch a glimpse of what this pedestrian and driver mean by examining Photo 1.1.

Photo 1.1. UO Bookstore

There does appear to be a good deal of chaos reigning at the corner of Kincaid Street and 13th Street, where the majority of the University of Oregon's students, faculty, and staff enter and depart the campus each morning, evening, and whenever they need to visit the UO Bookstore, a bank, or one of the many restaurants and shops next to campus. Pedestrians jaywalk back and forth all day long, paying little attention to the endless stream of vehicular traffic that dead-ends at the campus and that is composed of cars, buses, ambulances, taxis, delivery vans of every size, et cetera. As these two antagonists vie with each other, cyclists and skateboarders weave their ways in between them, determined never to stop and with little regard for the one-way traffic lanes that were intended to render their movements predictable.

Persons new to crossing Kincaid occasionally suggest that "something should be done" about the chaos there. But as a matter of social organization, there is nothing at the corner of 13th and Kincaid that requires fixing. What is more, it is likely that no repair is possible. There may be some disorder, but the disorder there is durable, not amenable to remedy, reproduced all day long, and probably essential for the ability of the great many pedestrians and drivers who cross there to do so in an efficient and safe manner. Crossing Kincaid is a locally produced procedure that relies heavily upon the natural and learned expertise of the crossers who pay intricate attention to the task. Novices and experts concert themselves—experts teaching experts along with the novices—to ensure that the maximum number of crossers can be accommodated at all times. At first sight, the busiest crossing at the entrance to the UO campus may look like confusion, but despite hundreds of ticketable offenses per hour the people who staff those crossings know how to figure things out for themselves; moreover, what they are doing there is far too complicated for any set of traffic rules to handle or improve. For the most part—for the vast majority of tens of thousands of daily crossings—pedestrians and motorized traffic work well together in coordinating a local orderliness, and their crossings are efficient and orderly.

It is not just that the majority of crossers know how to cross well—it is that they are experts. There are many venues in our everyday lives where objective rules or laws can contribute to the orderliness of the social interaction. In addition to rules, the locally concerted practices of the persons who staff those occasions contribute to the orderliness. In most cases the locally concerted practices are more important than the rules, and even in those situations where the rules and regulations seem to be more important, it is probably the locally concerted practices that are doing the heavy lifting. Perhaps there is a place where rules and locally concerted practices meet regularly, or it may be that rules have their origins in locally concerted practices, or that rules are one of the locally concerted practices. But it is for certain that crossing Kincaid is one phenomenon of *local* order where the concerted practices are what is vital for the organization of affairs on-the-ground; however, these local procedures escape detection by most of the widely applied methods of professional scientific inquiry, methods that would include surveys, interviews, questionnaires, "content analysis," document coding, and historical research.

## THE HISTORY OF CROSSING KINCAID

The crossings at Kincaid are a well studied phenomenon. The first study that my students and I could locate was a 1952 survey of "the problem" there, which led to a decision to close off most vehicular traffic to the portion of 13th Street that runs through campus. This inaugurated the situation where the traffic on 13th Street dead-ends at the campus and must turn left toward the major thoroughfares or right toward the parking district, a decision that forces the flow of traffic to slow down, hesitate, and become congested just where the majority of the University of Oregon's students enter and exit the campus on foot, by bicycle, and by skateboard. In 1955, the student newspaper, the *Oregon Daily Emerald*, featured an article, "How to Cross a Street," that offered advice to students for making the crossing. This led the City of Eugene to formally acknowledge persistence of a "problem" there in 1956, when they requested an Oregon Highway Department study. Alarmed by the perceived threat of the vehicular congestion to some of the state's brightest youth and following accepted general practice at the time, the authorities provided additional protection for the students by installing stop signs for all vehicles and by clearly marking the pedestrian crossings.

This remedy did not change very much at 13th and Kincaid, and there were calls over the succeeding decade for further studies of "the problem." However, in 1973 a city report concluded, "The students already know how to cross. . . . So wasting money on a survey is pointless." In that same year, use of the "Manual on Uniform Traffic Control Devices" (MUTCD) was applied to traffic statewide. MUTCD was a remarkable piece of governmental policy in that it recommended experimentation as the driver of changes to traffic design rather than rational theorizing in the abstract, thereby acknowledging that at most of the locations where traffic flow is problematic there will be too much going on for rational prediction to be reliable. All applications for a change in traffic design were required to be accompanied by a successful experiment that employs the changes being proposed. Since most of the problems at localities with heavy congestion are resolved by local orderlinesses that are autochthonous, *solutions can only be discovered* and not simply applied in reliance upon one or another theory of traffic flow; the legal authorities in the State of Oregon came to recognize that it was problematic to manage the local orderlinesses with objective one-size-fits-all regulations and that even survey methods of field research may not be able to locate or accurately describe the local orderliness that is taking place, an admission that it is likely most mainstream scientific researchers would be unwilling to make.

Memos in the late 1970s began to entertain the notion that rather than the students of Oregon needing protection from the motorists, it was the motorists who required protection from the students. The problem the city was facing was that as the city and the university grew in size, the stalled traffic on 13th Street was getting backed up across the intersections one and two blocks west of the dead-end of 13th Street at Kincaid. Some of this traffic found itself stuck in the middle of these two intersections during red lights, freezing in place the city's cross-traffic at two vital north-south arteries there. Something had to be done to speed up the flow of vehicular traffic through 13th Street; simply put, the student pedestrians had become too successful at crossing Kincaid. So in 1988, the city removed two of the traffic control mechanisms that had been benefiting the pedestrians—the white crosswalk markings across Kincaid at the north corner of 13th and the stop sign that was restricting the flow of vehicles traveling east one-way on 13th. The resulting situation is depicted by this photograph of the situation today (Photo 1.2).

Photo 1.2

At the place where the pedestrian is crossing, there is no crosswalk; and the car attempting to turn from 13th Street onto Kincaid Street has the right-of-way, there being no stop sign requiring it to wait for competing traffic. Apart from continuous repaving of the area, made necessary by the heavy traffic there, the two white lines that are visible mark off a one-way bicycle lane (more imaginary than real for everyone concerned) from the bus lane to the right of the lines (lower left of Photo 1.2) and the vehicular lane to the left of the bicycle traffic flow (above the lines in the photo). Across the way, at the middle left of the picture, are cyclists who are riding across Kincaid into campus along 13th. While ordinary vehicles are prohibited from entering the campus (delivery and maintenance vans may enter), cyclists are allowed free access. Waiting at the south side of 13th (on Kincaid) for the cyclists to cross are cars on Kincaid who must stop at the posted stop sign on Kincaid. A quick glance at Photo 1.1 will clearly reveal the stop sign there and also the very largely drawn pedestrian crossing intended to attract the majority of pedestrian crossings; however, fewer pedestrians cross there than cross at the north side of 13th where there is no pedestrian crossing, and even the jaywalkers regularly outnumber the pedestrians who cross at the designated pedestrian crosswalk. Traffic flow is one-way on 13th Street, except for a very small one-way bicycle lane between the parked cars and the Bookstore, which runs in the opposite direction to the west along 13th. Traffic on Kincaid north of 13th is one-way going north, and the traffic on Kincaid south of 13th is two-way. While the traffic on 13th east of Kincaid is restricted to all but authorized vehicles, there is usually a steady flow of cyclists and skateboarders in both directions. In all locations, the pedestrians have the strength of numbers. The University of Oregon bookstore on the corner (see Photo 1.1), dominates the scene and receives a good percentage of the foot traffic.

Nothing that the city could do to enforce traffic law there could improve upon the pedestrians' and motorists' indigenous capabilities to manage their own affairs, and every time the city has tried to do to improve the flow of vehicles at 13th Street and Kincaid by enforcing the traffic laws the traffic jams only worsened. The city's traffic police told us that it was current city policy not to enforce city traffic regulations there and to keep away from the site (except for some daily observations on foot). They explained that when they do not enforce traffic rules the problems seem to resolve themselves! Something the people crossing there are doing manages to provide sufficient organization of the crossings and passings-through. With the added advantage of having no stop sign to impede the flow of traffic where 13th Street traffic meets Kincaid, the traffic flow along 13th was no longer backing up, while a maximum number of nonvehicular crossers could still get across safely. The solution rests in not enforcing traffic regulations.

So the question I posed to my students was "Why?" What is it that the people crossing Kincaid were doing that solved the problem without recourse to supervision and enforcement? More than that, supervision and enforcement only slows things down. Who are these people? They are bus drivers, skateboarders, bicyclists riding outside of the bike lanes, bicyclists riding in the bike lanes but in the wrong direction, especially bicyclists who will not stop under nearly any circumstances, pedestrians who keep stepping into the same bike lanes while staring at their iPods, other pedestrians jaywalking, still other pedestrians waiting dutifully and sometimes perplexed at the curb, a stroller who wears flip-flops in the winter rain and drinks his coffee as he casually seizes a right-of-way that is not lawfully his (and in the face of which the motorists sit frozen), law-abiding motorists who come to a stop at the corner where there is no stop sign, mothers with baby carriages using the carriage to help block vehicular access to the lane, and so on. The coherence of these people occupied with concerting their crossings is a unique kind of coherence. It is not just that there are one or two methods for crossing Kincaid, there are numerous local systems operating together, predictably and repeatedly. It is not the confusion that is amazing, it is the orderliness of the streaming flows of participants. To better understand the orderliness there, my students and I—armed with video cameras—recorded some 20 hours of crossings, divided up into teams, and analyzed the data carefully, crossing by crossing, on a digital video platform.

Generally speaking, human affairs proceed better when they are orderly; and laws, regulations, and local rules can assist in achieving an organization that provides efficiency, predictability, and safety. But not always. My students and I discovered that sometimes a local orderliness will proceed more effectively when rules are not adhered to slavishly; and there are common situations where the *smooth functioning* of affairs—a government office, a queue for service, an international crisis—makes it necessary *not* to follow rules. It is not as if rules exist so that God can be happy. Rules exist to facilitate a local orderliness, and wherever the local orderliness can be better served by not following rules, the rules may not be enforced. The key insight here would be that *orderliness itself has precedence over rules*.

## LOCAL METHODS

Pedestrians dominate the crossings here, but cars, cyclists, and skateboarders also have their methods. Photo 1.3 displays an occasion in which both the car and the two cyclists failed to stop at their designated stop signs; however, if they concert their movements across the intersection, all of them can cross without stopping. It is all a matter of pacing: on this occasion, the car sped up and cyclists slowed down. The car sped up not only to be able to move out of the cyclists' way more quickly; the driver was

# THE LOCAL ORDERLINESS OF CROSSING KINCAID

Photo 1.3

also interested in displaying a certain inevitability to the car's crossing, an inevitability which thereby became more public and more compelling. The cyclists, who are more vulnerable to the rain, were primarily concerned with not stopping their bicycles' momentum, and slowing was an acceptable method for them to concert their crossing. It was no problem, despite two ticketable traffic violations.

The chaos at Kincaid is exacerbated by the wrong-way traffic of cyclists (Photo 1.4.) and skateboarders (Photo 1.5).

Photo 1.4. Wrong-Way Cyclist

Here the helmeted cyclist is traveling the wrong way against the designated flow of traffic in the one-way bike lane (the car is traveling in the correct one-way direction for its lane). Below (Photo 1.5), the skateboarder is traveling the wrong way and sailing seamlessly between two cars who have the right-of-way. Just as with the case of the car and the two cyclists, they are all concerting their movements perfectly and efficiently.

The skateboarder in Photo 1.6 would be traveling in the correct direction if he had been in the one-way bike lane, but that would have entailed him stopping to wait for the car who is turning left into the flow of pedestrians; skateboarders care to stop even less than cyclists, so instead the skateboarder moves into the vehicular lane, traveling in violation of the one-way designation there, but no one is delayed by his doing so; on the contrary, the pace of traffic flow is increased by his actions. Here scrupulous attention to the regulations can result in hanging everyone up in long delays, and the end result will be the backing up of the traffic along 13th Street.

The car in Photo 1.6 has no choice but to wait for the pedestrians, and it will be necessary also for it to wait for the jogger who soon steps off the curb (remember, there is no crosswalk here for pedestrians) to cross in the opposite direction, and for the couple who takes advantage of the latter delay, as well as the swarm that arrives just in time to join in behind the couple. These swarms can involve *heavy flows* of pedestrians, and so the

Photo 1.5

# THE LOCAL ORDERLINESS OF CROSSING KINCAID

Photo 1.6

most sincere negotiation gifted to a lone pleading pedestrian by a friendly motorist can halt the flow of traffic for several other pedestrians, and then a bursting floodgate of foot traffic, leaving the kind motorist with plenty of time to contemplate the fate of motorists.

A good deal of the traffic flow is not reasoned but mimetic: people copy what they see happening, and methods for crossing wax and wane in spurts of reproducibility. If one car stops dutifully where there is no stop sign, it is common for the succeeding car also to stop, without ever having spied a stop sign; and the car after that. Rarely is there time for making a "rational choice," and the compliance-oriented crosser will simply replicate the embodied looks of affairs. One's actions are not strictly personal but part of an emerging public event, in which the parties collaborate in making one or another method for crossing Kincaid observable and publicly witnessable. The local collaborative displays, and not any regulations, signal the objective methods for organizing the crossings.

Old hands at crossing know how to handle the challenges, and many of them are renegades. Take the case of three female friends most probably returning to campus from lunch. They are standing in front of the bookstore, two of them with umbrellas protecting them from the rain. They wish to cross Kincaid at the same time that a city bus with the right-of-way is moving to turn left from 13th Street onto Kincaid, where a bus stop is located. Two of the three friends are veteran crossers and one is a novice. As the three commence to cross, the novice crosser spies the bus barreling into the intersection and hesitates, making a bid to catch the gaze of the driver in hope of securing his permission to cross. The veterans brook no such illusion, and lunge straightforward into the wet crossing, the one with an umbrella shielding her head from the driver's gaze and the other in a rain jacket staring steadily at the opposite side. They know from experience that this driver will not run them over and that if they hesitate they will lose the opportunity to cross. The novice stands paralyzed at the curb as her friends move across without her (see Photo 1.11)—and for a moment she is left alone to vie with the bus and the rest. After a bit of indecision, she hops across the street and quickly catches up with her friends, and the three reunite while the bus driver sits in the intersection waiting for them all to complete their crossing.

## SALIENCES

There is no need to overdo the rational aspects of crossing Kincaid. The persons traversing the intersection do not depend upon any analysts working out a theory of crossing, nor do they have a theory themselves. A person crossing Kincaid does not even need to make sense of what everyone is doing—one only has to get across. So there can be no question of any "grand theory of crossing" having to be worked out rationally and then stuffed into the heads of the crossers before they will be able to cross. While rational agency is not totally absent, the bulk of the actions are responses to one or another *salience* of a gestalt contexture and are largely unavailable to rational planning. By "gestalt" is meant a coherence that "detaches itself as an organized and closed unit from the surrounding field" (Gurwitsch 1964, 115), or in other words a salience is an opportunity that is segregated from the phenomenal field and seized upon. Gurwitsch (1966, 432–4) came to question "Husserl's egological conception of consciousness" and contended that the phenomenal identity of things matters more than what can be worked out formally by a synthesis of meanings. The looks of the world involve more than what is strictly rational, and organization is more public than it is personal.

There is no single method for crossing Kincaid, there are all manner of methods taking place at once. And there is not one phenomenal field but heterogeneous fields, reflecting the perspectives of the persons who are intending to cross. The situation is not one that is easily amenable to modeling or rational analyses without the model grossly ruining the intricacy that is the local achievement. There is a swarm, perhaps at first undifferentiated, and out of the chaos an opening "emerges from the camouflage" (Garfinkel and Livingston 2003, 24) and a crosser moves through it. A "salience" of a particular pattern emerges authochthonously and disappears suddenly, and usually there is insufficient time for thinking about it. As Garfinkel (2002, 281) observed, "Salience abbreviates the endogenous coherence of a figure of organized gestalt contexture that emerges upon its background, disengaged from its background." Saliences are worldly things like an opening to skate through. That the open zone on the left, into which one is skating in order to avoid a car, is designated as one-way against one matters less than snagging that salient opening before it closes. A cyclist, willing to adopt any method that can be used to avoid coming to a complete stop, will embrace the space adjacent to a self-absorbed cellphone user who suddenly appears and gains access to the intersection, and no advanced planning was necessary or possible. Pedestrians face a continually changing complex of developing possibilities. They have in view a phenomenal field of possible routes as *emerging things* with which they contend.

"Salience" is a notion that Gurwitsch borrowed from William James, and it refers to a self-organizing phenomenon whereby "some part emerges from this chaotic and inarticulate mass and stands out" (Gurwitsch 1964, 28). A salience is *not an interpretation* projected by a crosser; *neither is it a representation* of crossing in the mind of a crosser; rather, it is a self-organization of the flow of traffic that is "immanent to and not superimposed upon the stream" (Gurwitsch 1964, 31). It is arises authochthonously.[1] Gurwitsch writes (1964, 34), "Organization emerges out of the experiential stream and thus proves a feature immanent to and exhibited by immediate experience, not bestowed upon the latter from without," and so here there is an emphasis that departs somewhat from Husserl's original constitutional phenomenology. Gurwitsch adds (1964, 31), "If salience is admitted, it follows that not all organization is derived from a selective and organizing activity working on the chaotic stream." The point of our addressing the phenomenal field is to cease our quest for finding solutions by examining the mind of the person crossing and instead to examine the world. The methods for coping with the traffic here emerge from the world and are presented to the crossers as worldly opportunities. Let us examine some of the methodologies cultivated by the persons who cross Kincaid.

## LOOKING AND RECOGNITION

Among the methods for crossing Kincaid, the use of looks and gazes to concert the crossings is the most refined. The very first step is to [Look] at the other party (see Photo 1.7). The brackets that surround the gloss "[Look]" are for reminding the reader that one should not interrogate the *name* for the ethnomethod but examine the worldly practice itself in its course, and as its course, of the worldly activities that compose it. In Photo 1.7, in addition to wanting to cross Kincaid, the pedestrian is attending to the need to produce an orderliness there. The orderliness is responsive not just to his looking but to the way his head is turned, the casualness or tension there, the rich gestural arsenal that may be employed, and the body's orientation. The pedestrian is not only looking but doing so in a manner that renders his looking as witnessable and recognizable as looking. It is a public display of looking, an engagement in social interaction, and not just any social interaction but a diligent concern for the interaction that remains to be organized by the parties there. We cannot see the look of the driver, but it would not be unreasonable to imagine that there is a similar look and diligent concern there as well.

In Photo 1.8a the head-turn is so slight that it is best studied in slow motion on the videotape. There is some soliciting of the driver's recognition by the young woman in white (the car is partly visible beneath the foliage of the tree), which they seem to have received since in Photo 1.8b the pair is able to cross Kincaid without having to wait.

In Photo 1.9 only one of the two parties turns her head, but it is sufficient for slowing the advance of the car. What is consequential is not what one does or what one intends to do but what is *observable* by others as one's intended movement. An analyst could divide the act into subjective and

Photo 1.7. The Look

Photo 1.8

objective phases, but it is really only what is objective that matters, and the parties who staff these crossings work at making what they do objectively available to parties present.

The second key component of the ethnomethod here is that following the [Look] there may or may not be a [Recognition]. In most cases, as the looker is soliciting a recognition of her look the other party will look back. Not only will the other party look back but in that look back that party will make it publicly available that it sees her looking, that she is being looked at. This is made increasingly difficult by modern windows that are glazed

Photo 1.9. The Look

with a heavy gray or green tint, making eye contact difficult to establish. We may have entered an historical phase during which persons in sunglasses will not be reciprocally looking at people behind tinted windows. During [Recognition] there may be a struggle while their attentions converge. It is a very subtle phenomenon; for instance, it may be a struggle to avoid their attentions converging. The victory here can depend upon an eye-blink, with the first to blink ceding the right-of-way. And if no [Recognition] is received, it may be that the pedestrian will need to cede to the vehicle. Here in Photo 1.10 it seems that the struggle between the car and the pedestrian has yet to be won or lost, and the [Recognition] may be still up in the air. The pedestrian who shoots a [Look] is just stepping off the curb in front of the sedan.

In our story of the three women crossing in front of the bus who had the right-of-way, the novice crosser was stalled in her wait for the [Recognition] of the bus driver (the bus is approaching just outside the right of edge of Photo 1.11). But of course it is a [Recognition] that never came, for there are few practices at Kincaid more hopeless than waiting for the [Recognition] of a bus driver. Bus drivers are too experienced and know better than to give away their phenomenal field, which is why the old-hand crossers that were her friends had to steal it.

Photo 1.10

Photo 1.11

The final stage of this ethnomethod is that once a [Recognition] is received, the person who originally commenced the [Look] is advised to [Acknowledge the Recognition]. This serves the public availability of what they have coordinated, minimizes surprises, and contributes to the objectivity of their affairs. The [Acknowledgment] can include a gesture, however slight, and it is common for the gesture to be one of gratitude, even when it is the gesture itself that becomes the tool that is used to ensure one's ability to cross (Photo 1.12).

Photo 1.12. Acknowledging the Recognition

While this entire process—from [Look] to [Recognition] to [Acknowledgment]—can take place quickly, it does consume some time, and so it tends to be employed more commonly during off-peak hours. During periods when the traffic is highly congested, there is considerably less recourse to this ethnomethod for crossing Kincaid. The details that compose the three stages of this method vary widely, but overall it is a safe and secure method for gaining a right to cross. In one case there was a car who wished to brook no such negotiation, and so the pedestrian waved slightly to get the driver's attention. The pedestrian hardly paused long enough to secure the [Recognition], but once he got it, even fleetingly, it was over for the car's designs on the right-of-way. When the traffic is heavy, such negotiations are complicated by the fact that the different pedestrians and cars may be employing different methods simultaneously, and there may be multiple sequences of [Look] – [Recognition] – [Acknowledgment] in play. One pedestrian may successfully capture the [Recognition] of a car; however, a succeeding vehicle's driver may have missed the entire show, cut inside of the turning car that has been made to wait for pedestrians, and threaten to inadvertently mow down the pedestrians who had already pocketed the acknowledgments. Indeed, accidents may be caused by drivers who were not part of an already completed and publicly acknowledged negotiation procedure arriving late with their own competing strategy; however, here at Kincaid there are nearly no accidents. But if there are not, then these pedestrians each of whom has a method, and these motorists each of whom has a method, must be doing some very elegant work concerting their methods.

## BEING OBLIVIOUS

If the age-old advice, "Look both ways before you cross the street," is to be found at one pole, then at the opposite pole is the ethnomethod of [Being oblivious], and there are many occasions where looking both ways would only complicate a crosser's passage. *Being oblivious is a skilled practice* that is widely employed by vehicles and pedestrians alike as a method for securing rights to the intersection at Kincaid Street. Among the methods for never having to look at a competing crosser are staring at the ground or at an object across the street, talking with friends in an engaged manner, being absorbed in a cellphone call, keeping one's hood draped over the eyes, selecting a tune on one's iPod, and so forth. Rummaging around in one's bag or backpack for a cellphone all the while crossing in the middle of traffic is a very effective method; it is possible the motorists will question the person's sanity, which will work further toward the pedestrian's gaining access to the crossing. In fact, acting unpredictably crazy is another reliable ethnomethod for securing the right-of-way, and in a city that is filled with street people—whose expertise at crossing streets exceeds that of other pedestrians—motorists are accustomed to ceding the way to people who do not appear to be completely sane. Not that the students at the University of Oregon are slouches at appearing to have a touch of lunacy, an appearance they are willing to use to their advantage when crossing Kincaid: any method for crossing will do; however, [Being oblivious] is one of the best.

The pedestrian in Photo 1.13 is a decent example of being oblivious. Probably a student of architecture or graphic arts, he pays no attention to the car whatsoever and even uses the side of his folio bag to his advantage. Of him, one of my students commented, "The pedestrian never seems to give the car a second thought." There does not seem to be any first thought either.

When perambulating across the center of the intersection while being oblivious is accompanied by a large poster, as happens frequently during the course of any day, even taxi drivers are rendered powerless. On our videotapes there are times when the jaywalking-with-poster crosser is too absorbed with a cellphone conversation to even notice there is traffic, let alone make eye contact with it. On those occasions when the cellphone is being held between the crosser's chin and shoulder, making eye-contact with a driver would necessitate the cellphone falling to the ground. Crossers like these always gain the right-of-way. In sum, if one wishes to cross Kincaid

Photo 1.13. Being Oblivious

without any delay, then simply entering the intersection without glancing toward the cars is an effective ethnomethod.

Photo 1.14 features an expert crosser who brooks no compromise with the cars who had been queuing up for the right to cross. The white car managed to make a left turn from 13th onto Kincaid before the crosser arrives, and the darker sedan, who had been waiting dutifully at the stop sign on the other side of Kincaid and had allowed some pedestrians there to cross, after deferring further to the white car (who had the right-of-way) is relatively determined to make it across before another group of pedestrians block the way. It appears that at least one pedestrian had lost the [Look] negotiation with the sedan and is pausing at the curb waiting for it to pass, just as the man in the dark jacket, accepting no prisoners, came out of the doors of the Bookstore and headed directly into the intersection with his cup of coffee in hand. As a method for crossing, staring at one's coffee while savoring a sip will do nicely. The sedan had no recourse but to allow the man with the coffee to slip in front of his passage.

A person accomplished at doing [Oblivious] is featured in Photo 1.15, who takes advantage of the space produced by the pair who had negotiated their passage by means of the [Look] method (cf. Photo 1.9). That he may not truly be oblivious is suggested by the fact that his gait is quite fast, which suggests that he knows that the opening behind the pedestrians is closing down.

Photo 1.14

# THE LOCAL ORDERLINESS OF CROSSING KINCAID

Photo 1.15

The actions of this oblivious crosser illustrates that there exists a difference between "being oblivious" and "doing oblivious." Some crossers are really oblivious, and it is obvious that other crossers are simply pretending to be oblivious, and there are all shades of methodologies in between. It is a simple matter, for instance, to feign distraction by becoming preoccupied with the controls of one's iPod. Doing [Oblivious] is a simple but effective practice that the reader can experiment with at any 4-corner traffic stop: the next time you come to a corner where several cars reach their stop signs at about the same time, do not [Look] at any of the other cars, just wait *without looking at them* until they cede you the right-of-way. This also works very well when one is walking on the sidewalk toward a group of three or four persons moving in the opposite direction, none of whom is ready to cede any space to for you to pass them: just cast your eyes to the ground and proceed as if you think there is no obstruction. You will gain access every time! Avoiding eye-contact, as a motorist or pedestrian, is roughly equivalent to the discovery made by some early conversation analysts that the most secure way to obtain a turn for talking is to simply to keep talking, ignoring the other person who is also trying to get the floor, no matter how long that takes. Even an interlocutor who is determined to win the floor will persist only for a few seconds so long as you keep talking also and do not stop. In part, they are unable to hear what you are saying, and the length of your utterance offers the possibility that what you are saying may be important or be offering some justification for getting the floor; so they stop long enough to take a reading of what you are saying, and by then they have lost the struggle. The rule of thumb is that the last person to stop talking will have the floor. Similarly, among those doing [oblivious] at Kincaid, the last person to look up to gaze at what is happening will win the competition for the intersection.

For this reason, when crossers look to assess the congestion in the street, they may do so with only the slightest head motion, or with none at all, so that they can preserve the option of doing [Oblivious]. It is like having one's cake and eating it too. At times the gaze, occasionally required to verify the unlikelihood of imminent destruction, will be hardly more than an eye-blink. The real world-class virtuosos with this ethnomethod are people from the Indian subcontinent. During more than five years of residence in India, I have never ceased to be amazed at the way *no one*—not pedestrian, motorcyclist, rickshaw driver, cyclist, taxi driver—will ever gaze at another traveler. It may be considered a sign of weakness, and it is for certain that anyone who tries to [Look] will become the one prevented from gaining access to the street (I am an expert at this way of failing). What Indian drivers and pedestrians are doing may look like something chaotic and dangerous, but they know just what they are doing, and since they have such highly congested flows of traffic I can only presume that it is a procedure necessary for the tasks they face regularly. Knowing this, I never drive in India but hire vehicles that come with knowledgeable drivers.

A similar phenomenon of orderliness transpires with queues in India, which mostly appear to the novice visitor to be an absence of queues. Every line in India is a swarm—ticket offices, photocopying machines, stores, taxi stands, service lines, etc. are under siege by more parties than can be serviced in the available time. So, in most venues the potential clients crowd around the focal point of service, and lines there are nearly nonexistent. Take the queues for the many photocopying machine shops that line the streets of Indian cities: there is no apparent order of service, and being "first-in-line" can be an achievement without any consequences. The task of the server is to process as many people as possible in the shortest possible time, and so they are taking readings of who will be quick and who will present complications. The conversations of foreign visitors when they finally get back to their hotels for lunch commonly turn to how there is no order to the queues in India, and the probably racist sentiment is offered that Indians seem to be unorganized or uncivil. This is not the case at all. Inside of the swarms that compose Indian queues, like the figure that is still lost in the camouflage, are intricate methods of social organization, and a corporate orientation is in no way lacking there.

THE LOCAL ORDERLINESS OF CROSSING KINCAID 31

The complaints of the Air Emirates hostesses who staff the entrance to the free breakfast that Air Emirates offers to all its air travelers transferring planes at the international airport in Dubai sound much like the complaints of the American and European visitors to India. It seems that the Indian travelers, even when relocated to an international venue where they are no longer in the majority, crowd around the entrance to the busy free meal cafeteria just the way they do in India, and they present persons who are unfamiliar with this way of organizing affairs with a difficult task, a task that goes on every day at the Dubai airport. Part of the Indians' method is to coordinate their pressing with their fellows in line until together they can collaboratively squeeze the entrance until a point that the authorities are compelled to release the pressure by letting some of them stream in. So, it is not a strictly individualist procedure in the way that some of the people who complain think; rather, it is a collaborative, collective, and even civil activity through and through.

The conflict of differing methodologies and civilizations can become quite comical. One Air Emirates stewardess asked me, "Why don't they know how to form a straight line?" I replied that they do, only that it is not always the most effective method. I had learned that they know *just how* to form a strict line when during a long overlay in Doha, Qatar, I observed Indian passengers attempting to apply the standard Indian queue to a line supervised by an airport transport security officer, who was checking bags for dangerous items. All day long the Indian passengers attempted to crowd the point where one puts one's bags on the belt that runs through the scanner, but each time the officer in charge of the security check warned them to behave, they reformed themselves swiftly into tidy strict lines, revealing that they were indeed accomplished practitioners of that method as well. So it was never a matter of their not knowing how to queue in a straight line, it was having other competing and on occasion more efficient ethnomethods for concerting rights to an order of service.

The difference between being oblivious and doing [Oblivious] is illustrated well in Photo 1.16. The driver in the white car (whose motor is gunned up and is reverberating loudly) commences his right-of-way turn without paying the slightest [Recognition] to the student wearing a white cast, who is making an attempt to [Look] at the driver. Brooking no negotiation with the student with the cast, who cannot have been missed, the driver is stalled by the second student in the white baseball cap, who is absorbed in a cellphone conversation and appears to be unaware that a vehicle is heading his way. The motorist is doing [Oblivious], whereas the student in the white cap is simply being oblivious. It is evident on the videotape that the driver employs the method of doing [Oblivious] perfectly and has prevailed over the student with the cast, but runs aground when he

Photo 1.16

reaches the other student whose oblivion is more perfect because it is real. Usually, being oblivious will trump doing [Oblivious]. In Photo 1.16, the stall forced upon the car by the oblivious student blocks the projected access across Kincaid of the student with the cast, who, much like a cyclist, has no intention of stopping his gait and instead circles behind the car, having timed the car's likely exit from the intersection. But for a time the passage that way is blocked, and the student with the cast is forced to circle further around behind the car, almost to the middle of the intersection. Possibly already annoyed by the unwillingness of the motorist to engage in a losing negotiation, the student's frustration turns to a moment of anger when the car's stall delays him even further: as the car finally exits the intersection the student gives the car the finger.

While cases of being oblivious are abundant, cases of doing [Oblivious] seem even more common. Bus and taxi drivers are excellent practitioners, and it may be a skill that is required of professional drivers. The ambulance drivers we observed never acknowledged anyone and refused to become involved in the dialectics of recognizing and being recognized, even when there was no emergency and no siren. Doing [Oblivious] is an accomplished practice.

Moreover, doing [Oblivious] is not the anti-social act that at first glance it appears to be. Much as in the case of the Indian queues, there is full participation in the sociality of the occasion because *one is continuously oriented to the public observability of the action one is taking*. Properly considered, they are not merely actions—they are *demonstrations*, exhibits of obliviousness as a way to organize the local orderliness of affairs. And so the obliviousness of our crossers is a social activity. As each party attempts to out-demonstrate (or out nondemonstrate) the other, and these displays contest the scene—withholding any recognition that might objectify the other's demonstration as the acceptable practice, while providing one's own demonstration for others to react to—there is continuous engagement in coordinated activity. It certainly cannot be asserted that there is *no* interest in collaboration or in *somehow* concerting their activities together. Out-demonstrating another entails some degree of the other having recognized them, and so has entailed the other's participation in spite of appearances. These displays are made not only for the sake of receiving confirmation, thereby objectivating the practice, but also to help clarify *for oneself* the reasonableness and public availability of a method one has come upon.

## CONTINUOUS MOTION

Another ethnomethod for vehicles we observed is difficult to appreciate without any videotape, and that is the method of attempting to merge into the flow of traffic by slowly, but inexorably, moving into the flow of traffic. What is involved here is not just merging but merging-while-engaging-in-a-public-demonstration-of-merging: there is *no* space for you, and no one is willing to make any space for you; however, you demonstrate the facticity of your merging (i.e., its purported objectivity) by keeping your car moving, even if it is at a pace as slow as a snail. [Keeping oneself moving] to ensure that one remains a part of the emerging gestalt contexture of the scene is the ethnomethod here. Buses rely heavily upon this method. The key aspect is that the merging must be made witnessably there; it is not a matter of simply moving slowly but of *demonstrably* moving slowly. One's barely perceptible movement is an accountable action, part of the orderliness of crossing Kincaid. One wants to present one's partners with the inevitability of a real world that includes the merging as one of the facts of life.

Formulating accounts of affairs is an important tool for organizing a local orderliness, and there is a great deal of ethnomethodological scholarship about accounts and accountability (cf. Garfinkel and Sacks 1970, Garfinkel 2002, 169–92, and Heritage 1984, 135–78). There are two essential aspects to being accountable: first, one is addressed to the receptivity of local affairs to an account and to the potential utility of the account for organizing the local orderliness of those affairs; second, one is continuously oriented to the possible ways that one might get into trouble and be held accountable for something one does or says. One is abidingly concerned for the ways that one or another's account can crystallize the intelligibility of some interaction, and at the same time one is rubbernecking the responses of one's associates to learn not merely the feasibility of an account one might offer but also to learn its sense and consequences. Merging into a flow of traffic presents to everyone at the scene a candidate for reasonable traffic behavior, and can be an effective means of gaining passage through at an intersection, honks notwithstanding.

## NEGOTIATING

While [Look] and [Recognition] are a species of negotiating, the crossers at Kincaid have ways of negotiating that exceed those facilities. And a note of caution is required here: some theorists have a fondness for the language of "negotiation" that is mostly unjustified; when the details that compose "negotiation" are kept general and unspecified, it may be assumed that the term has more coherence than it actually bears. In the context of this study, we are using "negotiation" to refer to interaction between contending crossers that is more complicated than [Look] and [Recognition]. Motorists entering the intersection survey the scene for any sign among the pedestrians of a willingness to yield. Whether through politeness or with another strategy in mind, pedestrians will signal their cooperation with a motorist and indicate a sort of permission with subtle gestures that include nose-scratching, stuffing the hands in one's pockets, craning their necks to gaze beyond the drivers (an indication that they are resolved to commence their negotiation with the succeeding motorist), a nod or flick of the head, etc. These are all methods for exhibiting permission to cross, and sometimes they are like vaudeville performances in that the gestures are exaggerated in order to ensure their observability. During negotiations a driver can nonverbally plead a case, be rejected, plead further, and finally have the pedestrian cede. Because negotiation typically includes a more extensive social interchange, it is not unusual for some cooperative courtesy to be displayed, such as the pedestrian speeding up to demonstrate a concern for the inconvenience of a motorist. During one noontime, two student jaywalkers were strolling directly across the center of the intersection with the intention of visiting the corner pub, and their path placed them directly in front of a loaded bus that had the right-of-way and was in the process of turning right, ahead of them (see Photo 1.17). One of the students graciously flicked his left thumb to indicate that they were willing to cede to the bus driver.

THE LOCAL ORDERLINESS OF CROSSING KINCAID    35

Photo 1.17. Courtesy

The heavier the traffic flow is, the less opportunity there will be for negotiation. One student observer commented, "During the high-traffic time of day, everyone—pedestrians, bicycles, cars—just keeps moving." In fact, safely negotiating the priority of passage is an inefficient way to handle traffic flow. Occasionally, a negotiation will become a kind of "After you, Alphonse. No, after *you*!" routine that will stall traffic for a considerable time and cause the crossers to lose their patience. Once when a car stopped for the sign that doesn't exist (on 13th Street), a car and a pedestrian waited for the car to pass anyway, insisting upon applying the regulation there; but the stopped car deferred, gesturing for the others to go. The others again insisted that the car go, and the pedestrian motioned severely with his hands; this may have been considered competitive, for the car decided to stand its ground and for about half-a-minute the traffic there was paralyzed. It was an unsafe situation in which there was no clarity. Negotiation is not without its problems.

The most damning aspect of negotiation is that the complicated procedures that the people at Kincaid regularly use to concert their crossings cannot be reduced to a rational process. It is a noble idea, but the actions there are not calculated analyses. The orderliness there mostly consists of gestalt contextures that appear suddenly and without planning, and disappear before the slightest rational intercourse has time to commence. The local methods there do not derive their authority from any logic about how crossing can best be done but from what is immanently observed and witnessable. The details of the phenomenal field that compose the event of crossing do not represent anything more than their own tangible presence, a fact that some researchers may regret. Waiting for the resolution of an "After you, Alphonse" routine consumes too much time and is not worthy of recommendation.

A much more efficient method is that of the coffee-sipping crosser of Photo 1.14. In considerably less time than it would take to follow a rational procedure for negotiating the right to cross, the coffee sipper had already crossed. The critical benefit of his methodology is that the orderliness there was communicated without any consumption of time. For the motorist, it was a case of not getting one's cake but eating it too. What by appearances was a case of mindless self-absorption was an intelligent and efficient means of crossing Kincaid. As Garfinkel (2002, 97) has written, "The coherence of things is that of the phenomenal field properties of figural contexture." The coffee sipper *made it plain* that he would be there, and gone, before any other crosser could even entertain ideas.

Time and again, negotiators are trumped by events that are faster moving, and end up being left at the curb. Attempting to follow a formal protocol for *conceptually* working out a procedure for crossing is not the most effective strategy. An occurrence in one of our videos is not really communicable via still photos, but it displayed this phenomenon along with its intricacy: a pair of students was walking south along Kincaid across from the Bookstore and were engaged in deep conversation when they reached the corner at 13th and had to separate. One of them began to enter the crossing while still engaged with terminating his conversation and with making his farewell (his left hand waving good-bye as he made his away across the street, his eyes fixed only upon his departing friend who was continuing down the sidewalk). In the intersection, a female student jaywalking across with a large poster was negotiating passage with a taxi driver, a negotiation that had gone in the taxi's favor; however, during this time the parting student unknowingly moved into the projected route of the taxi. Only when two of them nearly collided, did the parting student notice the taxi for the first time. He froze there, startled. The student was ready at once to defer to the taxi driver, but the taxi driver was equally startled and halted mid-intersection. The student with the poster used the pause as a serendipitous opportunity to slip in between them. Taking advantage of that poster that then came between him and the taxi driver, the parting student also made his way across, and the driver—who had won the preceding negotiation—ended up being the last one to pass.

## PIGGYBACKING

The final ethnomethod we will examine is used by all crossers, but is most effectively used by those attempting a vehicular crossing in the face of a swarm of expert student-pedestrians. My students gave to this method the name "piggybacking." It involves skillfully taking advantage of crossers-in-progress who have already forced competing traffic to make way. Although vehicles usually piggyback vehicles and pedestrians usually piggyback pedestrians, anyone can take advantage of any preceding crosser who provides a salient opening. Piggybacking is one of the principal methods used for crossing Kincaid Street.

Frequently a car, van, or other vehicle will closely hug the rear bumper of a preceding car in order to slip through the same opening a preceding car locates before that opening shuts down. It is also common for cars to gear up for piggybacking a car that is proceeding across from the adjacent street; most typically, a vehicle traveling north that is stalled at the stop sign on Kincaid south of 13th Street will attempt to squeeze in behind a vehicle on 13th with the right-of-way who is turning into the north side of Kincaid. Successful piggybacking here may require that an alert vehicle on Kincaid *not* stop at the stop sign, for the reason that the driver needs to remove any space between itself and the preceding car that pedestrians might be capable of utilizing. The stop sign is not a major factor in the hierarchy of the orderliness here. (Remember: as a matter of city policy, no traffic regulations are enforced at Kincaid and 13th Street.) One of our videos shows a van riding through the stop sign on Kincaid to enable it to piggyback another van that is turning from 13th Street just as a jogger was timing his entry into the intersection following the 13th Street van. The car refused to surrender his piggyback, and the jogger swiftly adjusted his pace so he could dodge the second van and pass it immediately after it had moved through. As one of my students described it, "The runner seamlessly dodges the van and continues across without a pause."

Vans have professional drivers, who tend to be more proficient at piggybacking. UPS drivers are brilliant at this ethnomethod and brook scant generosity. The task of any UPS driver is to use its size to intimidate pedestrians while denying pedestrians a phenomenal field into which they could insert themselves. It is reminiscent of a hockey game. Photo 1.18 illustrates a "triple piggy".

On this occasion the second car was beginning to veer to the right in order to safely hug the first car, who had just turned onto Kincaid, but when he was forced to veer left and slow down in order to avoid a competing pedestrian ahead, the third piggybacker (who had run the stop sign) nearly collides with him and is compelled to move to the right as well, and also

Photo 1.18. A Triple Piggyback

to veer left again to avoid the oncoming pedestrian. Given the wetness of the streets, this swerving left and right was less than ideal.

Above all, the objective of piggybacking is to prevent the floodgate of pedestrians from opening. In Photo 1.6 (shown earlier), an SUV with the right-of-way is crawling into the intersection and is followed closely by a square-back who is attempting to piggyback. When the SUV is forced to stop for three pedestrians, the sedan who had been waiting at the stop sign at Kincaid, moves behind the SUV without any hesitation, leaving the square-back to piggyback the sedan as the third vehicle of the series and in spite of a skateboarder who is traveling the wrong way and who successfully inserts himself between the SUV and the sedan. All three vehicles (and the skateboarder) make it through before the flood of pedestrians recommenced.

Bus drivers piggyback regularly also (see Photo 1.19) and confessed to us that if they did not piggyback they would be unable to remain on schedule. If one cares to learn how to piggyback, one can go to school on the bus drivers. The issue for a bus driver each time the driver reaches this intersection is how will the driver avoid having to stop for the assertive pedestrians here. Bus drivers enter the intersection at Kincaid already searching the field for something that can be piggybacked, the most likely candidate being cars proceeding across 13th on Kincaid (see Photo 1.20).

Photo 1.19. Bus Waiting to Piggyback

Photo 1.20

In order to be successful at piggybacking, buses must not allow intervening space to develop while being careful to avoid rear-ending the vehicle they are piggybacking. It works best when the bus driver is able to present the bus's movement as "natural" as if it was simply the way of the world. Doing so requires the driver to *maintain a steady speed*, for the steadiness lends to the driver's movement the aspect of being natural and inevitable. We have collected from our videotapes some fabulous illustrations of near-misses involving buses (see Photo 1.21), which would be entertaining if were not for the perilous situations they display.

On occasion it can seem that the drivers are too vigorous, but their skills are standard and routine, and no drivers or police officers were aware of any incidents that involved buses. Skateboarders and cyclists are also skilled at piggybacking and will exploit any available mother with a baby carriage or student with a poster. For instance, the wrong-way cyclist in Photo 1.4 sped across using pedestrians (visible in the photo). Pedestrians themselves will jump behind any salience, which could be other crossers, a lagging elderly pedestrian, or someone absorbed with their cellphone. A person crossing in a wheelchair will serve as a magnet for all pedestrians waiting for an opportunity to flow across (think Peter Piper). In Photo 1.22, the sedan had already waited for several pedestrians, and then a jaywalker who had become self-righteous about having to walk around the car, when

Photo 1.21

Photo 1.22

a Johnny-come-lately spied the salience offered by the jaywalker (her dark hair is barely visible above the car), and skipped across as well.

Despite the many violations and recklessness of the crossers, there is not a problem at Kincaid. The orderliness there works satisfactorily, and anyway, it is too complicated to organize by means of one-size-fits-all regulations. The 1955 *Oregon Daily Emerald* article observed, "We hope that there will not be a lot of needless spending on a problem that perhaps is not serious at all. . . . The students already know how to cross the street themselves." The cars may have a more difficult time of it, however, but the permission to occasionally violate the traffic code is probably all the assistance they require. The local methods are uniquely adequate to the occasion, which offers up a phenomenal field that is remarkably stable over time. That a car planning to piggyback may illegally pass a too scrupulous law-abider who is stopping where there is no stop sign or has not yet learned how to find a way though a pedestrian swarm, or that another vehicle may find it necessary to run the stop sign in order to piggyback successfully, contributes to the efficiency of the traffic flow and conforms to the local orderliness, if not to the letter of the law.[2]

It seems possible that the situation examined here at Kincaid Street may be typical of a great many localities where traffic is impeded on a regular basis. Drivers at certain intricate intersections may have devised routine, uniquely local solutions that speed up the daily flow of traffic there, and any novice driver will need to be observant in order to avoid causing problems. When the vehicular interaction becomes not only intricate but intense, it can be grounds for a novice driver to comment, "Drivers here are very unfriendly," although it may be simply that the motorists there have a system that the driver is not yet able to fathom. The orderlinesses are local.

## A CLOSING NOTE ON THE NON-CONCEPTUALITY OF SOME OCCASIONS

Throughout this study we have emphasized that the work of crossing Kincaid is oriented behavior that has more to do with the looks of a local gestalt contexture than with conceptualizing. This is a perspective that is at variance with most philosophical and sociological studies of ordinary action, including those by phenomenologists. It seems that academicians throughout the world only feel competent when they have reduced affairs to concepts. For this reason, I have included in this present collection of studies several ethnomethodological studies that seek an orderliness in phenomena that does not rely upon words. This does not imply that phenomenological inquiries into the synthesis of concepts are unimportant. I only want to insist that studies of affairs that center on how concepts are developed and organized should not eclipse any nonconceptual matters that are critical for organizing any local orderliness.

What fascinates all phenomenologists is the birth of meaning, but there is a danger of too narrowly constraining what meaning can be. Especially, I try to locate myself in the moments just *before* sense congeals, an achievement I first came to appreciate by considering carefully the descriptions of Merleau-Ponty. I attempt to infect at least a portion of my studies with a degree of non-knowledge, since we phenomenologists may presume far too much about what our subjects are thinking, even when they may not be thinking anything. Sometimes people function blindly and act without thinking anything through. It may be the case that for ethnomethodology to make further progress, it will need to more deeply explore wordless phenomena, so it will be less tempted to focus its analysis upon ideation. University researchers are too adept and too eager to convert what they find into events where concepts are always driving the interaction, whereas in everyday life concepts are only one feature of mundane interaction.

Garfinkel himself took up a number of studies of wordless situations. These include his examination of Helen-the-blind-woman's kitchen (Garfinkel 2002, 212–14), orientation while seeing through inverting lenses (Garfinkel 2002, 207–10), Agnes' practices for passing as a woman (Garfinkel 1967, 116–85), formatted queues (Garfinkel 2002, 245–61), Polynesian navigation (Garfinkel 2007, 23–26), a study of freeway driving, "What's

Holding Up the Traffic?" (unpublished), and several others. This way of undertaking social phenomenological investigations has become increasingly rare. Nevertheless, it is for certain that the coherence that most things have is *not an analytic coherence*—most coherences are authochthonous. It is even more important to observe that the coherence of most things simply is what it is. The coherence of these crossings we have been studying is not representative of a theory of social organization; it is not the result of an interest in good government; and it has nothing to do with discovering the proper techniques of traffic control. The coherences are more practical and less fully reasoned than that. Similarly, the assertiveness displayed by some drivers or pedestrians is not to be attributed to quality of personality, culture, or any deficiency of character; rather, the assertiveness is a product of the contingent features of the scene's orderliness.[3]

The coherence of things is usually unpredictable, serendipitous, and relies upon the saliences of particular patterns that emerge and become available for resolving local problems with organizing affairs, saliences that are snatched up just as quickly as they appear. They do not need to fit into any theory, and they offer the local practitioners solutions just the same. The formal analytic solutions to traffic flow that constitute the professional expertise of traffic managers (and which was reformed by Oregon's 1973 MUCTD manual) could not provide the solutions needed to prevent the backup of traffic on 13th Street because their survey and even their observational methods did not take seriously enough, nor were they informed by, the local ethnomethods that are in play there. Garfinkel (2002, 96) insists that because these ethnomethods are procedures that take advantage of the saliences in the local gestalt contexture, they are nearly impossible to imagine but can only be discovered and described, and must be studied "in their unmediated details" (Garfinkel 2002, 97). In order to imagine them one would have to lean too predominantly upon one's conceptualizing.

Alfred Schutz wrote to Aron Gurwitsch (Grathoff 1989, 263), "There isn't a transcendental ego, but only a thematic field which isn't egological," and Garfinkel took up the phenomenological notion of the phenomenal field and Gurwitsch's notion that intelligibilities were "autochthonous," and sustained this insight through the entire course of his career. Especially, Garfinkel challenged conventional social phenomenological inquiry with the observation that the orderlinesses of ordinary society were not so much socially constructed or deliberate as they were "self-organizing" and serendipitous. The notion that social affairs are self-organizing is a betrayal of the Lockean version of affairs that has motivated most academic theorizing. What is it that is self-organizing? The essential matters cannot be clarified adequately by theoretical summaries; that is why I have offered clarification by presenting the details of one perspicuous setting that is self-organizing: crossing Kincaid.

TWO

# FOLLOWING SKETCHED MAPS

> not as land looks on a map
> but as sea bord seen by men sailing.
>
> —Ezra Pound, Canto LIX

Ethnomethodology shares with phenomenology an interest in examining the immanent activity of thinking, which includes how ideas are shaped and formed, shared and objectivated, and when necessary evaded and transformed. It has been customary for philosophers and social psychologists alike to idealize thinking so that it can more readily be tamed by their theoretical models; however, ethnomethodological researchers mostly eschew modeling and try to restrict themselves to describing how thinking is actually done in practical circumstances. Accordingly, the ethnomethodological task is concerned more with description than theoretical explanation. Ethnomethodologists are fascinated when they are able to follow some practical reasoning over its course and provide a dynamic account of its worldly work. While static accounts of thinking can be suggestive, they will never provide radical access to the roots of the ordinary expertise that is required to make sense of the world, in just the way that people make sense.

In his undergraduate course during the winter of 1977 and the graduate seminar that followed in the spring, Harold Garfinkel took up the topic of how people use occasioned maps. There are few topics better able to capture the creative range of practical reasoning than just how people make intelligible the route directions to unfamiliar locations. Occasioned or sketched maps are filled with uncertainties and confusion that lead those trying to follow them to repeated aporias where their thinking becomes congested, clogged, and finally stopped. Yet such journeyers somehow manage to transform a map into advice adequate enough to guide them to their destination. The topic is one of several seminal studies that Garfinkel never wrote up in comprehensive full-length form, although brief accounts appear in Garfinkel 2002, 129–30 and 179–81, Garfinkel 2007, 23–26, and in an article-length grant application in 1996 ("A Comparison of Two Analytic Formats of Occasion Maps and Way Finding Journeys"). In 2006, when Prof. Garfinkel asked me to turn my seminar notes into a book, we decided that I should include extended accounts of the studies that my students and I have undertaken as part of my teaching and research. I used the topic twice for class projects in my own course on ethnomethodology, and I discovered that it was a pedagogically sound way to introduce many ethnomethodological issues. I divided the class into teams of four students, of which one student (or sometimes a friend of the students) would draw the map and wait for the other three students to arrive at the destination while one drove the car, another navigated, and the last one video-recorded the way-finding journey. This chapter offers an account of our findings; in that regard, Garfinkel, my students, and I are co-authors of these ideas, whose plausibility and validity were developed collaboratively.

There are at least four kinds of direction-giving (see Psathas 1992): sketched maps, whose sense must be achieved by the readers working off of notations on a page; occasioned maps (a.k.a. occasion maps) that are drawn in the reader's presence; face-to-face verbal instructions; and route directions given over the telephone. They share many common features, but my students and I (and Garfinkel himself) mostly examined sketched maps; and we examined them for what "the work of reading a map consists of as a *part* of the work of getting the journey done" (Garfinkel 1977a). We were not interested in studying the map alone, for in a journey there never is any such thing. Nor were we studying the map and the landscape together, since that also misguidedly suggests that a map by itself can have an intelligibility apart from the landscape. Rather, we were studying the event of reading-the-map-while-journeying, a lived activity. We were less preoccupied with assessing the geographic accuracy of maps than we were interested in a map's utility for and fidelity to the journeying work. We were seeking to identify "just what there is about a sketched map that persons in fact make use of in order to get done the work of journeying" (Garfinkel 1977a). The maps were used to locate features of the terrain that in turn made intelligible the map's notations.

## WHAT IS AT STAKE

Maps purport about themselves that they are complete "without any further explanation thought to be required" (Psathas 1979, 204); that is, they are thought to stand independently of their production. The map is used, and it is essential; however, its sense cannot exist apart from the practices that accompany its use. A map does not provide for those practices *prior* to an occasion—instead, it is the occasion that affords the map its coherency, a coherency not of ideas but of a collection of practices. Our disciplinary aim here is not to develop a theorized version of these practices but to identify the practices themselves, as rooted in *the looks of the world* for the parties who are following a route: "We want the looks of the practices of which the map-in-use is an integral part" (Garfinkel 1977a). These are investigations of what the being-done of a journey looks like, which demands a unique kind of disciplinary rigor that is capable of retaining its fidelity to *just what* the parties are witnessing at each step of the journey, a phenomenon that deserves to be a component of social research however frequently it gets reduced or ignored. An ethnomethodological investigation restricts itself to the endogenous account of the way-finding journey that is relying upon a sketched map for its sense and direction.

The map is part of the journey that it is consulted to get done (Garfinkel 1977a); it is not something that has its life as an in-itself. The map's "coherent, *contingent*, factual exposition" (Garfinkel 2002, 179) is the result of the contingencies of real worldly driving, journeying in which the journeyers keep "reading the display to find thereby in and as the reading, what it could be the reading of" (Garfinkel 1977a). If it sounds crazy, it is the mundane craziness that everywhere keeps occurring naturally in our lives. Apart from an actual journey that involves some map-readers' skills, it is impossible to say whether a map is good. Just as in the case of linguists who overlook the phenomenon of communication by concentrating exclusively upon speakers and without examining closely the work of listeners, here the competency of a map already implicates the competency of the map-recipients. Some research designs lose and read out of relevance the embodied, *in vivo* aspects of the phenomenon. Losing the fact of our participation—our production of the phenomenon as a reality—is an error widespread in modern lay and professional analyses.

One of the outstanding features of maps is that they only have the cogency they are able to collect from the landmarks they address. In the way that the rules of games collect the specific sense that they have during the players' game-play with rules, a map develops the clarity of its sense and reference only over the course of an actual journey. The map's correctness can only be a correctness in and as it is applied to a journey, and that correctness is something very tangible—hands-on, as it were. The map is used to find the mapping in the map, and the first task that way-finders face is organizing the coherency of the map. The landscape is used to find the sense of the map while the map is used to guide the way-finders' survey of the landscape. The situation provides us with a field study in which practical reasoning is richly available as a dynamic, emerging reflective activity, and the thickness of the way-finding problems that travelers face makes it difficult to for us to turn their practices into another social taxidermy. The practices of way-finding require that way-finders always remain open to what may be lacking, and the way-finders are so wild in their interpretative creativity that they do not become myopic easily. That is to say, the coherence way-finders develop for, and with, a map is a coherence that must keep itself *open* to what it does not yet know while at the same time *keep tamed* the very wide-ranging, perspectival orientations that proliferate during the map-reading. This is practical reasoning.

Unfortunately, many researchers "would just as soon ignore the real world, wanting nothing to do with it" (Garfinkel 1977b) because of how cumbersome it is to faithfully capture the complexity of such analytic work *in vivo*. The preference of many social researchers is for questionnaires and interviews, but those methods are inadequate, first of all because *the people themselves frequently do not know what they are doing*, or may not have commenced to reason about their affairs, so one cannot straightforwardly interview them or have them fill out questionnaires about it. Questionnaires are designed perfectly for obscuring this fact, by never failing to turn a subjects' confusion into something definite. Most of the time people think and act effectively in the midst of affairs that are ambiguous, and this is only a problem for researchers who wish to analyze their actions. Karl Mannheim (1952, 79fn) keenly observed, "Ambiguity is an offence to the analytic mind, but a source of rich insights for the synthetically oriented scholar."

Another problem is that the understanding of way-finders is *not deductive*, and the coherence of the maps they use is often a self-organizing gestalt-contexture (Gurwitsch 1964, 134). A person driving from Tijuana to Ensenada, Mexico, for the first time will have to locate the toll expressway that will make the journey a piece of cake; however, none of the advice contained in the written directions provided by a friend or in the American Automobile Association's official Baja California road map will tell him just how he managed to get onto a minor, toll-free coastal road that seemed to accommodate nothing but slow-moving vehicles, until during their continual surveying of the landscape the travelers locate a superhighway in the distance climbing a hill, and understand at once that that is where they need to be. The map's intelligibility is reestablished in a flash; however, it was not deduced analytically in a methodical fashion as realists might suppose, *nor* was it formulated or "constituted" in the way that idealists might suppose. Instead, the cogency of the map is grounded in the *tangible* contingencies of the worldly traveling, a cogency whose truth is not amenable to realist nor idealist versions of way-finding but to the developing and ongoing worldly work of way-finding. Merleau-Ponty (1962, 57–58) describes such an immanent, embodied appropriation of a gestalt: "The sensible configuration of an object. . . . 'is understood' through a sort of act of appropriation which we all experience when we say that we have 'found' the rabbit in the foliage of a puzzle."

What is the truth of the map? Docile models, whether realist or idealist, fail to capture it adequately. The way-finding involved in following a sketched map is a non-calculable practice, and the truth of a map is more an event than it is a datum. Alfred Schutz appreciated that humans are not as rational as many epistemologists and social scientists assume they are. He was original in giving full scope for the ways that our understanding of the world is shaped by nonconceptual factors. Schutz (1970, 19) praises Carneades for starting "with the observation that there is no pure representation existing in our mind," and he castigates the idea that most human activity is warranted in advance by deductively rational schema. Schutz (1970, 99) ridicules the notion that humans always have "to start from the basic definitions and fundamental concepts. . . . and then proceed to build up *more geometrico*, deduction by deduction." And he rejects the idea that most interpretation "belongs to the predicative sphere and occurs in a chain of logical steps passing from premises to conclusion" (1970, 43). Schutz's thoughts remain most welcome today. Schutz (1970, 153) contended that knowledge "has to be conceived in the broadest possible sense; not as the result of ratiocination," and he broadened the scope of phenomenological inquiry by being attentive to "all forms of acceptance" (1970, 76) and by insisting that knowing is not necessarily grounded only in clear conceptualizing. Finally, Schutz even offers us his best wisdom when he suggests that a sage "will not look for guidance to 'comprehensive representations'" (1970, 18).

Truth is not a correspondence of representation to fact: it is worldly. One does not so much follow a map as follow the developing looks of the world as it is configured with the aid of consulting the map, and *the critical answers to the truth of the map lie only in the map-in-use*: "For the map-in-use the issue of completeness is posed only on the way to the destination" (Garfinkel 1977b). There can be no completeness (or incompleteness) of a map that is not used, and fidelity to analytic geometry is not the same thing as fidelity to way-finding. It is a sign of our culture that we are ever ready to surrender our own embodied worldly expertise and replace it with a formal sounding analytic version that may able to foster improved (objective) communication but may miss *just what* will offer us the clue to the destination. In such a way the pressures of keeping society (writ large) orderly may cause collateral damage to more local orderlinesses.

Garfinkel (1977b) insists that "issues of decidable truth and correctness turn specifically on the map's circumstantial use as part of the journey it is consulted to make" and that "map reading is *chained* to the world in the world's particular looks of things." In this regard Garfinkel (1977b) always maintained, "There is nothing hidden behind the ordinary looks of things. Instead, the world is indeed what it appears to be." This is a programmatic tenet that was motivated by the guidance Garfinkel found in Husserl's emphasis upon inspecting things "as these are given in actual experience" (Husserl 1970c, 6).

From the time of his *Logical Investigations* to the *Crisis*, Husserl's goal was to locate, identify, and describe "the complete self-manifestation of the object" (Husserl 1970a, 765), a project that he claimed in his *Ideas* was to be guided by "the principle of all principles"—that the things immanently before us are the source for all claims to knowledge. According to Husserl, "Every originary presentive intuition is a legitimizing source of cognition," and analysts should accept only what is there, immanently before them, without applying theoretical notions that are extraneous to what is "originarily offered to us" (Husserl 1982, 44). The contemporary phenomenologist Dan Zahavi (2003, 45) comments that no extraneous authority, not even modern science, should be allowed to question the knowledge we gain from our immanent witnessing. In fact, rigor in applying the principle of all principles is Husserl's vision of science, a science that should remain uncompromised by theoretical or methodological preferences. The Husserlian commentator Henry Pietersma (1977, 42) translates Husserl a bit differently when he says that "every primordially presentative seeing" is the source for true knowledge. This "seeing" became for Garfinkel a technical concern for identifying—and sustaining contact with—"the looks of the world" for parties engaged in the affairs of ordinary life. If anything, Garfinkel radicalized Husserl's principle of principles, commencing, sustaining, and concluding every inquiry with the mundane looks of the world for parties engaged in the affairs of everyday life. Garfinkel (1977b) was interested in how people make the world orderly—"Our interest is in orderliness's work, its *own* work"—and his rigor was to always keep the details of that work at the center of his inquiries.

## THE MAP IS NOT A REPRESENTATION

A map invites the reader to set out on an adventure, some key particulars of which the map may elucidate. Nevertheless, it is common for people to think that a route is "provided by the 'map itself,' as if little or no work on the reader's part were needed" (Psathas 1979, 224). It is really inaccurate to say one is "following a map" since whatever may be there to follow is necessarily the handiwork of the person who is reading the map. The fundamental reflexivity of the situation does not offer any scope for a subjectivity that could stand apart from what there is to follow, and hence neither can there be any objectivity in-itself. There is surely nothing like a one-to-one correspondence, and most sketched maps offer not much more than chicken scratches whose intelligibility must still be arranged, and whose significance keeps changing as travelers proceed along a route.

Psathas (1979, 218) observes that the places on the map "stand in a relation of inexact correspondence to the places and objects of the world," and it is this inexactitude that confronts the reader's competence, a competence that is capable of turning the map into something useful. The term "correspondence" barely covers the phenomenon, and offers little help in specifying what is taking place. It is not a situation in which a subjectivity confronts an objectivity; this would be a grade school science class's way of addressing the problem. The situation is that the subjective always has its eye fixated upon the objective; and without a keenly operating subjectivity what is known to be objective will be impoverished. "Experience is the mutual 'openness' between interior and exterior, which *precedes* the dualism of subject and object" (Carbone 2004, 22; my emphasis). That first instant of seeing the toll expressway on the hill from a secondary road is an immanent, tangible fathoming that precedes any representational calculus.

A map's sense and relevance emerges from a reflexive engagement with the landscape while using the map; however, the eloquence of the notion "reflexivity" can just as easily become a distraction here, and we need to disavow speaking of reflexivity in a principled way. Garfinkel developed the topic of reflexivity during the 1960s in the course of undertaking several empirical studies, and during one ethnomethodology conference at UCLA in 1972 he celebrated its discovery and elucidation; but by 1977 he was reluctant to introduce the term whenever it could be used as an excuse to abandon deeper inquiry and description of the actual *in vivo* details of some affairs. He was irritated when it was introduced as a slogan that substituted for scrutinizing *just what* is taking place or when researchers introduced the term without including full description of some local details, and especially when the development of theoretical discourse about reflexivity was turned into a positive project of its own. Reflexivity is not to be talked *about*, it is to be discovered as worldly activity, as any ethnomethodologist who has tried to teach the phenomenon to students has quickly discovered; offering students an opportunity to follow sketched maps is a better pedagogy here. The fact that reflexivity, too, is capable of being turned into a discussion of generalities severed from a lived experience reveals the insidiousness of theorizing and the ease with which worldly inquiries can get distracted. So let me try to explain what is going on with sketched maps.

At first, the chicken scratches on a sketched map are barely intelligible (see the selection of sketched maps included in this chapter). One is not only unable to recognize what it is they signify, one is unable to distinguish just which components of the drawing are doing some signifying. One uses the map to interrogate the landscape and locates terrestrial candidates that might turn some marks on the map into signs that could be referring to them—and into the kind of thing that could serve as a sign in the first place. De Saussure has offered a semiotic theory in which a sign is made up of two components, a signifier and a signified, and he has keenly observed that there is not only a relation between the two (with the signified capable of isolating what is serving as a signifier) but also lateral relations among the signifieds and among the signifiers. That is, the things on a map that signify are part of a system that at first may not present clearly which marks are acting as particular units in the system and which ones are not. He speaks of the *differences* between phonemes as contributing to our being able to distinguish one phoneme from the other, thereby affording it the capacity to signify.

Saussure (1959:,118) writes, "The important thing in the word is not the word's sound alone but the phonic differences that make it possible to distinguish this word from all the others, for differences carry signification." Accordingly, it is not anything positive in a "p" sound in "pad" or a "b" sound in "bad" that allows them to signify different words; rather, it is the difference between them—the way that they differentiate themselves from each other—that distinguishes them as unique units. Saussure (1959, 119) observes that the actual character of a phonic unit, take "r" for example, is not as important as its difference from other phonic units ("l" for instance), and that in some languages it is inconsequential whether the "r" is dorsal, retroflex, or a tongue-tip trill. "Language requires only that the sound be different" from the other phonic units in that linguistic system. As soon as trills or retroflexion (as in Sanskrit or the Aboriginal languages of Australia) announce that they are separate phonic units that can be used for signifying other things, the pertinent differentiation is not simply with an "l" but also with the varieties of "r." Any free variation of the "r" will then begin to impinge upon the clarity of the signifying tools, and the utterances will become vulnerable to ambiguity and confusion. However, in cases of synonyms, or in cases like Latin American Spanish where the fricative "v" begins to impede upon the labial "b," the meaning itself can assist the listener to distinguish the signifying units.

Each language has its own unique body of phonemes that are capable of distinguishing themselves as elements that signify. For example, in Tibetan the sound "nga" can be uttered in three different tones (low, medium, and high) with each tone referring to a completely different signified (e.g. "*Nga la nga nga yoe*" means "I have five drums"). Only the differences of the tones mark each "nga" out as a distinct signifier. Once one recognizes this, one's ear begins to attend to the vast tonal field of Tibetan discourse, recognizing new "things" that must be related to signifieds; but the task is made easier by there being a worldly context with affairs that can be allocated to the emerging string of signifying elements, *and these signifieds assist one in parsing the phrase.* Like the map, gradually the locutions gain additional clarity and depth, and the semantic field provides us with information about the semiotic system itself.

The located sense and the signifiers are mutually determining. When a string of words is being uttered it can be extremely difficult for a non-native speaker, even one who has spent years studying a language by analyzing its grammar, to hear the phonic units. The readers of sketched maps are like non-native speakers. It can be "extremely difficult to disentangle the interplay of units that are found in a sound-chain and to specify the concrete elements on which a language functions" (Saussure 1959, 106). Apart from the sense, sounds by themselves do not readily yield predelimited entities, and the same is true for the notational marks on a sketched map. The units of sound are reciprocally delimited (phoneme contra phoneme) as they engage with a flow of thought, and the marks on a map (figure contra figure) are reciprocally delimited as they are used to collect terrestrial features. "Language works out its units while taking shape between two shapeless masses" (Saussure 1959, 112), the two shapeless masses being the sound-chain and the thought-chain, the signifiers and the signifieds. And each is used to progressively clarify the other.

Over the course of a journey, as one works from the landscape to the map and back, the notations of the sketched map become more clear and distinct and one comes to recognize that a given mark does indeed indicate something, even when one is not yet aware of just what that something might be. The terrain traveled helps us to parse the marks of the map, which gain integrity, and one comes to recognize a formerly indistinguishable mark that obliges us to search for something more. One learns to "read" the map even when what it is intended that one find is not obvious. Locating things in the landscape that can be matched with notations on the map informs us about what is and what is not a notation in the map: *the landscape* that we locate with the map *transforms the face of the map*, which gains an intelligibility, a depth of detail, and a clarity thereby. The landscape discovered with the map *reflexively* transforms the map which, so amended, can be used to locate more terrestrial details. By the time we reach our destination, the sketched map has become a deeply textured array, rich with advice—but an array that we had our hand in making. It is not a vicious circularity but a productive one. Garfinkel is fond of citing Merleau-Ponty's use of the notion of chiasm. In the "Working Notes" to his posthumously published *The Visible and the Invisible*, Merleau-Ponty (1968, 266) has noted, "The idea of *chiasm*, that is: every relation with being is simultaneously a taking and a being taken, the hold is held, it is inscribed, and inscribed in the same being it takes hold of."

Let us give this more definiteness by inspecting briefly some details of a way-finding expedition undertaken by a group of my students. The map, which is poorly drawn especially in the zone where these students find the most difficulty (see Map 2.1), has to contend with a district in which not every street crosses the thoroughfare; moreover, some of the streets are really alleys that have posted street names ("15th St. Alley"), and so it is difficult for the students to determine just what constitutes an intersection as depicted on the map.

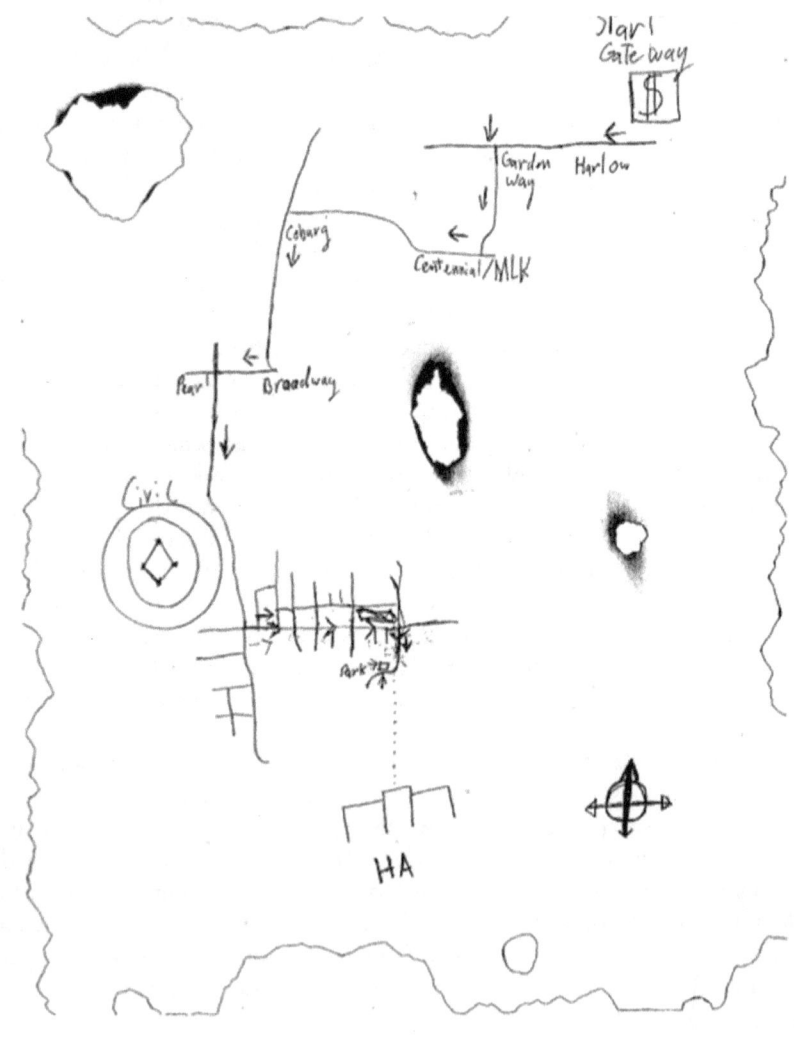

Map 2.1

Further, the two in the backseat of the car, who are reading the map, must communicate directions verbally to the driver and the videographer who are sitting in the front seat. Q uses the gloss "juncture" (line 2) to handle the fact that the map graphically indicates alleys as well as streets:

P: All right, very first left.

Q: First left, and then we have to count junctures, right?

M: Yes.

Q: Nine of them?

M: Si.

P: Junctures.

The use of the gloss is collaboratively confirmed by M's "Yes" at line 3 and by P's repeat at line 6; however, the local organization of the sense and reference of this term will not end there, since the emerging meaning of "juncture" in the terrestrial context will intrude upon the map, and so it is a term whose meaning will necessarily evolve. The travelers count the junctures on the map and confirm that they will need to turn right at the ninth juncture. As they travel along the thoroughfare, they notice some well-paved driveways that equal or exceed the alleys in substance, and since neither the alleys nor the paved driveways cross to the other side of the thoroughfare, the driver (B) wants to know how the gloss "juncture" should be applied:

B: Are we counting *these* as /junctures.

Q: /That is not a juncture.

P: All right, is this a juncture?

10   M: No, no. It doesn't count. I am looking at the map. That does not count as a /juncture.

Q: /No.

So the terrain, with the help of the map, is elaborating the sense of the group's glosses for the map notations, and as the landscape is defining the notations, the notations are read to witnessably exclude some terrestrial features and include others. In line 10, M derives some authority from the fact that he is looking at the map; however, any notion that the map could validate M's counsel independently of M's interpretation must be rejected (even though it is quite common to refer to "the map" or "the rules" as capable of serving as objective reference). The phenomenal details of the terrain are always developing, but since the map-readers (in the backseat) also face the problem of communicating verbally with the driver (in the front) they must keep concretizing publicly their changing contextual understanding of the map; that is, the need to communicate requires them to continuously make objective their observations.

> B: Are we counting driveways?
>
> P: Maybe. Maybe he [the person who drew the map] was counting /driveways.
>
> M: /No.
>
> P: Oh, one right here. Alright, number one.
>
> M: No, that's not a road.
>
> B: That's a road.

As the context changes, so does the potential sense of "juncture." We can witness the uncertainty of the gloss in line 13, where P is ready to remain open to any reading of it (and of the marks on the map it distinguishes) that may be necessary to provide for the map's coherency; however, M with the map in hand opts for restraining the sense of the term until such time as that proves unworkable, and he modifies the gloss by offering a new term, "road," to emphasize that the map has acquired some standards that need to be maintained. What is significant and reflexive in this case is that M is using the map, which has been transformed by the landscape that it found, to further interpret the terrain, a process that continues until a destination is reached. And this is so even when the party notices that the map-drawer has made a few minor errors. These errors (mostly on the left side of the thoroughfare, which by their convention was not included in their making the count of nine junctures) do not undermine the integrity of the map, if only because the map, while perhaps not the last word on the route they are taking, is the only word they have at hand. What guides them is the way the map can be used to witness the terrestrial traveling, not some map that stands as an authority that is independent of that witnessing. It is not the analytic map they are using: it is the way-finders' map.

As Garfinkel (1977a) has summarized the situation, "It's not that the map is correct in that certain ways of drawing it have consequences. It's quite the other way around. Its definiteness *consists* of its consequences." This would be to say that the notion

Map → Consequences

would have to be rewritten

Consequences → Map

or at least Map ←→ Consequences. The map acquires its cogency from what it collects. Maps suggest to people what to look for, and what they find permits them to arrange the orderliness of the map, which then is capable of providing them further assistance in how to scrutinize the landscape. As we will learn in chapter 8, the coffee flavor descriptor "blueberry" can be used to locate corresponding tastes that are objectively there in a cup of coffee that, once located, inform the taster about *just what* the descriptor "blueberry" really means; flavor descriptors gain their efficacy in this way, just as the notations on a map gain their sense and reference from what they find during the way-finding.

## CASE-STUDY: A WAY-FINDING JOURNEY

In order to better ground ourselves in some of the worldly practices of way-finding we will take up the details of another journey attempted by a party of my students. The group reported that their sketched map alternated between being completely ambiguous and having a sense that was readily available to them. They do not begin by following the map from the beginning; typically, route-finders do not start from the origin point. Instead, the party takes a shortcut that was made possible because the early portions of their route were familiar to them. This gave them a sense of confidence that they could find their way. As they drove they began to parse the map, which had a straight north-south line drawn through the middle of it, identified as "I-5," the Interstate Highway:

J: That's I-5.

A: Yeah, that's I-5.

P: That's I-5.

Their repetition displays to each other that the members of the traveling party understand something in common and know that they have understood it in common. It is interesting is that I-5 here travels northwest to southeast for a spell and has some curves that are not reflected in the perfectly straight line of the map (see Map 2.2); nevertheless their organization of the map facilitates their traverse of the left half of the map; however, it is the right half where their troubles occur. After crossing under the Interstate, they approach a stop sign, and the driver (J) asks a question:

J: Left or right?

A: Take D-E for half a mile.

P: D-E?

J: D-E?

A: Yeah.

5) Take 1st R road after passing over I-5
6) Take 1st RD to East.
7) Turn South on Aspen.
8) Take D-E for around a ½ mi.
9) Go R on Water
10) Park and go to the Park
11) Walk through the park, past the playground, up the road to the "Contax" building.
12) Go down trail on E side of the building
☆ the little waterfalls are your finish

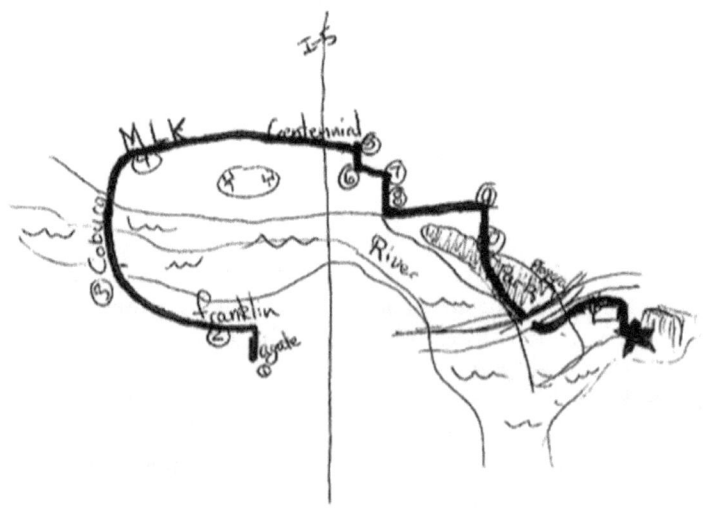

Map 2.2

It is not certain to them just what "D-E" could mean, and A's gratuitous concurrence does not offer any clarity. The ambiguity does not disturb A in the least, but it leaves them at an aporia, which is disturbing for the driver as he approaches the spot where he must make a decision.

    J:   What? What?

10  A:  It says, take D-E.

    J:   I don't know what your talking/

    A:                              /Take D-E.

    J:   [Car stops at stop sign.] What do you, oh wait, D!

Having reached the stop sign (line 13), the party is offered a chance to more calmly inspect the terrain, and J has located a street that is named "D." However, that still leaves the "E" to be explained. A offers an explanation, but J is not convinced:

    A:   So wait, "D-E" would be D-east.

    J:   Uhh, D.

    P:   Yeah.

    J:   But there is no D-east. In fact, that's "West D."

Next, A offers an interpretation to satisfy J's doubt, but P at first does not find it to be satisfactory until they collaboratively and publicly work out their interpretation:

    A:   But if we turn that way won't we be necessarily going east?

    P:   But that [the mark on the map] is not necessarily east, though.
20       It's just an "E" with a star next to it and a box around it. He wrote out the "east" for the one before that.

    J:   That's "West."

    P:   Oh wait, later there's another "E" with a box around it meaning east, so this must be east too. Yeah.

    J:   East on West D?

    P:   "D-east."

They are facing some confusion because of the fact that by having taken I-5 as true north and south, what should be true east on the map is not true east in the terrain. There is further confusion because there is an inconsistency in how the drawer of the map has represented "east," first by spelling it out [instruction number 6 on Map 2.2] and then placing a box around it [see instruction number 8]. There is an additional problem of how to interpret the asterisk [E*] next to the "E," a matter *that is never resolved*. It is not a bit unusual for route-finding to present map readers with dilemmas that never get resolved. But P, the map-holder, notices that there is another "E"-with-a-box-around-it at instruction 12 where it clearly means "east," and this becomes the clue that affords them a way to understand the "E*"-with-a-box-around-it that perplexes them. A common feature of map reading is that maps will elucidate their own conventions,[1] and some consistency in the drawer's practice is assumed. The lack of consistency here only adds to their difficulties,[2] and they end up less than confident as they continue their way traveling generally east on West D. The group reported to me, "E with a star next to it could mean anything, especially since the map creator has elsewhere already written out 'east'" Ultimately, West D has become "D-East." Mapmakers, both lay and professional, are unable to anticipate the many possible ambiguities that their instructions will inevitably suggest.

The travelers are next confronted with a new ambiguity when they reach the point where they must go right on "Water":

J: It looks like the river.

A: I think so.

J: Alright, so half-a-mile-ish?

30  A: -ish.

J: Whatever that is.

P: And right on water.

J: Water is a street?

P: We don't know. It must be a street.

J: Okay.

A: Yeah, it's the river.

Here P displays a healthy open-mindedness about ways that the map can be read; however, it turns out that "Water" is both the name of the street and refers to the river. The group reports that their finding the river, which was the next orientational reference point after West D Street, helped to *retroactively confirm* that they had successfully navigated the previous difficult directional reference point at D-E*. Just as in intercultural communication one portion of an utterance can be used to restrict the sense of another portion that could otherwise bear two possible interpretations, here the later directional location serves to clarify their reading of a previous directional point.

They locate one more confirming detail when they spy the street sign that reads "Water St.":

> P: It says right on water.
>
> J: Alrighty, "Water" it is.
>
> P: "Water Street."
>
> 40 J: And we just park?
>
> P: Park near the park.
>
> A: Is that the park with the green thing?
>
> J: I guess so.

Although they find Water Street, the group reports that they had little confidence that they had arrived at the correct location. Route-finding typically occurs amidst indeterminacies that are natural to the occasion. The final part of their journey is made on foot: they are to find a "trail" on the "E" side of a building and go to the little "waterfalls" that is their destination. Their problem is that there are a number of footpaths, so it is not obvious to them which one is the "trail." Moreover, they don't see or hear any "waterfall;" in fact, it is only a small cascade and not a waterfall properly speaking:

> J: Maybe that trail, is that a trail?
>
> P: Uh huh. The waterfall is what we have to eventually get to, right?
>
> J: Oh yeah.
>
> A: There.
>
> J: Go down "the east side of the building to the little waterfalls."
>
> 50 P: Oh. East side of the building.
>
> J: Hey, maybe this is it.

In any semiotic system, the signs will function in a coordinated way. While one determinate element is able to restrict the semantic field of an indeterminate element, when *both* elements *are indeterminate*, the potential solutions increase geometrically. In this case, they are confronted with two indeterminate elements—a "trail" that is not obvious amidst a variety of footpaths, and a waterfall that is not really a "waterfall." They report: "At first, we were unsure whether or not the trail off the side of the building was the right one. After coming upon the Contax building [see instruction 11], the location of the trail seemed difficult to find. We weren't sure whether or not the map was referring to a trail leading off the side of the building, which would have required us to step onto Contax building property or another trail entirely." But as they reached the cascade, the notation "little" in "little waterfall" loomed larger for them than it had at first (it had previously been overshadowed by the idea of "waterfall"), and they decided that they had in fact reached their destination, which retrospectively rendered the path that they took the "trail." It was the tangible discovery and experience of the cascade that gave the way-finders the confidence that they had understood the previous directions, rather than any formal analysis of the map's representations. They never once reconsidered what the asterisk in "D-E*" was meant to signify, which they left behind along with other ambiguities of their journey. The analytic features of the map were not their interest.

WAY-FINDING AS A PRACTICAL DISCIPLINE

With this case study in hand, let us examine more closely some of the components of following sketched maps.

*Confidence*

Garfinkel (2002, 179) describes the confidence of a driver setting out on a way-finding journey: "The driver 'remembered' the instructions he had been given. It didn't make any difference that he forgot whether it was *one* street name or *another* street name. He was more or less confidently on the way." Here the phrase "more or less" is an accurate description of this confidence, since in way-finding journeys it commences by being "more" confident, and then becomes "less" so as the typical journey proceeds. Most of the expedition that Garfinkel describes was a struggle with being lost. Of *just what* does the confidence of the way-finder consist when it is built upon so rickety a framework? Part of the dynamic can be attributed to the nature of the face-to-face social interaction between the person giving the directions and the one following them, where the recipient may feel obligated to gratuitously grant to the direction-giver that the directions are clear. When a direction-giver declares, "Ya really can't miss it" (Psathas 1986a, 235), the recipient may develop a false sense of confidence, or at least will have some reluctance to interrogate the direction-giver about uncertainties that remain. For the sake of social harmony, a recipient may reassure the direction-giver by saying, "Oh, that sounds easy" (Psathas 1991, 212); but what "sounds easy" is hardly ever quite so easy once the route-finder's journey is actually underway. Here the parties may only be collaborating in some self-deception:

> Direction-giver: We're half a mile from the exit at the most, it's very easy to find.
>
> Direction-recipient: Okay, I'll find it. (Psathas 1988, 4)

There is a ubiquitous confidence that recipients have about directions, perhaps deluded by the confidence of the direction-giver, but it is a confidence that fades the moment the direction-giver is no longer present. It is not unusual that after only a dozen steps further down the block the certainty of the recipient will turn into vapors.[3]

But even when there is no direction-giver present and one has only the sketched map, frequently the map-follower experiences some confidence, so there is more to this phenomenon than social pressure. A docile map lends itself to anything that the map-reader can make of it when there is no one and nothing to contest the point. These initial readings are almost always superficial and full of themselves, with little corroborating data. Only the brute demands of the journeying throw the confidence under the bus. The coherence that a sketched map will come to have is rarely the coherence that readers grasp at the outset when they first take hold of "these endless, inexhaustibly coherent details making up the facticity of the map accountably available as, 'Okay, we've got it. We're on the way'" (Garfinkel 2002, 180). However, what is critical for the way-finders is that they get on their way.

*Getting on the Map*

One of the important early tasks of map reading is "getting on the map" (Garfinkel 1996). Map-readers rarely commence at the origin point of a sketched map; instead, they usually scrutinize locations on the map in order to locate a landmark they recognize, thereby omitting some of the more tedious sections of the route-finding. As one group of students reported, "David is looking beyond where the directions begin and focuses on where they lead." It is a kind of search for a global solution to the route-finding, in which the route-follower does not have to proceed slavishly step-by-step but can simultaneously be scanning the directions for ways to make shorter work of the task. Following a map is not like a decision-making algorithm, and the tactic of moving directly to a recognized feature is a sound one, provided that the map reader can *preserve the directionality* of the location found, since its directionality may be difficult to recover when the site is approached from a direction other than the one presumed by the mapmaker. A landmark does not anchor a sketched map so much as it anchors the horizon of the driving that accompanies the landmark, and missing a landmark's directionality in just the way that the direction-giver intended may complicate the route-following. Psathas (1986, 239) describes the tactic of globally interrogating the map: "By virtue of this maneuver, the direction giver can 'jump' from any previous last mentioned places *to* the [known] place." Some maps do not even indicate clearly where a starting point is, and frequently the more obvious "jumps" are worked into the directions already; however, they carry a risk of segmenting the directions in ways that can get a follower lost. Some maps are drawn on a presumption that a landmark or street is so well known that it is unnecessary to provide elucidating information. In one case, a way-finder begins to complain about the lack of literal-mindedness of the map's drawer, but he is dissuaded from his criticism by his fellow traveler who was considerably more attentive to how indeterminacy can be compatible with route-finding:

P:  He didn't write out instructions from the start.

A:  Well maybe he figures everybody knows where that is.

No matter how they find themselves on their way, getting on the map becomes a critical task.

*Staying on the Map*

A second task of way-finders is *staying* on the map, which involves soliciting from the map a "next" point that must be located. The drivers on my students' videotapes could be heard providing a chorus of "What is the next turn?" The orderliness of the map, which is not available in the map in-itself, not even in a cartographers' map, consists of identifying in the map a sequence of particulars that is composed of one "next" after another "next" ("a route as a set of next events," Garfinkel 1977a—perhaps a golf course on the right, a school on the left, etc.). One's task becomes finding these particulars in their sequential order, and this orderliness is termed by Garfinkel (1977a) "the sequential organization of the journey's events" and is something mostly provided by the map user: the sequential components have a *definiteness* of sense "only and entirely in the way in which they're situated in the action." The heart of the way-finding competence here is to connect the "sequential particulars" (Psathas 1979, 224) given in the directions into a directional sequence, i.e., into the "nexts" that will compose the route. Having a particular sequence of travel is essential to keeping the map organized.

The map-readers continually monitor the map and landscape for each "next" that will preserve the directionality of their route; the map directions have a direction. Each "next" landmark certifies the correctness of the route-follower's reading of the previous landmark, a reading whose certainty is not really complete until it has carried the follower to a "next." Psathas (1987, 101) observes, "The appearance of the second landmark retrospectively furnishes the first or prior landmark its property of having been prior to the 'next.'" If the "next" landmark is not found, it may put into question the operative interpretation of an ensemble of landmarks. Until a "next" landmark can be located, readers may lose confidence in their understanding of the directions or in the direction-giver's competence, or both. Once the reader is following a *pathway*, the reader is directionally oriented, an orientation that informs each of the notations on the map and is essential for finding and recognizing the places that "correspond" to the map's notations. So *finding each "next" becomes an important task*. As parties of map-followers reported, "We constantly read the street signs to see if they matched what was drawn on the map;" and, "We know we are on the right track because we are finding all the landmarks on the map."

Commercial street maps lack this directionality or any conventionality of usage, and in order to be used effectively map-readers must provide the directionality along with their readings. Indication of the well-traveled thoroughfares may be more clear on a sketched map than on a cartographic map, which is why cartographic maps sometimes introduce as many problems as they resolve. An important feature of pathways is that they compose an important part of the practical, everyday organization of the city's navigable spaces (Psathas 1976, 121), and every city's navigators are familiar with the conventional routes for finding one's way less painfully through the usual congestion and street organization. That is, a city is not composed simply of streets and landmarks, but of courses-through-districts or "thoroughfares."

When way-finders do use a cartographic map, it is necessary for them to reconstrue the map into a pathway, into a directional series of "nexts," by scanning the map for directional or orientational points (a post office here, a park there; "three streets after the cemetery there will be a left turn"). Sketched maps feature both *directional reference points* and *orientational reference points*. Directional reference points are "places at which one is to turn and proceed in a different direction" (Psathas 1988, 5), that is, they are not just places but a change in directions. And orientational reference points are "nexts" that are helpful for reassuring the way-finders that they are on the right path. Cartographic maps level out all experience, even "passing over in silence the decisive moment in perception" (Merleau-Ponty 1962, 53). Travelers using these maps must "return to the world of actual experience which is prior to the objective world" (Merleau-Ponty 1962, 57) and reconstrue some of the points on the map as directional pathways, worldly things that are rarely apparent on commercial maps.

In these ways "the directions" include not only streets and landmarks but a direction, and on sketched maps "roads or pathways are depicted as 'already in progress'" (Psathas 1979, 209). Naturally, the drawer of a sketched map cannot present each and every pathway, so a reduced selection is inevitable; but readers understand that, which is why they give some scope for the map designer's ways before becoming critical about them. A reader or directions-recipient will frequently assume that the map designer's selection reflects some familiar knowledge about which route is the easiest one. Psathas (1979, 218) comments, "[Paths] noted are noted as the ones *to take* and these set the ones *not* noted into the background," and sometimes this can lead to the map readers making unwarranted judgments about the routes indicated. They may not assume or insist that the pathways indicated be the fastest ones, but they usually expect that they will be the simplest ones, and when map-followers themselves discover a pathway that is simpler than the route provided by the map's maker, they may feel a sense of betrayal.

Of course the landmarks one sees while traveling do not bear these orientational distinctions on their rooftops; instead, these distinctions are provided by the reading of the map while way-finding. One is compelled to always be searching for the next "next" as a method for continuously monitoring one's way. If one becomes too myopic, either in reading the map or in scrutinizing the landscape, one may find oneself not knowing where to look or where one is with respect to any given "next" that is ahead, and defining that "ahead" and its distance can become a problem. Analytic accounts of route-finding do not address this—they cannot even recognize what is really happening in terms of a phenomenal field or what the way-finders' problems really consist of. An analytic rationalization of the journey can sometimes make it seem that the analysts must be examining matters with field binoculars that are turned the wrong way around. The perspective in play is exclusively the analyst's perspective, and the journeyers' perspective is missing-in-action.

How would an analytic account of traveling gain access to this not uncommon experience reported on camera by one of the groups in the course of their way-finding adventure: "We think we are going the right way when we are actually going the opposite direction of where the map is supposed to lead us . . . The mapmaker said it was 'in the middle of nowhere,' so we thought we were on the right track when we were not." Would turning the map upside down solve the problem? What interrogation of the map could reveal a solution? The most common way-finders' method in such situations is not to engage in reasoning about the features of the map's construction—that will only lead them further astray by "the placing of spirit into an axiological dimension having no common measure with nature" (Merleau-Ponty 1962, 56). Their preferred method is to go back and retrace their steps. *This is done in order to recover an embodied sense of the horizon*, and to pick up the fringe meanings of what the map might have been suggesting at that last moment when they knew where they were. One of the principal discoveries of my investigations of following sketched maps is that *more thinking* rarely provides travelers the solutions to their way-finding problems; instead, the way-finders resort to placing themselves *embodiedly* into the horizonal perspective of the journeying and take their leads from there. Way-finders keep relocating themselves on the sketched map (again and again, sometimes more than seems necessary) in order to regain and retain an embodied sense of the looks of the journeying, that is, to "restore to things their concrete physiognomy" (Merleau-Ponty 1962, 57). When the reading becomes too calculative and deductive, the journeyers become carried away with analytic structures, further removing their bodies from the scene. In this fashion thinking can get in their way, something that thinking is prone to do.[4]

## THE NONCALCULABILITY OF WAY-FINDING

Most solutions to problems with following sketched maps are not the result of determinate, deliberate calculations. As we witnessed in our case study, the party's solution resulted from two indeterminate features (the "trail" and the "waterfall") mutually determining each other to the extent that enough certainty was reached to render the way-finders' practical decision regarding the equally ambiguous "Take D-E*" the right decision after all. The resolution of that journeying was more serendipitous than it was formally reasoned, and much of the success rested in the journeyers' remarkable ability to keep proceeding in the midst of persistent ambiguities in the route they were traveling. Each territorial detail did not by itself bear inside it its reality but found its intelligibility as part of a larger complex of orientational markers, whose sense kept emerging as a phenomenal field. The landscape gradually became populated with pathways and landmarks, "territorial objects [that] are observed as a phenomenal field of *ordered* details" (Garfinkel 1996). The phenomenal field is "this immediately present world, the only one we know" (Merleau-Ponty 1962, 59), and is first described by Merleau-Ponty in a chapter by that name in his *Phenomenology of Perception*, a book considered seminal by most ethnomethodologists. Merleau-Ponty (1962, 61) illustrates the notion by offering the contrast between the circle of the geometrical analyst and the circle as it is experienced: "The Gestalt of a circle is not its mathematical law but its physiognomy," and he emphasizes (1962, 59) that "The phenomenal field is not an 'inner world,' the 'phenomenon' is not a 'mental fact,' and the experience of phenomena is not an act of introspection or an intuition." Accordingly, the phenomenal field is neither an objectivist naturalism nor a variety of subjectivist constituting of things; instead, "Perception presents the object," and if there is a rational tradition it is one that arises from what perception presents.

In the epigraph to this chapter, the American poet Ezra Pound (1970, 324) writes,

> periplum, not as land looks on a map
> but as sea bord seen by men sailing.

This is Pound's way of insisting that some seventeenth-century Chinese sailors had an efficacious method for navigating the seas by knowing how to read the way rather than by depending upon abstract maps, a topic that Garfinkel took up after reading the ethnographic accounts of David Lewis, Edwin Hutchins, and Geoffrey White about Polynesian sea navigation.[5] The neologism of "periplum" was Pound's way to name how sailors operate with an embodied grasp of the surrounding terrain; and it is this intelligence that composes these navigators' expertise, an expertise that cannot be reduced to formal knowledge.

Merleau-Ponty (1962, 61) elucidates the notion of *field*: "This word indicates that reflection never holds, arrayed and objectified before its gaze, the whole world and . . . that its view is never other than partial and of limited power." The expertise at work here is always practical, is rarely clear and distinct, and will be deceived by any proliferation of abstractions that becomes too divorced from the phenomenal field. On many occasions when my students began to over-think their problem, they lost contact with the phenomenal field for a time and were only able to make progress again when they set aside their abstract examination. This was usually when they decided to retrace their steps until they could find again a place where they had an embodied grasp of the terrain. This is similar to what persons in intercultural conversations do when they become confused—they return to a phrase where there was some adequacy of communication and keep repeating the phrase until they can relocate and reestablish their bearings. This helps the interlocutors to recover the phenomenal field of the conversation. Rarely do problems of communication in conversations get resolved by the parties formally analyzing the logic of their discourse.[6]

The territory that the parties operate with is an empirical one, but most social researchers today misunderstand what is "empirical." The empirical realm is not a subjectivity-starved plenum. Perception presents humans with real objects. What some researchers define as empirical are situations that are reduced exclusively to what their analytic methods are able to distinguish. With some contemporary methodologies the scope of human experience gets leveled off to the lowest common denominator that is capable of being measured. Reality is segmented, and each segment is reinterpreted by the theorizing, to the point that phenomena are able to bear *only* an analytic sense that substitutes for its actual, phenomenal sense; then that reinterpretation, or reduction, is offered up as an "empirical" finding. How odd it is that what is empirical comes to be only those things that can trace their origin to what was in the researchers' heads! As Merleau-Ponty (1968, 268) keenly observed in one of his final working notes, "Every analysis that disentangles renders unintelligible." It is unintelligible because the lived world is no longer in sight.

*Waiting*

The noncalculability of sketched maps is particularly evident at the start of a journey when the way-finders decide to set out *before* clearly grasping the orderliness of the map. Much as is the case with the players of games, way-finders set out happily, and not unlike The Fool of the Tarot deck they are confident while knowing very little. A reason for this is that directions do not make sense until one gets to the point where one is actively using them; moreover, the sense they have is a sense that is organized by the way-finders. Brown and Laurier (2005) include in their transcripts of following sketched maps a way-finder who resolves a dilemma by saying, "Ah well. Let's just drive, see what happens." There is a kinship between the way-finders who say "Let's just drive," and the game-players who frequently say "Let's just play." The mundane world is lived *before* it is analyzed. There is a role for formal analysis to be sure, but *just what* that role is must be made a topic for further ethnomethodological investigations and not simply assumed by a preferred cultural mythology about reason.

One group of travelers were confronted with a portion of their sketched map that contained a squiggly line ["Marcola Rd." on Map 2.3], and they were uncertain about its intent. Their solution was to wait until they reach that part of the route, which will then become what squiggliness means: "I think we'll figure it out once we get down there." The waiting that is introduced thereby sets up a method of route-finding in which the parties do not expect or insist upon knowing just where they are at all times. They are able to sustain searching while having something less than analytic clarity. It might be said that way-finders spend more time following passively than they do deliberately planning their route.

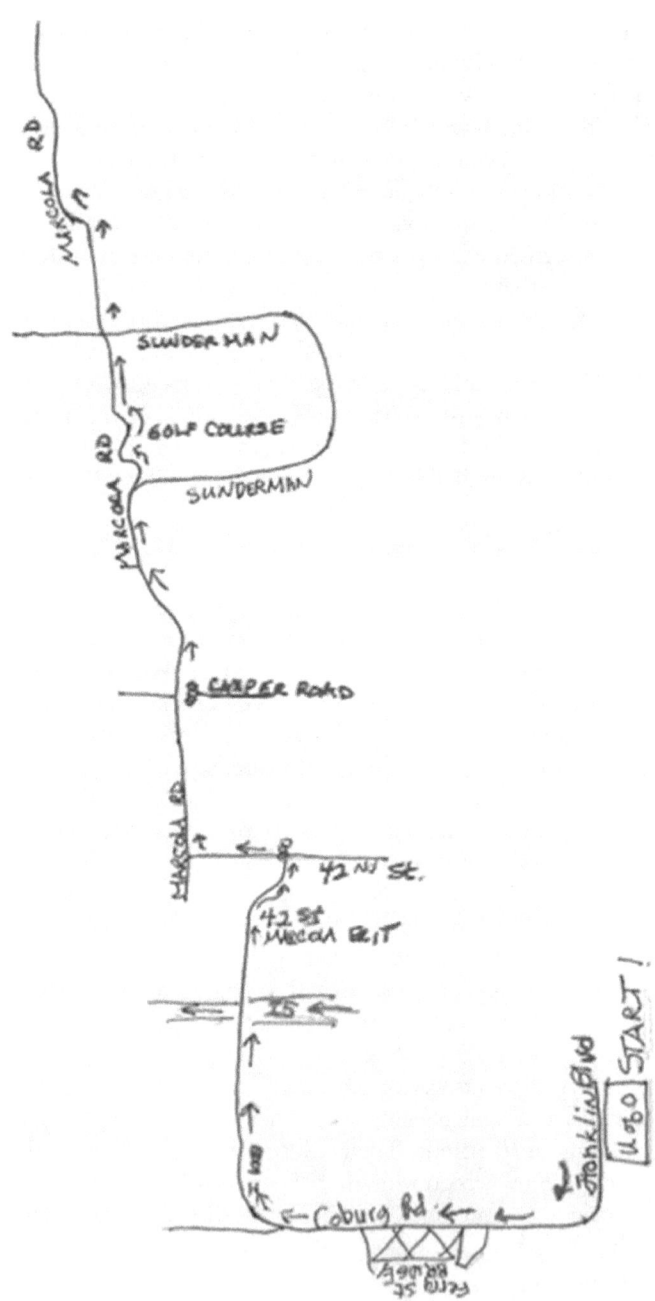

Map 2.3

## Thinking Amidst Ambiguities

A sketched map consists of a selection of undecidable indicators that become clarified only over the course of the journey and gain definiteness only when the destination is reached. This is not the definiteness to which formal analysts are accustomed. These maps are filled with conventions that are yet to be deciphered—things like arrows, dotted lines, a sweeping arc, etc.—and yet way-finders are not deterred. If they were deterred, few journeys would be attempted. In a medium-sized California city off of Interstate 5, I was given a brief sketched map with the directions to the local library: "Go Right—Follow Lane to Left" it said. I had no idea how that "right" would be relatable to that "left," but I headed off quickly into traffic again, eager not to miss the green light before it changed. When I reached a Y-junction, I became paralyzed, since there was no sufficient time there in the congestion of traffic that knew where it was heading for me to resolve the problem analytically; so I simply followed the bulk of the traffic flow. I went to the right and discovered that the entire right side of the boulevard made a sharp left turn shortly after the Y-junction. It seemed to me that the directional problem solved itself.

Curves are interesting features since there is no way that a map, even a cartographer's map, could encode reliable information about the number and severity of the curves that a single arc on a map could be made to bear. We have witnessed how even a straight line on a sketched map can disguise a curve. A veer to the right and a veer to the left will end up being "straight," so the veering can be considered to reside inside the straight line; its straightness results from the fact that it is impossible *not* to veer left and right. One way-finder complained on the videotape: "You'd think that with all the curves in this road, the line on the map would not be straight." Moreover, a single bend on a sketched map can turn out to be a very winding section of road. While one may be surprised by it, it is a simple matter to retrospectively reinterpret the single arc to be a reasonable indicator for that state of affairs. But such reasonableness can also lead one to convince oneself that a convenient but erroneous reading is correct. In just this fashion, maps can gain some cogency that they do not necessarily deserve, and not infrequently the map-readers must readjust their understandings and interpretations as earlier coherences come apart. This is not the exception, but is typical.

There is a great deal of information that a sketch map is unable to indicate: "That there are other paths which may intersect, crossover, under, parallel, merge, or whatever is not noted in each and every case" (Psathas 1979, 209), so the way-finders come to accept the unexpected and do not always become troubled when their pathway is less than distinct. Whether it says so or not, a sketched map is not drawn to scale, and "the warning that 'this is not to scale' does not even come close to saying what the map is not" (Psathas 1979, 218). This necessarily leaves gaps and incongruities, the very existence of which encourages followers to postpone the doubts they may have regarding the adequacy of the directions. Some of the incongruities and inconsistencies that recipients overlook are errors in the cardinal directions, conspicuous absences, and disconnected pathways. As we witnessed in our case study, in a region where all the major highways run north and south, a map-drawer may write "north" for a direction that is actually northwest, overlooking the fact that for a short distance the highway makes a bend in a certain sector. Accordingly, map-recipients will attempt a reasonable guess and do not fault the direction-giver for every mistake. One direction-giver studied by Psathas (1976, 115) warned the recipient, "Well you could call it south but everybody calls it east," a case where the incorrect cardinal direction had become an objective local practice, to which the direction-giver is simply conforming.

Absences or lacunae on a map can include missing street signs where an important directional reference point is located, a one-way street that interferes with the supposed route, or street-name changes that may be unknown or considered irrelevant by the direction-giver (after all, there is an infinity of detail that could be provided, and an explanation must cease at some point). There are occasionally times where every one of the location guides on a sketched map can become unclear, but even then the travelers make their way with them since those ambiguities are the only things they have to work with. Brown and Laurier (2005) cite a story written about a small Hungarian detachment of troops in the Alps that had become lost in a snowstorm. They had considered themselves lost "and waited for the end. And then one of us found a map in his pocket. That calmed us down." When the unit arrived back in camp three days later their worried lieutenant examined their map and discovered that "It was not a map of the Alps but of the Pyrenees." Somehow the troops had been able to read the landscape into their map and thereby find their way home. What more than analytical map reading could have been operative?

*"How Far?"*

Another often heard refrain on my tapes was the question, "How far are we supposed to travel?" While a sketched map may indicate a next "next," the lack of scale of the map makes it uncertain just how long it will be before that next "next" will be encountered and just where "too far" might be located.

A: I still don't see a fire station.

B: We still have a ways to go.

A: It's funny how we think we have a ways to go.

C: Yeah, like we have no scale.

The logic of the "nexts" can become quite complicated when one finds oneself in a spot where one is unsure whether the sought for orientational location point is ahead of one or behind. It may happen that a succeeding orientational point will be reached that will render the problem of the lost location point moot. Way-finders may give the mapmaker (and themselves) the benefit of the doubt, and keep moving the "next" orientational point further into the distance ahead, only to find that what was assumed to be ahead of them will suddenly need to be shifted to the rear, presenting them with some practical problems for how they have become accustomed to orienting themselves to the landscape with the map. What is valuable about these investigations is that they afford abundant opportunities to undertake social phenomenological analyses that are *not static* but are able to witness *the working of ongoing doings* over-their-course, lending to the study of knowing a dynamic quality that better reflects what actually takes place.

Here is part of an account of a videotape of some *in vivo* way-finding in which the way-finders find themselves having lost their direction:

> The group continues driving not knowing where we are headed . . . At 19:58 the entire group is telling M. to go forward on what turned out to be the wrong road. . . . At 22:37 we now have proceeded about 3 miles in the wrong direction and J states that we are not going the wrong way, but she is not completely certain. At 23:50 we have gone 5 miles in the wrong direction, and still no one is suggesting we should turn around. At 24:34 M. finally turns around.

How many times have you decided to turn around, done so, only to learn that you turned around too soon? One can get vertigo from this sort of repetitive back-tracking; not only this, but the natural inclination to follow a direction rather than actively determine each step one step at a time can work against an early decision to turn around. Sketched maps like these, which may for a time seem clear on their face can become for a recipient one aporia after another.

## INTERPRETING THE DRAWER'S INTENTIONS

Part of the ambiguity of following a sketched map is that the way-finders are not simply directly applying the notations on the map but must keep accounting for several possibilities at once for what the mapmaker might have really meant by the notations used. The authors of these maps are not traffic engineers, and their notations depend upon the many horizonal features that compose the maker's orientation; therefore, it is necessary for a map-reader to recover some of those horizontal perspectives that sit at the fringes of the mapmaker's understanding of a route. On an occasion where a group found themselves wondering whether they had driven past a key directional location point, one of the travelers asked, "How far would John send us this way?" In this fashion the drawer's motives, orientation, perspectives, etc. are always being constructed in a sort of documentary method of interpretation[7] and figured into their map-reading.

A colleague and I once found ourselves following a sketched map (Map 2.4) from Trento to a location on the outskirts of Verona, Italy. The directions were "Take the Autostrada to Verona, turn right onto the Autostrada to Brescia, and take the first exit." However, the first right turn led

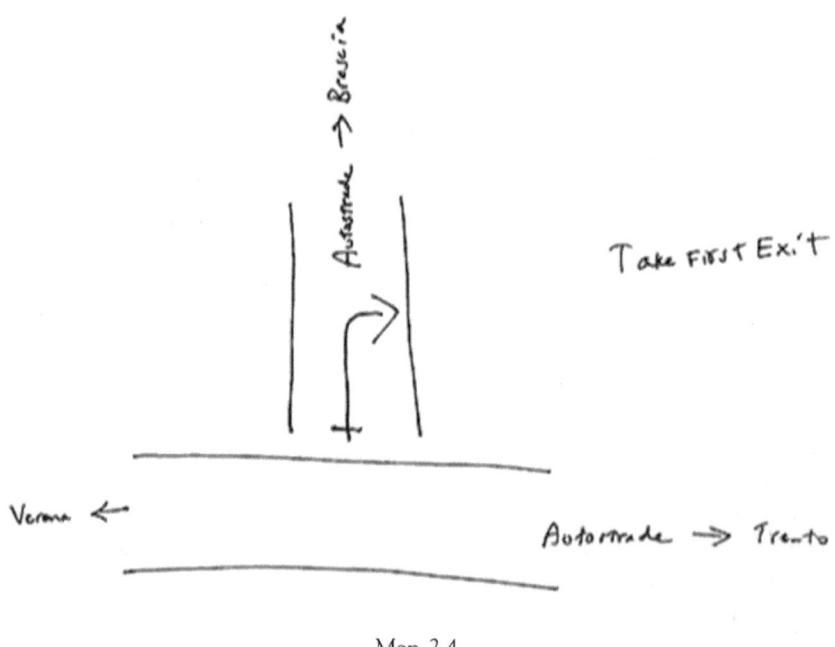

Map 2.4

us onto an access road that itself led into a highway maintenance yard, so we at once reinterpreted the words to mean our mapmaker's "first exit" and not the actual first exit. The correct exit proved to be the second exit. Reinterpretations of the drawer's intentions like this are common when using sketched maps. The correct turn turned out to be the second exit.

Another set of directions said to turn "left" at Franklin Blvd., but the emerging sense of the way-finding seemed to indicate that a right turn was what was sensible, so "We figured it was a mistake and disregarded it." One map to a distant picnic relied heavily upon highway mileage posts for orientational location markers. When the name of one of the roads bore a question mark, it became necessary for the way-finders to interpret the sense of the question mark. Did it mean that the one who drew it was uncertain of the precise name of the road, or that she was unsure of which mileage post was adjacent? After they had been traveling a considerable distance and had still not reached a park that was indicated on the map, they reinterpreted the question mark to apply globally to that entire section of the map, something that was not likely. We freely employ our capacity to tweak the particulars we have in hand into an interpretation that can be made to seem reasonable. Given this capacity, along with how our interpretations can be projected into the documents at hand, lending them the intelligibility they come to bear, sometimes we find ourselves following pathways of our own invention, pathways that keep revealing their correctness like a self-fulfilling prophesy, right up to the point where we become lost. One driver asked the rest of the group whether the map-reader had the map upside down because it seemed that everything was backwards. Her partner replied that everything was alright, "The person just drew it wrong." One way not to reach the destination is to hang on too tenaciously to one's perspectives, and so any flexibility of the hermeneutic practices of way-finders can be salutary.

What is the sense to be made of the selection of possible roads that a drawer has chosen to include? And how are omissions to be understood? "Although there were other significant landmarks between Sunderman Road and the Fire Station, the map creator did not include them." Another mapmaker included only one of two existing exits to a destination; was it the intention that the one included is better, or did the drawer only know about one? When a turn connecting one part of the route to another is not included on a map, one might think that the drawer forgot the turn, considers it such a simple matter that no one could become lost there, that the drawer is incompetent after all, or perhaps think that not making any turn at such an equivocal point is the intention, according to the rule, "The absence of a point, expressed or implied, *at* which direction will change does indicate, however, that a 'straight' course is to be followed" (Psathas 1976, 124). What is reasonable keeps shifting.

Many difficulties occur because despite a direction-giver's expertise with a route, he or she may lack the most critical expertise: the looks of the route for novices. "As a competent member able to locate his own home, the explication of the procedures followed in the process of locating it is a task not regularly undertaken" (Psathas 1979, 219), and so the map-readers may be unable to find in the map the looks of the world they have. A person accustomed to finding his or her home as a matter of habit week after week, year after year, may be the last person who should be consulted to offer directions for a novice seeking to find the location for the very first time. I once prepared a sketch map for people finding their way to my mountain cabin, and I drew a large bridge at the only point where three creeks come together at a confluence; the map included the direction "Turn left just before the large cement bridge." More than one party reported to me upon arriving at my cabin that they held debates about what was "a bridge" at each culvert and creek overpass the county's road builders had constructed. When I scolded them that none of those locations were adjacent to three creeks, I was informed by one that they didn't know how to tell a river from a creek and by another that they were unaware of more than one river.

Signaled intersections, where it is possible to turn right or left, are left off of many maps when no turn is required. It may be presumed that straight ahead is the intended instruction, but this interpretation may be doubted when the lane one is in turns into a left-turn lane and the majority of the traffic flow begins to move to the left. When the car behind honks when one does not make the turn (and instead of turning left, one considers merging into the lane to one's right), one can find oneself without a clue, wondering why the person did not draw *that* signal. The person who drew the map did not anticipate the potential local crisis (a problem that only occurs during the five o'clock rush hour), *nor can the map be consulted to solve it,* at least not without causing an accident.

A map-in-use produces its own organizational principles, which are always in the process of emerging, and map-readers do have some expectation that a map will remain consistent at least with its own standards and conventions. Just as a map that skips the details between one "next" and the subsequent "next" will be given wide latitude when judging "how far" it can be to the next "next," so will maps that provide scrupulous details, like the one that included intricately drawn traffic signals at each corner that has stoplights, be expected to include some indication for each intersection that has a traffic light. Only after the party of way-finders following the latter sketched map found their way to a subsequent part of the map where the drawer's standards became lax, was a critical left-turn missed where there was a traffic light but where none was suspected because there was no drawing of a stoplight there. But even inconsistency can become a principle, and once one inconsistency is demonstrated, then inconsistencies can be worked into the reading of the map's organization and become a standard by which a map is read. Way-finders' skills are remarkable, once they are identified.

One group reported that their trust in the person who drew the map kept waxing and waning. The protean nature of these sketched maps is one of their ubiquitous characteristics.[8] A second group wrote, "Trust came into question, and we shifted the idea of the map from a dependable document to placing more emphasis upon our interpretation." And still another group that had become "a little worried that maybe we weren't going the right way" discovered that these worries began to infect every part of their reading to the extent that their way-finding began to get away from them, a problem they blamed exclusively on "the map itself" and not to any reading of the map that they had provided. The way that people usually are unaware of their own hand in the production of the ordinary world is a common aspect of social affairs.[9]

## THE PROTEAN NATURE OF SKETCHED MAPS

The coherence that a sketched map has is peculiar in that it keeps shifting over the course of the journey. This coherence is continuously provided by the map-reader and must be flexible and protean in order to keep being relevant for the emerging details of the route events that occur during a journey. No aspect of the worldly tasks that make up way-finding better identifies the work of following a map than the task of continuously transforming the coherence of the map itself; taming these transformations while remaining alert for the need for further changes to the map's intelligibility is a central interest for ethnomethodological investigations of way-finding. One group following a sketched map reported as follows: "The journey would morph after each single event. . . . The map indicated that Interstate-5 at one point took a sharp left turn. Most highways and interstates don't make sharp turns (see Map 2.5), so we interpreted this as an exit we needed to take. What looked like a left turn in the middle of the interstate morphed into an exit, which in turn morphed into a bridge, which ended up as a transition road to another freeway. Like this, the journey would morph after each single event." The map they are following draws their attention to a terrestrial situation that can clarify the ambiguity on the map, and if everything goes well the map will gradually gain clarity with each newly deciphered orientation point.

Maps being what they are, one is not always addressed simply to what is ahead but to all degrees of the compass, and the scope of the map can

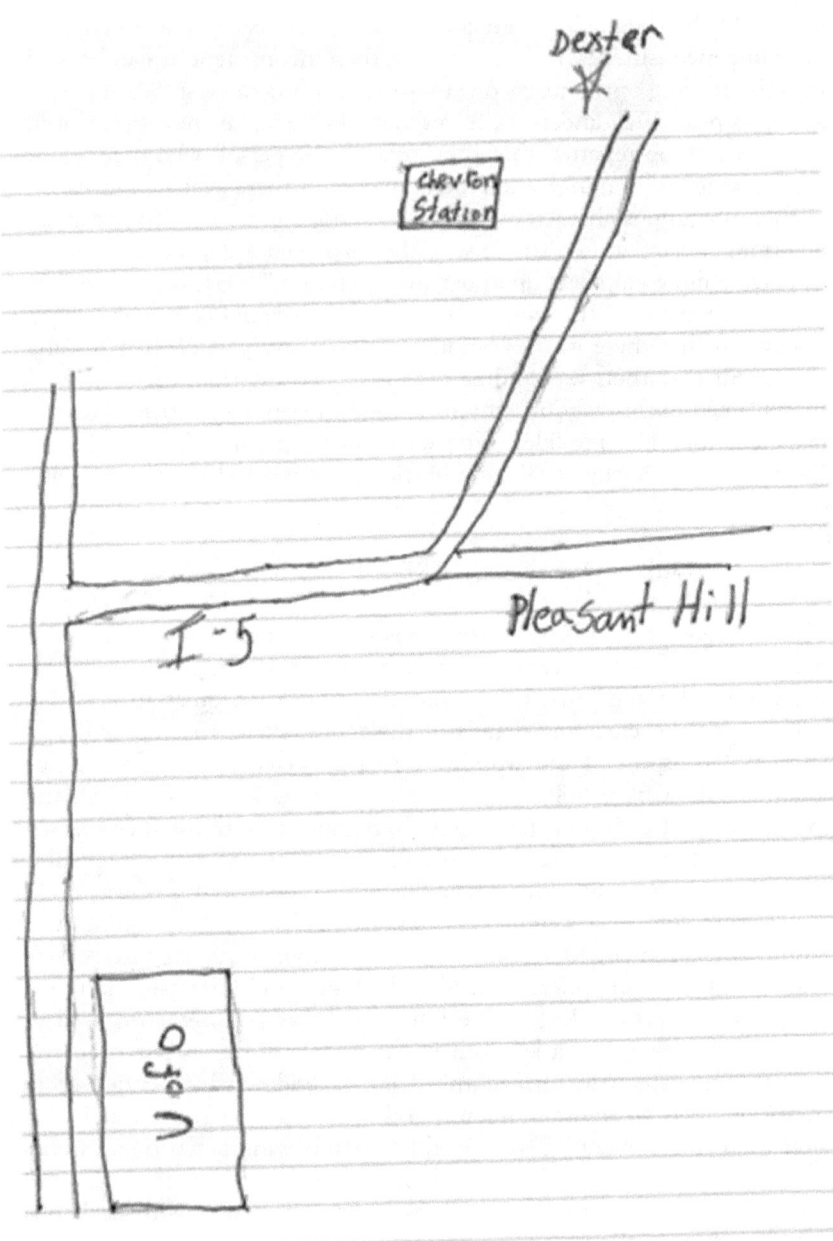

Map 2.5

wax and wane to collect larger or smaller portions of that landscape. Garfinkel offers this account of a way-finder who is traveling along Los Angeles's winding Sunset Boulevard:

> It could be that it's Palisades High, but if it's Pali High what is it doing here so soon? Pali High should still be two miles further on. And now here's the Bay Theater, when the Bay Theater was to have *preceded* Pali High. Then what is it on the map that was Pali High that wasn't Pali High? That could have been a junior high school or something like that. These features of the territory can become increasingly detailed in such a fashion as to require revision of what it is they consisted of in the first place.

Or, alternatively, Garfinkel suggests that in other way-finding journeys the matter that one is addressed to becomes increasingly that thing that the details add to without requiring essential revision. The point is that one must be prepared, simultaneously, for *either* case. One way not to succeed would be to hang on obsessively to one coherent reading of the map that has emerged. Only with a maximum flexibility of perspective can one resolve aporias like the situation where one must admit that the landmark that one has not yet reached was passed long before.

The protean character of route directions became a feature during the way-finding using this paragraph of written directions:

> Take the Crater Lake HWY exit and turn left, over the freeway. After Fred Meyers on the right is a road called Poplar—turn right (Taco Bell on the corner). Go down about a mile (through one light) and the road dead ends at McAndrews. Turn left on McAndrews, travel about 2 miles; past Royal (1st light), past Crater Lake BLVD (2nd light), past Springbrook (3rd light), then take Modoc, 4th street on the right after Springbrook. Turn right on Modoc and travel about 200 yards to the first right (Juanita). We're the house on the corner.

The first thing one notices about these directions is that "HWY" and "BLVD" are capitalized. One realizes at once that the composer of these directions is trying to anticipate a possible confusion that could occur by mistaking one road named "Crater Lake" for another road bearing the same name, with only the "HWY"/"BLVD" designation distinguishing them. The directions win some respect by the way it emphasizes this matter, and when the way-finder approaches "Crater Lake BLVD" additional caution is exercised. In this case, "Crater Lake BLVD" turned out to be Crater Lake Avenue, causing some hesitation and confusion. There were other details in the directions sufficient for resolving the aporia and deducing that "HWY"/"not-HWY" was the pertinent contrast intended. However, the directions forfeited much of the trust of the way-finders, who became more ready to submit other features of the directions to possible reinterpretations. In this way, the sense of the document has a protean character

The situation is not unlike how expert mountaineers read topographic maps. It is not unusual for a "reading" of the surrounding hilltops and forested slopes—represented by rings of increasingly tight concentric circles as the hills grow steeper, and by the color green wherever there is forest—to seem compatible with however one has construed the topographic lines of the map. Upon reaching the top of the steep hill ("That was easy!"), one's partner observes a peak towering in front of them that had previously been obstructed by the hill and asks, pointing, "What hill is that?" As soon as one refers to the map and studies its orientation, with the increased benefit of gazing from a higher elevation, one recognizes that the second mountain is actually what one had initially thought the first mountain to be: "Ohh! That must be the one we are climbing." The way that the very same topographic map can be read to be compatible with either of the two configurations of hills and/or mountains demonstrates the protean character of map-reading. The climbers experience a kind of Doppler-shift in their perspective, at which each of the terrestrial details—which must sustain their orientation together as an ensemble of particulars—are drawn into a new coherency. This may occur not merely once during an expedition, but when it happens frequently it can lead to a disorientation that undermines the mountaineers' confidence that they can find their way. In fact, it is this challenge that makes orienteering so compelling a sport. An orienteer can find delight when the topographic map becomes inexplicable for a time, requiring the orienteer to keep his or her mental awareness very open to possible solutions that exist just beyond the limit of understanding; at such times it can seem like the proprioceptive attention of the way-finder jumps out of the skin and enters the terrain.

The continuous remaking of the coherence of the environing landscape with the aid of the map, each addressing the other, can be a key that unlocks the praxis of thinking itself, exposing its bare wires to our observation. Witnessing the worldly work of the practical rationality of a map-reader who is faced with a series of aporias—while in the middle of them—is an ideal location from which to make ethnomethodological observations.

## WHAT HAVE WE LEARNED?

After hearing a brief account of these matters, my friend and colleague wanted to know, "So what's the big deal about these maps? I'll grant that some maps are poorly drawn, but is that really news?" I think my friend does not have it quite right—*all* maps lack completeness and contain the sorts of "errors" we have been examining, because the crucial problems arise from the in-courseness of their use. While cartographic maps may offer different benefits and liabilities, they can lead travelers to as many aporias as sketched maps do, and there is no perfect map in itself since the critical matters are what people *do* with the maps. There is hardly a map that does not become incompetent at some point. Garfinkel (1977a) describes a map used by American soldiers in Vietnam that was as formally accurate as any map could be; however, no interrogation of the map-in-hand could provide the soldiers with the information about their route that they needed most, which was where were the places that the Viet Cong might be lying in ambush? The soldiers reported that the map was no good. It may have been incomplete just where the soldiers wished for completeness, but the map was used anyway since it was the only map available to the soldiers. Much the same may be said of every map. At some point the problems are without remedy, but even so the maps are used.

Garfinkel (1977b) describes what following a map involves: "Traveling's work of reading the map reveals the map's properties in, and as, the territory's observable coherent order." That is to say, the map's properties are not only locatable in the coherency of the terrain that is the developing practical achievement of the travelers; the map's properties *are* that achievement, and could be nothing else. These properties do not lie in the map! They lie in a course of action in the world. As part of a way-finding journey, there is no territory in-itself, there is no map in-itself: the map's identity is the territory's identity. Dividing them is an artificial analyst's technique that in no way accurately reflects the affairs of the real world. Somehow we must find a way to get beyond the dualist reductions that distort our lives and make us blind to the ways we live.

A vision of maps as formal analytic objects requires that a map be disengaged from the *work* of way-finding, and there is a sort of massive cultural compulsion to everywhere respecify local courses of activity as isolatable, objective phenomena that yield to their principled versions. When such a strategy is successful in the case of maps, it will lose the phenomenon that is responsible for any success in the way-finding: the phenomenon of the procedural journey, the creativity required to locate each new "next" point in an ensemble of nexts. And it is easy to lose the phenomenon this way, since it is simpler and more orderly for analysts to deal with formal analytic schedules and criteria—"analytic formats whose adequacies in empirical details are obtained and warranted by the methods of formal analysis" (Garfinkel 1996)—than it is to keep oneself addressed to the complicated but specific worldly details that identify a phenomenon. The analytic practice, then, is to divide up the map into its units, sever it from any journeying, and develop formal criteria for assessing them. Garfinkel describes this praxis by which the world is lost:

> Signed objects are objects whose entire specifications are found and demonstrated by treating them as a collection of marks, indicators, signs, and symbols [the sense and reference of which only the analyst is privileged to know] and then assigns to them their interpreted significance. The reader need not leave the page in order to find, formulate, and decide any issues of adequacy.

How can a map be judged good or bad apart from a journey? It may be this sort of thinking that leads the U.S. Army Corps of Engineers to design canals and levees that not only fail but cause the problem they are designed to prevent, or digital hospital record systems IT experts to develop software programs that fail to capture the nuances of practicing medicine, or British Petroleum to use "fail-safe" back-up systems that have little likelihood of preventing an oil leak. The confidence of all of these professional analysts is not unlike the confidence of the way-finder who has just been handed the sketched map before taking a first step on a journey that is sure to be longer than anticipated. We need to spend more time paying attention to the world in and as it is lived, especially when its natural orderlinesses offer up excesses that keep going beyond what formal analytic versions of the world have made provisions for.

The American Automobile Association provides splendid cartographic maps and "TripTiks" that include enough formal features of a route to overwhelm the ordinary way-finder. What the map may not make readily apparent to the journeyer is where they need to go. Recognizing the absurdity of this situation, the AAA long ago began to staff their counters with assistants whose specialization was to the turn the cartographic map into a way-finder's map with the use of highlighting pens, arrows, underlining, circling, etc. In their offices one finds an army of coaches whose job it is to make formal maps intelligible because they recognize that "The map's order and meaning is embedded in territorially affiliated practices of traveling" (Garfinkel 1996). They provide such services so that their traveler-members can actually make a journey.

THREE

# THE REFLEXIVITY OF RULES IN GAMES

It is widely supposed that ordinary life is more organized than it is, a supposition that itself is helpful for making our daily affairs seem less chaotic. Social researchers, in the business of making successful careers discovering hidden orders in the world, subscribe to a similar supposition that does not always hold up to close scrutiny either. In most societies there is a kind of "just-so story"[1] that daily affairs are governed by rules and that these rules exist externally to those who "follow" them. That is, these rules are accepted as preexisting the social activity they organize and as bearing within themselves—and by themselves—a coherence that assures orderly social interaction. Here we are interested in inquiring into *how* (and identifying when and where) any coherence of rule usage comes about. There is a further corollary to this just-so story, which holds that following rules is a general public good because rules foster smooth-flowing social interaction, ethics in daily life, and make it easier to stabilize the methods people use for living their lives together. While rules do sometimes work this way, they do not always do so.

That rules already bear a coherent order prior to the moment when they are applied is a shared belief, a kind of social mythology that people actively sustain. This belief can itself be a tool for making social interaction orderly. If at times obeying rules takes on religious dimensions, this is because it operates at the same depths at which the social solidarity that motivates religious sentiments operates, at least according to Durkheim.[2] If a culture adopts a mythology of rule-governed behavior, then theorists would be happy to be the priests.

For more than a decade my students and I undertook an open-ended inquiry into the nature and operation of rules. We did so by having the students organize themselves into teams of four, each of which purchased a commercial board game that none of them had played before. They videotaped themselves from the moment they opened the cellophane wrapping on the game box, through the reading of the rules, initial game play, and mature game play until one of the players had won a complete "first-time-through" run of the game. At that point their study began. Once each team had their videotape in hand, they digitized it, produced a written transcript of the spoken dialogue, and then analyzed the interaction in agonizing detail in labs by viewing the video repeatedly on computer terminals turn-by-speaking turn, while following along closely with their written transcript. This method of watching the interaction *at the same time* one is consulting the written transcript is the closest tool that social phenomenologists have to an electron microscope: the practice can reveal the fundamental phenomenological workings of any occasion, in their constitutive details. These films and their phenomenological analyses taught us how board games are made orderly and how rules are made to serve as a means for stabilizing the particular orderliness that game-players develop in the course of their play.

## LET'S JUST PLAY AND SEE

In all of the students' games, two features are ubiquitous. First, none of the teams ever read all the rules. They do not even read *most* of the rules. They open up the box, remove the game parts and game pieces, lay out the board, and are already at the work of organizing the game before a single word of the instructions is read (in fact before the rules are located and distinguished from the manufacturer's advertisements for other board games). Someone does locate and pick up the rules. Occasionally there is competition for this role of rule-reader, who can become "rule-master," but usually there is not. That person begins to read some of the rules out loud, while the remainder of the players at the table are already engaged in collaborative work to make the game orderly and enjoyable. After hardly a couple of paragraphs of rule-reading, one or more players typically calls out, "Let's just play!" and the reading of the rules is suspended in favor of commencing the game.[3] In a minority of cases particularly fastidious rule-readers persisted in reading the rules, defying the peer pressure, but this persistence held sway for little more than an additional paragraph, when the rule-reader submitted to the general demand to play the game before completing all the rules.

Players do not read all of the rules for a very good reason—rules are not intelligible. In themselves, divorced from the context of play that affords them their sense and reference, rules cannot be comprehended. They are nonsense syllables. They might as well be written in Greek. As one group of players expressed:

> Pablo: Do you want to read them *all*, like we could listen to all of it, and then play, we could try to play.

Diane: Fuck!

Pablo: Just read it all and then try to play.

Kaleb: Well, the thing is, I can't retain the information.

Mick: I'd like to actually play it.

Kaleb: Yeah.

Pablo: Yeah, that sounds good.[4]

Kaleb cannot "retain the information" since rules by themselves are incomprehensible. They are not self-interpreting. Accordingly, the second ubiquitous feature of playing games-with-rules is that the players do not understand the portion of the rules that they do read. Or, to describe the situation more accurately, they understand the rules senselessly. It may be that "understanding," located here as a real-world phenomena, is something other than what philosophers know about "understanding;" but in these documented cases, the players nod knowingly as they listen to nonsensical syllables, smile to each other, laugh embarrassedly, and stare at the board together *senselessly* in hopes that the game will suddenly materialize before them in a single gestalt. And sometimes it does, but more commonly as they are staring at the board in frustration one player will say, "Let's just play and see."

See what? See what the rules mean, in the only place they can have meaning—in the context of game play. It is here that a game-with-rules begins. At this point, players begin to offer accounts that turn the nonsense syllables into rules. These candidate formulations[5] of the rules are heard, assessed, and reflexively applied in the game. They become the game. This means that instead of dictating the game's procedures, the rules are used as a fabric for collecting procedures of orderly play; and the procedures they collect become just what the rules mean. The players' *in vivo* accounts do not bear their meaning within themselves any more than the rules do. Their lexical meaning may be among the less important things about them; rather, it is the context in which the players' accounts are applied that is important, a context that they also contribute to establishing. But it is not just some general and unspecified "context," as so many theorists' mentions of contexts are; it is a context that has the peculiar feature of having its specific sense only when it is worked into the play, by the play, and as the play. In fact the rules and the context each provide the other with whatever sense and coherency they are going to have.

If rules are senseless, if they are indeterminate, open to contesting interpretations and even confusion, that is all the better, since the more open-ended the rules are the more scope is offered to the players for organizing the orderliness of their game play. The essential reflexivity of the players' accounts, whereby they use what they have found in the game after consulting rules to make coherent the rules they have in hand, is not the property of any individual player; it is a corporate reflexivity that offers itself to cooperative interpretations and continuous public clarifications. The work of providing a unity for the "interpreted" rules, and the work to continually stabilize that unity of sense, operates at the heart of games-with-rules and is an example of how the stabilities of ordinary society are "produced" on any given occasion.

One of the reasons for the impossibility of the folkloric notion that rules provide for an order in advance is that rules cannot ever be complete. They cannot account for every unforeseen game contingency. They cannot come even close. Every game the students played bore contingencies that fell outside of what the rules provided. These game-furnished conditions[6] included such important matters as how to decide who goes first, how to properly roll dice, how to end the game, and a large corpus of game-relevant strategies. A rulebook the size of a dictionary would still be incomplete, and subject to further strategic reinterpretation and the serendipitous transformations that are *necessary for players to organize and maintain a smoothly functioning, orderly game*. What is more, while rules can never be complete, they can also be *too* complete: some games have rule books with so many pages that players are resistant to reading them. Given that rules are inherently incomprehensible, they are enough of a burden upon players that even in an abbreviated form they are not read thoroughly. Accordingly, it would be foolhardy to try to design rules that are "comprehensive," and only game designers who do not know their business would attempt to do so.

There was one set of rules (to the game, "Fluxx") that at the outset advised players that the rules should not be read but that it was better they just begin playing the game. This was a game designed by people who understood well what the game players will do anyway. Except that you need a few rules to get started; and so players read just that much—a few rules.

Many rules commence with a section that is titled something like "Object of the Game," as in this excerpt from the start of "Settlers of Catan":

Brenda: Do you want to just start? [Despite her suggestion or propaedeutic to it, Brenda herself decides to locate the object-of-the-game in the rules. She reads aloud . . .] "Winning The Game: The first player to accumulate ten or more victory points during his turn immediately wins the game."

Aaron: Oh, so we're just trying to make settlements to get ten points.

Brenda: I think so. I. It always helps to, like, read the object-of-the-game.

Carol: Or cities . . . 'cause a city replaces a settlement and is worth two points.

Aaron: Ohh! Okay.

Brenda: [Continues reading the rules] "This player is declared the 'Lord of All Catan.'"

Even when there is no official section like this, rule-readers quickly scan the rules for this information. Usually the first accounts to be voiced about how a game should be played are summary accounts of what the point of the game is. Even when the rules clearly stipulate the object-of-the-game, the players must work collaboratively to organize their understanding of what must be done. Once some vision of the object-of-the-game is in hand, subsequent rules are understood in the light of that vision. As with any organization of our thinking that we project onto experience, the game will become a self-fulfilling prophecy and begin to conform with whatever way the cohort of players is interrogating it.

## OBJECTIVATION AND THE OBJECTIVITY OF RULES

It is inherent in any notion of "rules" that they apply without variance across persons; some intersubjective validity is implied, as well as some consistency in their application. This intersubjective validity (i.e., the congruency among individual perspectives) can come to be considered "objective," but it does not acquire this objectivity by itself. It is necessary for the players themselves to concert their interaction to objectivate—to make a tangible object that can be used in common—each of the rules they employ. While some objectivity may be implied in any notion of a rule, generally speaking, it is not some objectivity that *already* exists inherently in any particular collection of rules; rather, *the real objectivity emerges from the collaborative displays of game players* who coordinate their play and their game-accounts as they play so that they can all be on the same page. This is the initial work of playing a game-with-rules. The worldly presence that a game has for players is more than a list of rules; it is a competent order of developing activities.

How are rules *objectivated* and how does rule-governed play become competent? The work of deciphering how the game proceeds begins even before the rules are read. As the players are emptying the box, they may announce to each other the parts as they remove them:

Player: These are the directions, apparently. And these are the other games they have. Okay. I don't know why we have play dough, but apparently we have play dough . . . I have no idea what these are for. I'm going to take these cards out of there [a box wrapped in cellophane]. I don't know what these do, sooo, we'll have to figure it out.

In this case, the objectivation of the play dough—making of it an object that can be witnessed in common—begins even before the players learn what to do with it. This player is collaborating with the others by exhibiting each item, one at a time, and offering a name or gloss for what they could be. These glosses already imply possible uses for them; and even when no use can be determined, that null fact is itself made a publicly observable phenomenon: "I don't know why we have play dough, but apparently we have play dough." Even the idea that there is hermeneutic work that the group will need to perform *is made a public object* so that the group can begin to develop a common understanding of the game. Objectivation is worldly work, and the objectivation of a game-with-rules proceeds like this. In game after game, similar public announcements were made, and they consisted largely of items that did not yet make sense; but it was a non-sense that was made the public property of all the players. While this preliminary organization took place, other players would set up the board, unfold the rules, and switch their seats around so that there was a uniformity and consistency to the players' orientation to each other, an equity to the seat locations, and so that all players were in reach of the game. At the end of this unspoken collaborative choreography, all the players were usually sitting around the game board, conveniently oriented to the spectacle of game play that unfolded with all eyes being oriented to the game board and pieces.

As the player with the rules begins to read, other players continue to pick up the game cards and pieces and rifle through them in an effort to flesh out the import of the rules that are being read. These first rules are necessary for providing an initial structure so that some play may begin. By the time the setting-up of the game pieces is completed, players become impatient with sitting and listening to more rule-reading. The rules that are read are open, flexible structures, and according to one ethnomethodologist who studied rules (Wieder 1974, 168 ff.), they require this flexibility in order to offer the players scope for keeping the local orderliness organized. *Rules do not provide a structure that is fully fleshed out*. Even when orderly play gets filled in by rules that are read later, the rules do not provide a ready-made structure that is complete at the time that play begins. *The rules are a resource* for the organizational capabilities of the people who play the games. These rules provide a scaffold that guides players to a basic method that players can use to configure their initial play. Much of the subsequent structure unfolds from the activities that the players will only discover by observing the spectacle that results from the succeeding play, activities that the players then cooperate in making routine and predictable. Any rule is an open-ended invitation to discover what more it can mean, and despite the players' reluctance to listen to more rules, they are extremely skilled at developing intricate ramifications from what few rules they do read, and they are able to work with those few rules they do read to take them a long way.

## SKIPPING RULES

As we have seen, not all the rules are read in their entirety. Instead, the rule-reader accepts it as his or her task to choose parts of them to skip. As one reader of rules remarked, "You play the game, 'Settlers of Catan,' on a variable game board. For your first game we suggest that you use . . . [skips the rest of the paragraph]." Given the unintelligibility of rules, only a player who is socially incompetent would persist in reading sentences that bear no sense for anyone. On those occasions where it was ambiguous whether or not the rules bore any sense, readers would read the passage in a tone that plainly reveals they are being read without comprehension. Frequently the reading of such a passage is followed by a pause when all of the players stare dumbfoundedly at the board.

Following the pause, the reading usually continues non-sensically, and the reader will take even further license to skip more rules. The most commonly adopted strategy is for readers to read any of the rules that seemed important and to skip any of the rules that did not seem essential. In a game played by another group, a player remarked about what was observed on the videotape, "The directions are long and the reader comments that we will not likely read all of them; instead, she reads those directions she determines will be of most benefit to initiate play." Another player reported, "She skipped reading some of the rules because she didn't think that certain rules were important." One rule-reader just says "Blah, blah, blah," which reflects his in-the-course assessment of the value of the rules, and then he offers a severely reduced account of what he was the only person to read:

> Aaron: Okay. "Each player chooses a color." I think we Ace'd that part. Um [reads rules]. "Blah, blah, blahhh." Okay. So basically, put all your pieces in front of you. You can, like, divide them up.

The matter of reading only the essential rules raises a vital question: if the players have never played the game before, do not know how the game is played, and have not read very many of the rules, *how* is it possible for them to recognize which rules are the essential ones? This question has two conflicting answers: first, they cannot know; and second, somehow they seem to know pretty well. It is certainly one of the core hermeneutic skills of a game-player to be able to recognize an inessential rule when they come upon one. Rules are not read any which way. There is an *economy* of rule reading according to which only "important" rules are read. *Their primary aim is to read every single rule that is absolutely necessary for playing the game, and not one rule more,* and their estimates in this regard are minimalist.

In their analytic reports students did not spare many words when complaining about the rules, faulting their inadequacies, and remarking about how unintelligible they often were. They even express some sense of betrayal that rules, once investigated closely, are so flawed. As will be argued below, such complaints reveal a disappointment that has its birth in a naïve and uncritical adoption of folklore about rules. The attitude holds that rules are already competent in themselves and straightforwardly provide for orderly play, a mythology that is part of what Edmund Husserl called "the natural attitude." Most of these flaws are a necessary component of all rules; moreover, they are flaws that, in the end, are without remedy since the game's events will always outstrip what the rules seem to have provided for. The competency of a collection of rules is an achievement of the players, not the accomplishment of instructions that arrived in the box.

In the course of their collaboration in providing some sense to the rules, players had these comments about what to do when rules were bereft of sense:

> "Should we read all the rules? I guess we should go through this . . . There is a lot!"
>
> "The rules just continue on and on."
>
> "Do we have to read the entire thing?"
>
> "Let's just see what we have to do to start the game."
>
> [After some minutes of listening to the rules], "Are there any other *important* rules?"

A game of "Mousetrap" commenced this way:

> Rule-reader: [Reads] " 'Object of the Game': take turns building the mousetrap as you move around the game. Then use the mousetrap to capture your opponents' mice. Be the last uncaptured mouse on the game board and win."

THE REFLEXIVITY OF RULES IN GAMES 91

Jerome: [holding one of the two plastic mouldings in which a mousetrap might be found] So we build the mousetrap right now?

Rule-reader: [Consults the rules.]

Jerome: That doesn't make too much sense though.

Rule-reader: [Gazing at the rules] Oh my God!! [Laughs, while unfolding a massive amount of rules.]

Beth: Are you serious!

Rule-reader: [Laughs; sighs; begins to read] "The player turns the crank 'A' which rotates the gear 'B,' causing lever 'C' to move and push the top sign against the shoe 'D.'"

[All of the players look at each other and grimace at the incomprehensibility of what is being read aloud.]

Rule-reader: "The shoe tips the bucket holding the metal marble 'E.' The marble rolls down the rickety stairs 'F' into the gutter 'G,' when . . ."/

Beth:       / Is this all something to do about the game? Or do you −//

Rule-reader: // And then it just continues and continues.[7]

Because rules like these are senseless apart from the relevant game-play, the rule-reader simply cannot keep on reading. To do so would be a sign of social incompetence.

The general befuddlement of players at the outset of any new game is a ubiquitous feature. One student reported, "Having exhumed numerous playing pieces from the game's box, it took us approximately five seconds to agree that none of us had any clue about what we were doing." Another comments, "We are having a hard time grasping the rules." After the reading of some initial rules, there are many blank stares. The 'What?'-s and 'Repeat that'-s abound. But even after the rules are re-read, the players do not always understand them, since rules are not very amenable to analytic comprehension. Everywhere on the videotapes, much shrugging of shoulders is observable. While this shrugging may not make it into formal analytic studies of game play,[8] there is so much shrugging that one hesitates to ignore it. One student reports, "There were times during the game in which every single player was confused by the rules." But *none of the players seem intimidated by their not understanding*, perhaps because not knowing everything is the familiar ambience of mundane life. While most indeterminacies get written out of ethnographic reportage, they remain a natural part of the quotidian existence of all persons. Indeterminacy is less of a problem for players than it is for social theorists; it is simply life as we live it.

## THE INDETERMINACY OF RULES

While many indeterminacies get resolved while playing the game, others are left unresolved. One group of players observed in their course paper, "What is amazing about this rule [where to discard] is that we as a group continue not to have a full grasp of it even into our second game." At various points during a game, one or another player will have a thought about the game and pick up the rules in order to pursue an inquiry. Typically, a player will study the rules silently, become confused by what is read, and then set the rules back down while shaking his or her head as if not a word of it made sense. It is not necessarily the case that all the problems of the game are resolved; it may not even be usually the case. As one player admitted, "The entire group walked away from the game still unsure about several facets of game-play." But they played; and they played well.

Clearly, a strategy besides interrogating the literal meaning of the rules is needed for rendering rules intelligible; and this is a serious task that players accept as a collaborative responsibility. Accordingly, the players are in active collaboration as they begin to play. Players explained,

> "We didn't seem to grasp the concept of the game because we didn't understand what the directions were referring to."

> "You can't understand rules until you actually use them."

> "Alright, let's just play for a minute, and we'll figure things out as we go."

> "We are to make this rule definite. But it has a specific context [that is necessary] for interpretation, so we are having a hard time making it definite."

> "Time was not wasted on over-reading the rules."

> "Even after some rules were read, we were still confused about exactly how the game was played, but we began anyway."

Having concluded that they have heard enough to be able to begin game-play, players rolled the dice into what begins as an oblivion.

Despite the fact that out-of-the-box rules are in large part incomprehensible, relatively few players ask questions or call for clarification. As one player reported, "During the initial reading of the rules, Robert gave an account of the rules and met with very few questions." Given the players' confusion, why would there be few questions? If you don't ask when you don't know, how will you learn? One reason is that one who is not following anything is not capable of formulating a competent question—one needs to know something already and be partly in the picture in order to ask a question that can be productive. Productive for what? Productive for establishing the orderliness of the game. In the same way, how can a player answer the question that is occasionally posed by the person who is reading the rules—"Do you understand?"—when the player has little grounds for knowing what sufficient comprehension could consist of? The replies are generally gratuitous concurrences, such as "Yeahhh," nods, smiles, or "I think I get it."[9] During their reading of a section of the rules of "Mousetrap" that dealt with the function of "the loop," every player gazed at board. But no one found the loop. Finally one player declared, "O.K." What does "O.K." mean here? Certainly not "I know what the loop section is."

Generally, people who understand little do not ask questions. But there is a more important reason for the inutility of asking questions, and that is that the amount of time that is required for working out analytically a literal explanation for what a rule means far exceeds the time it would take to recognize the sense and reference of a rule in the natural flow of the game's play. The meaning of a rule does not lie in the correctness of a literal account of its meaning; instead, a rule consists of its consequences.[10] For this reason, the vacuously gratuitous replies serve as a capable method for participants to nudge the interaction along to the point where the game-play can begin, which is where the solutions to their confusions will eventually be found.

A rule collects its meaning over the course of the natural flow of the game play to which it gives rise. In order to know what a rule means *really*, and not just imaginarily, you need to witness the rule in the natural temporality of its occurrence. If you stop that natural flow to ask a question about it, only an abstract and apophantic-like account can be supplied; to know a rule is to know it in-its-course, as its course, and so to the extent that asking a question stops that natural flow in its tracks, questions can be harmful to the hermeneutics of understanding rules. In one game a player asks repeatedly, half a dozen times over the course of ten minutes of game-play, "What is the play dough for?" The question is ignored every time she asks it. It is ignored for the very good reason that no one knows, and because everyone expects that during the natural course of playing the game it will become evident; and if it does not become evident it probably is not important enough to bother about. Had players replied by offering various candidate accounts of what the play dough could be about and by discussing the merits of those accounts, a good deal of time would be lost, and the ultimate solution to her query—and the start of the game—would be delayed. In the end, as soon as one of the players picked a card that instructed him to design a snake out of the play dough, it was patently obvious that there really was no mystery at all to the play dough.

Similarly, in the game "Fluxx" Karla, the rule-reader, read through a section of the rules that explained the specific types of cards that were included in the game. The rules presented some technical details, including this section: "When a Goal is played, place it face up in the center of the table and disregard the previous Goal." The rule made no sense to anyone. No one knew what a "previous" Goal could be; they didn't know what a current Goal was either. Since no one knew how to make sense of what it was talking about, Karla skipped quickly through the rules without a thorough reading. This is not incompetent play; on the contrary, it is ordinary play. It is not a flaw in their methodology, since there was no way for them to grasp the rules that way. Instead, they started playing the game. Melissa dealt five cards to everyone, a procedure familiar to all; as she studied her hand, she asked the group what a Goal card was, recalling the term in the rules. Karla then re-read the rules, which began to make some sense to the players. It turned out that the Goal cards, and the way the Goal cards kept changing the objectives of the game, were critical to their play, but it was only in the course of the game play—or more specifically, in the course of serial disappointments to their strategic planning, which had to keep shifting its orientation (the designed idiosyncrasy of this game)—that players could appreciate the consequences of the rule about Goal cards.

The game of "Mousetrap" included a number of conspicuously cheddar-yellow soft plastic squares that the players quickly decided were intended to be pieces of cheese, prompting a player's query:

Jerome: What is the cheese supposed to do?

Julia: I don't know, we'll figure it out.

Rule-reader: We'll see l<u>aaaa</u>-ter.

This is a sound hermeneutics that recognizes that the elements of the game will only be intelligible in, and as, the course of their play. For example, the rules of "Cranium Congo" state that one should read the question card, push the button on the red timer box, and pass the box "quickly" to the next player. It would have been foolish for a player to ask what is meant by "quickly," since apart from playing the game no one could have had grounds for knowing its temporality. As it turned out, the "quickly" referred to in the rules was a good deal more quick than any of the players imagined it to be, and the first couple of occasions the time ran out before the box had been passed and before the players had settled into their seats to start their turns. Only when the natural temporality of the game was lived, could the meaning of the rules' "quickly" be understood. The meaning of "quickly" consisted of its consequences: it is not that rules have consequences, it is that they consist of their consequences.

The designers of computer software programs recognize this well. That is why they distribute beta versions of new products in order to learn from the *actual* uses of their program what it is that the program consists of. It is not just that they want to find the 'bugs,' which are always more than they can plan for; they want to learn what it is that they have achieved. The inventor of Post-Its, who conceived the product while on an airplane (and was wanting to hold his place in the index of a book he was reading) discovered what Post-Its were *"really"* only after the 3-M company sold many billions to people who hung small reminders to themselves; nevertheless, the fellow was happy to take whatever credit society offered him for his clever invention. In just this way, the writers of software look to the real world for the significance of what they have designed, and players look to the game-play to understand the sense and reference of the rules.

But what about games where certain rules are positively essential to the game play? Savvy game designers who are aware that many rules will be ignored have come up with narrative devices designed to catch the recalcitrant rule-reader's attention. Inset boxes, sometimes in red, can help to call attention to a rule. One game offered a "Special Rules Reminder" that communicated a couple of rules that were especially vital for the intended play. While even these rules were read in a cursory way, and without comprehension, this label kept calling attention to them so it was more likely that players referring to the rules in the midst of game-play would catch sight of them and read them at the very moment when they were hermeneutically more capable of grasping their significance. Here again, some game designers knowledgeable about the extent to which players ignore rules created this feature of the rules for this game. One day perhaps a game designer will create a rule that can hop up-and-down, calling attention to itself during the appropriate moment of the game-play.

## COLLABORATIVE ACTION

It is important to note about the citations above that the players frequently speak in a communal voice ("we") *and not as individuals negotiating individual perspectives*. The players' orientations commence and are sustained throughout as a corporate, intersubjective gaze. At the start of most games some procedure develops naturally according to which all members of the group kept stating aloud what was happening while it was happening, almost as if they were radio announcers for a sporting event. This was done in order to make each element of the game-play witnessable to every player. *Not as individuals* did persons remove each item from the game box and place them on the table in a manner that all could witness; rather, *a collectivity* was the agent of such pre-game organization. For example,

> Barry: [Reading] "After you're done, pass the dice to the player to your left/ who continues the game."
>
> Luke:  / [Picks up dice and displays it to all.]
>
> Celia: [Looks at Luke and smiles in a confirmation of understanding.]

The players' activities are closely coordinated. As the first roll of the dice occurs in this game, Luke calls out, "We're taking the first roll of the game." Since this fact is already obvious to all, what could the purpose be for such a comment? It is part of the way the players establish the orderliness of their play, so that they will be able to remain on the same page as the game proceeds. This same kind of collaboration is evidenced in this excerpt from the transcript of the game, "Are You Smarter Than a Fifth-Grader?" Note the collective orientation that is evident in the first line as the rule-reader makes an effort to read aloud the object-of-the-game:

> Pablo: Alright, let me read this. "Objective: answer eleven grade-school questions correctly. Prove that you are smarter than a fifth-grader and win one million dollars." . . . "The first time you play, remove the four money markers."
>
> Kaleb: Wait, the "money marker"?
>
> Pablo: [Continues reading] "Copy and Save pawns." (3.0) "In the pawn stands."

Pablo does not reply to Kaleb's question. Instead he avoids reading every line in preference for going for the global sense, trying to capture the essentials without dwelling on matters that would be unintelligible. The 3.0-second pause occurs when he is considering which parts of the paragraph to skip reading.

> Kaleb: That's a pawn? Is this a pawn? [He holds up a game piece that might be a pawn; while he does this, another player holds up

a slightly different piece; in their gestures they indicate that they are not identical.]

The players here face a dilemma regarding making the term "pawn" sensible. It is possible that they are trading on their knowledge of chess, in which all of the pawns are the same. The difficulty is that here the pieces are not the same, so which one is the pawn? There are no grounds yet for answering the question. Mick observes that there is another game-piece, which had been referred to in what was read, and that both game-pieces seem to require stands. He suggests that one of the pieces they are holding up is actually a stand for those pieces and not a piece by itself; however, he is still uncertain about which of the candidate-pawns is the real pawn. His announcement is part of the public work of organizing the players' understanding, work that is sustained as a collaborative task. He speaks out loud *so that all of the players can share in the witnessing*, a sharing whose importance may exceed that of understanding the matter correctly:

Mick: These are pawn stands.

Diane: Oh yeah!

With "pawn stands" in hand, it becomes easier for them to decide what "pawns" can be.

Throughout this collaborative work, players are constantly *looking to each other* in order to monitor the appropriateness of their actions. Here *thinking is a public activity* that is sustained by an intricate interconcatenation of gazes. After this group commences to play, the rule-reader himself becomes confused. His reply to a question was incorrect, and he was "Saved" by another player; but the players are still learning what it is to be Saved. Pablo thought that his term had ended, but in fact he still had a right to proceed to the subsequent question:

Pablo: I don't get the right to continue—I got that wrong.

Diane: No, he "Saved" you!

Mick: I "Saved" you.

Kaleb: Continue.

Mick: You roll!

Pablo: I can keep going?

Diane: You keep going.

Pablo: This is hard. I'm gonna lose. I'm gonna be the first to lose.

Diane: Wait. Because it—*do* you keep going? [Looks to Kaleb who is holding the rules.] Wait. Wait. Wait. We didn't check that [points to rules]. If you *do* keep going. [Kaleb picks up the rules.]

Mick: Oh, if he uses a "Save" and he is saved, does he keep going?

Kaleb: [Shuffles through the rules.]

Mick: I would think so [Looks to Diane for confirmation.]

In addition to the continuous looking to the others (e.g., lines 9 and 14), at line 12 Mick offers a summary account that collects concisely the events of the previous lines while offering a public warrant for Kaleb to consult the rules on behalf of the group. Summary accounts like this are a central part of the local organization of sense and speak to what ethnomethodologists call "accountability."

Accountability refers not only to the collective task of making intelligible and observable the essential understandings of a local interaction, including all of the reflexive properties of accounts whereby parties can use any account as an active tool to provide the orderliness that it was intended simply to describe. Accountability also involves a feeling "responsible for" what the response of the other participants will be to the candidate account (Schutz 1971, 274). That is, to describe the situation more precisely, following an utterance of an account there is a gaze that flows from the person making the account out to the faces of the cooperating parties. This gaze bears substantial dynamism: wide-eyed, the one who utters the account studies the response of one's fellows in order to learn what one's account has come to mean. Just as the rules of the game consist of their consequences, the meaning of a summary account consists of its consequences, and *the one who utters the account is not in command of that meaning*. Rather, one can only *witness* the meaning in the interaction (just as everyone else is doing) *and collect it* once it has been made apparent. As Merleau-Ponty (1964, xv) writes, "The germ of universality . . . is to be found ahead of us in the dialogue into which our experience of other people throws us by means of a movement not all of whose sources are known to us." We look to the others for what we could possibly have meant, and our spoken words "enjoy available significances as one might enjoy an acquired fortune" (Merleau-Ponty 1962, 197). We *look* to others not just because we have a stake in what we assert but also because *we need to learn what we asserted* since we will be held responsible for it, even if it turns out to mean something we did not intend. In the words of Schutz (1971, 274), "A person is responsible *for* what he did; on the other hand, he is responsible *to* someone—the person, the group, or the authority who makes him answerable."

Above all, each person wants to avoid getting into trouble. And so each person monitors events in order to not get into trouble for anything she or he has said. This is why the players' looks are continually shifting quickly from one pair of eyes to another—one is searching for any possibility of trouble and at the same time for what kind of sense might be lying behind any trouble. To this extent the sense of an occasion is the personal property of no individual, but is a public possession. Of course, typically players are eager to do what will be accepted as normal; *the problem lies in figuring out what normal is and communicating it to all of the persons present.* Whether they know what they are supposed to do or not, players wish to comply. "The power of external coercion" (Durkheim 1915, 10) is considerable. The players wish to satisfy expectations, and they are continually looking to learn what these expectations might be. Being cautious is never a guarantee that a player will not get into trouble. The players know they will be held accountable for whatever rules emerge, but they don't necessarily know what these rule-governed behaviors will be. Players report that some persons who are unsure of what an account means comply with them anyway. How do they do this? In one game Justin waited patiently for his turn, while Deirdre puzzled over the sense and consequence of what transpired in her turn. Finally, when Yoon calls out, "Let's just keep it going," Justin complied with his demand by finally taking his card. However, Deirdre's turn was not fully completed, since she had yet to discard; she had puzzled so long that Yoon and Justin had assumed she had done so. So Annie chastised Justin for playing out of turn, stopping him in his tracks, whereupon he became profusely apologetic. Despite his vigilance in staying out of trouble, he found himself in trouble anyway. Life is like that.

In the absence of an understanding of the rule or the existence of any precedent, there is a peculiar tendency for players to permit any action to stand for normal if they don't know any better; so practices can get to be normal in serendipitous ways. The objective meaning of a rule or of an account has a natural connection with the processes of being held answerable or accountable to others who make one feel responsible. This "feeling responsible" is a response to what are moral expectations, and it operates at the heart of any society. Here is where the social trumps the individual in what, ultimately, are epistemological matters. These interconcatenated gazes of query and expectations are the primal medium of social facts. Eye contact, nods, as well as monosyllabic verbal cues continually ratify displays of the rule-governed play.

Let us examine the delicate face-work of this interconcatenation of gazes in the game, "Mousetrap." The rule-reader, Janice, has played one of her pieces of cheese in a strategic move, landing on a square on which an opponent's piece is standing. Janice announces what she is doing so that her game play can be publicly witnessed and understood:

> Janice: I'm using my piece of cheese to roll her.

After she removes her opponent's piece, she plays again, announcing,

> Janice: I'm going to use my other piece of cheese to roll her again.

She looks to her principal antagonist not exactly for confirmation, but in order to maintain the intersubjective coordination. Jerome (incorrectly) takes this as an indication of some uncertainty on Janice's part, reading her gaze as a request for confirmation, so he responds to what he takes to be a weakness:

> Jerome: How can you do that, though?

Janice replies without hesitation,

> Janice: I can do that.

But her eyes are *still* up, and at, the eyes of the other players, in a bid for consensus; so it seems that the matter is still in the public domain. While her look is necessarily one that is evaluating the other's responses, she does not doubt the correctness of her game-play; however, since the other players do doubt the correctness of her game-play and a collective sentiment (Durkheim 1915, 9) builds against her, she begins to have enough doubt herself that she offers to consult the rules. The videotapes of game playing frequently reveal that a player who feels very confident about his or her understanding of the rules will nevertheless be so influenced by the barrage of questions and competing understandings that the certainty will become undone. It seems that certainty is a tenuous thing, and something that is highly dependent upon the confirmation of one's fellows.

> Julia: So you /
>
> Jerome:     / You can keep rollin'?
>
> Janice: Yah!
>
> Julia: Really, I can just say I'll keep rolling?
>
> Julia: I think that's what it says [consults rules].

As she consults the rules, the group begins to consider the matter as something that is up for general adjudication.

Jerome: Only when you're on that crank button.

Marge: You don't get another turn, though.

Jerome's attempt at a general summary account of a consensus that was building against Janice, specifying how the rule is to be applied in this case, falls flat since while he is developing his account; Janice is able to locate the part in the rules that warrants her additional turn, and so she prevails, much to the amazement of the rest of the players who had already congealed about a certainty of their own devising, even though it was antithetical to what the rules stipulate. The pertinent rule had been read and heard before, only it was not intelligible at the time, and only the rule-reader seemed to fathom its significance. In other games, when rules were not consulted again, the players' ad hoc emendation of the rules might have prevailed. Here, even though Janice was correct, her social sense demanded that she remain *socially accountable* for her game-play, and the *exposure* of her acts to others' expectations and evaluations is part of what sustains her need to monitor *the accountability* of her acts. So, accountability has this double sense: an account offers a cohort of persons a concrete means of coordinating the organization of local events; and it is also a continuous orientation to ways that one may be held responsible and accountable for compliance, and so it requires some *ongoing attentive monitoring* for ways that the local events are made orderly.

During the play of a game of "Parcheesi," the Doublets Penalty was read, and ignored. That is, it could not be heard comprehendingly since it stood without any context, so it was read and heard senselessly, even though the rule-reader paused and asked, "Does everyone get that?" The gratuitous nods and general good will she received were less than convincing, so she read the rule a second time. It is significant to note that asking players whether they understand is an equivocal means of ascertaining whether there is comprehension. For one thing, no one comprehends everything about a rule until play governed by the rule occurs, and even then the understanding will necessarily be incomplete, so there is always a question about how much understanding is required to warrant a positive reply. Claiming to understand in situations where the understanding is only partial is as reasonable as it is commonplace. Accordingly, the question regarding the adequacy of understanding is naturally converted in the course of mundane social interaction to a query about what constitutes partial understanding, lowering the bar for warranting an affirmation. While a player was reading aloud sections that described the rules regarding Doublets and the Doublets

Bonus, she herself cried "Wow!" at their complexity. She then continued to read the next rule:

> Rule-reader: "Doublets Penalty: the third consecutive /
>
> Marge:                                            /Doublets Penalty! What is that?
>
> RR: I'm going to explain now.
>
> Marge: Yep [giggles embarrassedly].
>
> RR: [Reading] "The third consecutive time you roll doublets you may not move forward. Instead, your pawn closest to home—even if it's on your home-path—must return to your start circle and reentered later. This ends your turn." [Looks to the others] Does
> 10   everyone get that?
>
> Marge: [Looks at Mai-li, and they laugh together.]
>
> Bud: [Nods] Alright [very softly spoken].
>
> Marge: [Groans loudly, pointing her index finger at her brain.]

As we have learned, it is interactionally incompetent for Marge to pose her question in the second line before the rule has even been read and some play with it has developed. The rule-reader mildly castigates her, and she publicly displays an apologetic attitude. Marge and Mai-li's laughter indicate that even after the rule has been read, their comprehension is poor. Bud's nod appears gratuitous too, and since he usually speaks with a deep voice his almost whispered "Alright" in line 12 may be further indication that his verbal assent was gratuitous. There is nothing for them to do but to continue past this moment of hearing emptily. The rule is indeed forgotten; and it may never have resurfaced in the players' lives except for the fact that 40 minutes later someone rolled doublets three times, and Marge recalled that there was some problem about doing that:

> Marge: Whoah! Another one. Penalty for third double! That was that thing you read that we got in the middle of. But what's the penalty for the third double?
>
> RR: You don't get to move it, the piece closest to your home has to go back to home.
>
> Marge: Oh WOW!!! [Frowns deeply.]

It was only at this point that Marge and other players finally were able to grasp the import of that rule that seemed so complicated before the game began.

## AD HOC RULE CONSTRUCTION

When the rules have been read, the game still awaits being made, and the players will be the ones who will make it. The players undertake this task as their collective responsibility. Some rules require interpretation, although the gloss "interpretation" does not adequately cover the variety of activities that players engage in to provide a local orderliness for their playing. Other rules require that players arrange some adaptation to the local contingencies. Some cohorts of players we filmed included small children among the players; other games, including a word-game, had players who had recently arrived from other countries and were taking English-as-a-second-language courses. Some players were operating under time commitments, which overrode any pursuit of perfection in understanding rules. It is life after all, which needs to look after itself; and rules are normally treated as standing in service of doing that living, rather than requiring that what was not fully comprehensible be followed slavishly. As one of the players reported, "The rule was changed because *everyone* knew the game was too hard." Sometimes rules are used only in an advisory capacity. Given a practical task, players do not feel hog-tied by the rules, but take it upon themselves to organize a game in a way that suits them. It is commonplace for players to innovate rules that they only subsequently learn contradict the stipulated rules of the game; and when this occurs the players mostly do not substitute the "real" rules for the ones they have initiated. They will say things like, "I'm pretty satisfied with this game," and feel free to ignore or second-guess any rule they conclude will not foster a convivial game:

> Al: It almost seems silly to go in here [they are required to enter a section of the game board].
>
> Barry: Yah it does.
>
> Celia: Yeah.

There is active rule-construction throughout most games, and rule-construction does not quit until the game itself has concluded. Players say, "So we're gonna make the rule be. . . ." Some changes to the rules are self-serving, such as when a player drew a bad card and offered to the other players that "We *all* get one chance to pass one undesirable card," an offer that was accepted. There is no shortage of excuses for rule changes, such as "This is our first time playing." Many if not most rules require some interpretation, since any rule relies upon matters that are not stipulated but are nevertheless presumed to be understood. Garfinkel (1977b) has observed, "At first, players cannot find from the rules what is not said but what is nevertheless being assumed by the rules." This ambiguity inherent in many rules affords players much scope for selective interpretation. One rule of a game required that a player roll a "five" before being permitted to enter a certain region of the board, but it was left to the players to rule whether a "five" meant a '1' + '4' or whether a "five" appearing on either die was required. Moreover, it is not abnormal for players to violate rules deliberately. One student observed about their videotape, "The group realizes they have been misinterpreting one of the rules. Despite hearing the actual rule described in the manual, they decided to devise their own reinterpretation of the rule as a mechanism for creating a more fluid game play." Providing a local orderliness is a responsibility that players collaborate in fulfilling. On those occasions when the realization that the rules have been applied improperly does not occur until the game is nearly over, it seems pointless to the players to revise their game-play, especially since the *repeatability* and *reliability* of their game-play has lent it a certain dignity that is part of what serves to assure its *orderliness*. In such an instance acting in compliance with the formal rules would work contrary to the players' interest in social order. In the game, "Settlers of Catan," it was not until the second hour of game-play that a player gained the insight that it was not permitted to build a City without first having built a Settlement. Since many Cities had been erected without there being Settlements preceding them, the players decided to permit all current Cities to stand but to require that henceforward new Cities have Settlements that precede them. Such ad hoc adjustments to rules continue throughout most game-play without relief.

In the game "Lost" it was also in the second hour of play that everyone finally appreciated the rule that "fate cards" were to be kept secret from the other players. This happened when one player drew a fate card that instructed him to show a certain number of his fate cards to the other players. Up to that point, the players had assumed that fate cards were "supposed" to be played in the open. Perhaps the rule-makers had assumed that this behavior was part of the unspoken expectations that accompany all rules, since in most card games players' hands are kept hidden from each other. Despite learning the "correct" rule, the players persisted with the procedure they had established.

It is significant that in their analysis very few players spoke of a correct game, while many spoke of work that was done "to make the game go smoothly." Players work skillfully to resolve problems quickly, in order "to keep the flow of the instructions moving along," and as a player figures out something that will make the game more efficient or entertaining, she or he will contribute this understanding to the game. Players will resolve any aporia that may occur—moments where players are unable to determine the local orderliness and activity comes to a halt—for example, when the rules stipulated that players were required to land "exactly" on the home space but did not indicate whether one needed to utilize one or two dice in doing so (this was a game that permitted one to divide up the dice between two different game pieces). The group decided that a player must roll both dice, but they did not anticipate the trouble that this way of resolving the dice rule would cause when a player's last game piece landed on the very last space of the game board. He could not enter home, since it was impossible to roll a "one" with two dice. The problem was resolved by awarding the game victory to the player anyway, since by then the time commitments of the players had overridden other considerations. It is *not* that these ad hoc provisions are exceptional. They are pervasive and ongoing, part of how players use rules to complete an orderly play of a game.

A player summarized, "As the game progressed, the rules also progressed," and there is usually some shift or "slippage" in the sense of rules as play proceeds. In one game the categories of pictures on the backs of the game-tiles were at first presumed to be very important, and players conscientiously organized their stash of tiles according to them, until over the course of playing they learned that the pictures had no game-relevant consequences beyond being decoration. Players are continually trying to "nail down" the game, and they are capable of sustaining many game-relevant orderings that turn out to be unessential, but they will not know which ones are essential until they play. Yet they must keep communicating with each other about these enlargements, reductions, and transformations of an evolving corpus of rules. This protean ebb and flow of the rules may be part of what makes playing a game engaging. Part of the work of players is to tame this slippage of meaning, but they will never be able to halt it altogether any more than one can use one's arms to prevent a stream from flowing.

## RATIFYING AND OBJECTIVATING ACCOUNTS

A student once made the comment that the talk among the players assisted them in improving their understanding of the game. Communication about rules frequently occurs in the form of *accounts*, which can be a matter of displaying, without anyone speaking, candidates for a course of correct rule-governed behavior; or it can involve verbal formulations. When indecision or confusion rises regarding how a rule is to be applied, players will entertain the issue by means of accounts. Here John is explaining one of the rules to "Adversity":

> John: If an advertiser has chosen beer as his product, "The Quicker Picker-Upper" as his slogan, the ad would be presented by reading out loud, "Beer, The Quicker Picker-Upper." Does that make sense?
>
> Paul: Yeah, so you say the first name, the word, and then you say your slogan.
>
> John: Yeah, with one of your slogans /
>
> Paul: / (Any of them, right?) You can pick the card up? Is that what the rules say? You can pick and choose?
>
> 10   John: Umm. You pick an ad-slogan card that you choose. Just one.
>
> Carl: Wait. So you have to look at them, so, if you choose it?
>
> John: Yeah.
>
> Sherry: So once you've chosen it, it's chosen. Do we all do that?
>
> John: Yeah. Now, I don't think we get to pick, like choose from five different ones, but I think we just pick, you know, the top one. Does that make sense?
>
> Carl: Random selection.
>
> Paul: Is it random selection?
>
> John: Whatever it says—it just says pick an ad-slogan card, so it's
> 20   like—
>
> Paul: Okay—
>
> John: / What do we want to agree on?
>
> Paul: / So, yeah
>
> Sherry: Umm.
>
> John: Random / selection.
>
> Carl: / Random—That way, yeah.
>
> Sherry: But then how do we . . . Okay, never mind. Because then they pick one, and they choose which one goes with it.
>
> Paul: And you guys have to guess based on which one I chose.
>
> 30   John: True. True. True.

The accountability of this effort to tame the meaning of the rules is in evidence from line 4 forward, when Paul offers a formal account of what John has explained in reply to John's request for some indication of how well they have understood what he had explained. John becomes entangled in the polysemic wording of Paul's effort to elicit some clarifying detail, which leads to ambiguity about whether one is free to choose among a number of ad cards. Carl's effort in line 11 is replete with indexical meanings,[11] a common feature of accounting activities; but John offers his assent anyway—"Yeah"—although it is far from clear what is meant. In line 13, Sherry asks for additional clarification, and she does so in a manner that is public, allowing her deliberations to be witnessed by all. The openness of her query and *her attentiveness to what the query will become* is part of the accountability of her participation. John rethinks his reply to Paul and offers the tentative account (lines 14–16) that the players do not get to choose the ad card but must just take the top card, and he asks whether the others concur and understand. In line 17, Carl offers a convenient label or *gloss*, "Random selection," for the account that John has presented. This is another important common feature of how groups handle accounting—a complicated course of behavior is given a name that will permit it to function economically in the group's deliberation about their reflections. It also makes possible a local semiotics that is efficient for communicating. That is, what is important about these shorthand glosses that are common in social intercourse is that they facilitate the collective thinking that is going on in public. However, they cannot serve to organize the intelligibility of an occasion unless they are understood similarly by a number of the parties. Developing a common language assists the ability of each participant to get on the same page. A gloss stands in for its meaning, and stabilizing the meaning of the gloss then becomes additional work for the parties, who are ever busy organizing the intelligibility of the occasion.

In lines 19–20, John distances himself from the rules, indicating that he is only concerned to abide by the rules ("Whatever it says—it just says . . .") just as soon as they are able to figure out what that is, and he opens up the meaning of the rule to general adjudication. Paul seems happy that the matter is being posed in an open-ended way to the group, but neither he nor Sherry suggests a solution. John himself endorses the "Random selection" notion in line 25, Carl confirms it, Sherry begins and then (in light of the growing consensus) withdraws a possible quibble, and in line 29 Paul adds something to the meaning of the account's gloss, whereupon Sherry indicates she is ready to go along, although she simultaneously remains oriented to learning just what it is that she will be going along with! In the last line, John firms up the confirmation, and the group finally has in hand a ratified account, *but they are still addressed to developing events in order to learn what it all will mean.* The process has proceeded like this: *Account* → *Ratification*. This can serve as a simple formula for how a rule gets legitimated.

But the confirming of accounts does not end here. Players not only want to produce rules that have a clear sense for the game play; they are also eager for the sense that they confirm to be capable of *standing independently* of the local contingencies of their production. The reliability of a social order somehow increases when all of the parties who produce the local orderliness contract a severe case of social amnesia that causes them to forget that they only then produced it. Accordingly, the rules that players develop become "the" rules, which quite rapidly come to offer the appearance that they have existed for all time. Even recent features of game-play quickly become "the way we've always done it," and thereby come to stand as an independent authority that is capable of authorizing proper game-play. This additional step is part of the work of achieving the orderliness of a local setting, and players collaborate in accomplishing this as well. A group reported to me, "We acted as though we were not the ones making the decisions, but that the rules dictated a form of play that we were unable to change." An independent social fact has been created. While social facts seem to exist independently of the players' collaborations, they are the practical achievement of the players' concerted game-play. Therefore, we need to acknowledge this additional step in our formula for rule-production, which provides for the proposal that the ratified rule is proposed to exist without any immanent connections to the players who produced it. The confirmed rule must be made an object in common, and this social work of objectivation is an important component of everyday life. Our formula now becomes

Account → Ratification → Objectivation

There are a number of objectivation practices that are effective in regularizing and making the game-play routine. As far as social order is concerned, what is important is that the rule-governed behavior be regular and consistent; it is less important just what those rule-governed behaviors are. The more objective a rule can be made, the more compliance there will be, and the more stable the game will become, even when the rule is not in conformity with what was intended by the game's creators. The existence of the social fact is made independent, which provides an opportunity for external coercion. This last step allows players to reconfigure their accomplishment so that it conforms to the prevailing social mythology that rules are fixed and exist independently of any local production cohort.

The confirmation or ratification of a rule does not mean that its indeterminacy has vanished, since most rules, even "exact" ones, will retain their open character. As Larry Wieder (1970, 109) has observed, there is a "lack of finitude in sets of rules." Garfinkel (1977a) has similarly observed that the orderliness of rules has the feature that whatever is determined is dependent upon clarifications still to be made. As in the case of the Doublets Penalty, the first reading of rule, even when it is indefinite, can cast a shadow over the future play of the game, and that something further will retrospectively come to fill in what was unknown. Orderliness does not demand that all indeterminacy be removed; given the many strategic ramifications of rules, all of their consequences can not be determined, though they are determinable as they are needed, by one or another procedure of cooperative accounting. Most of the more vital rules are developed by players in the context of some game-play. Players use rules to play the game, and their playing of the game reflexively establishes the meaning of the rules, which become "the" rules. As Garfinkel (1967, 78) phrased a similar situation, "Each is used to elaborate the other." Rules set certain elements of the game-play into motion, which players use to organize the meaning of those rules; and once any rule is interrogated in the light of a specific use of it, that use will reflexively be used to stabilize the rule understood in that way. It is like a self-fulfilling prophesy. Garfinkel (1977b) also observes, "Rules are part of the setting that they provide the directions for. They set up the very order in which they find their own intelligibility." If it sounds ironic, then it is our lives that are ironic.

All this constitutes a local means for producing the orderliness of a game, and it is no serious shortcoming when rules fail to provide direction for one or another aspect of game-play, which is something that occurs frequently. When the directions do not stipulate a rule that covers a certain game situation, players fill the gap without any disruption. After a first complete run-through of the game "Fact or Crap," two players ended in a tie, but the rules did not specify how to break a tie. The players effortlessly composed a "tie-breaker" situation that quickly resolved the aporia. Some game directions offer instructions for choosing who goes first, although such instructions are not always followed. Players can permit the oldest or youngest player in the game to go first (both methods were used), especially when a small child is playing. Some rules indicate that the player to move first should be decided by a "roll of the dice," but they do not stipulate whether the high or low number will prevail, so the players decide that. In one game that mentioned "dice" in the rules, a player contended that "you should always" roll one die when rolling for who moves first, and the players complied without argument. Another game directed that the one with the nearest birthday should be the first to move, but this was trumped by the qualifying person asserting that as the host of the house where the game is being played he should not be the one to go first, so the person who had the second closest birthday speedily suggested that she move first instead, a case of modifying the rule for convenience's sake.

Nearly every game that involved rolling dice at some point implicated the players in the task of adjudicating policy regarding what to do about dice that rolled off of the table, although no rules ever spoke to this issue. One group reported that they operated in accordance with an unspoken rule about re-rolling the dice if it lands on the floor, a rule with which everyone complied, even though it was never discussed by anyone throughout the entirety of the game. In other games there was considerable discussion about what to do with dice that roll off the table. The game of "Aggravation," featured a very conscientious rule-reader whose re-reading taxed the patience of an athletic player who kept shaking the dice in his hands for several minutes as the rules were being read. As his impatience grew, the shaking became more vigorous, and in advance of his first throw the players found themselves thinking that that he might very well miss the game board altogether; so the players discussed what to do if his dice miss the board:

> Crystal: So what do we do if the die rolls on the floor?
>
> Hal: Oh, that's / offensive.
>
> Crystal:        / Re-roll?
>
> Karla: Re-roll.
>
> 5   Hal: Re-roll. We're making that up, though? / We're making up that rule.
>
> Karla:                                                 / Yeah.
>
> Crystal: We're making that up.
>
> Sean: House Rule of "Aggravation."

Here we find a concise sequence of a candidate *Account* that wins *Ratification* in lines 4–7, and very quickly receives *Objectivation* as a "House Rule" (line 9). What is amusing is that in his very next turn Sean, the vigorous dice-shaker, rolls a die onto the floor, but instead of re-rolling, he attempts to play the number on the die since it was a favorable one:

> Sean: It's a five.
>
> Crystal: We decided to roll again.
>
> Hal: Yeah.
>
> Sean: No! That's right there!

Sean did not prevail, and when his re-roll hit the opposite wall, he rolled for a third time without complaint. In yet another game, "Mousetrap," Jerome rolled his die, and when it hit the floor he immediately picked it up and re-rolled; however, four minutes later when Marge rolled her die onto the floor she played the die since it had landed on the very number she required to successfully move her mouse onto a needed space. No one objected.

There were also some compliance issues with players who set the dice on the board rather than giving the dice a true shake, and these occurrences were handled differently by different cohorts of players, depending upon the local contingencies. In some games the players were required to re-roll. In another game ("Parcheesi") a very mild-mannered Vietnamese player, who spoke very little throughout the game, almost always set the dice on the board rather than shaking and rolling. The other players looked to each other, but none of them voiced anything, since it was obvious there was nothing deliberate about the player's behavior. In "Aggravation," when Crystal's dice accidentally rolled out of her hand, she picked it up quickly and was allowed to re-roll even though her re-roll was more favorable to her than the accidental fall. On many occasions there is considerable scope for manipulating that ambiguity. She was castigated by Hal, who teased, "I wish I could choose my rolls," and it served as an effective compliance production account that governed subsequent play—when Crystal's dice fell out of her hand again six minutes later, she allowed the dice to stand as they fell. It is not that the sides "negotiated" a settlement so much as that a procedure evolved in the public space of their play. The procedure became obligatory, even a matter of some moral consequence, but alongside many video recordings of other games that did not insist upon such a procedure, it constitutes a very limited moral universe.

## FAULTING THE RULES

All manner of contingencies are handled on an ad hoc basis by players, and there is a tendency for any procedure that emerges to become regularized as the rules of play. Students analyzing the process expressed much amazement at the malleability of rules. Most of the poorer student project papers include complaints, even bitter indictments, of the "inadequacies" of rules: "'Arne' has many odd rules," "The rules were unhelpful," "Our consensus is that the rules of 'Cranium' were minimal and unhelpful in most cases," and "The rules come up short in providing complete insight about what we needed to do." The missed point of the exercise was to gain an appreciation that rules are *necessarily* incomplete and will always require some players' work of meaning fulfillment. Since the rules are never read in their entirety, how would these players who fault the rules possibly know how complete they really were? Being minimal may be an asset when comprehensive rules are too lengthy to get read. Students who naively assume the rules are complete presume that the rules of a game always compose a preexisting order that merely needs to be applied straightforwardly. Under such a regime, any outbreak of disorder will be blamed on a "snag" in the rules, for which the game's creators may be blamed.

*What is the origin of the legitimacy of game play?* The rules? No. When properly viewed, the rules are only *a resource* that players can use for organizing the orderliness of their play. Players who fail to recognize their own authorship in the development of rules are trapped within "the natural attitude." Rules are indeed used to authorize play, but this "use" is an active, coordinated praxis that constitutes skill in playing games. One is able to cite rules, even selectively, to win agreement for what one wishes to do; one may even cry out, "It's the rule!" But more importantly, rules depend upon the skillful capacity of the player(s) to organize the game play in a manner that *makes its intelligibility available to all.* The actual sources of legitimacy are the players who learn to act in concert when organizing their rules. A rule doesn't come with its meaning instantly apparent to everyone in just the same way; rather, the rule is inscribed inside of a course of affairs that it helps to form, and any intersubjective adequacy of sense must be accomplished by the players. The intelligibility lies not in what the instructions say to do, but in the activities the players locate.

An important part of the work of legitimizing the rule-governed play that players have found, as well as the work of taming the perennial labile character of the meaning of rules, includes objectivating the solutions that players have discovered. Players will attempt to routinize the structure of their play by substituting objective expressions wherever they have been using indexical expressions (expressions whose richness of meaning is strictly local) to coordinate their activities. In Garfinkel's words, gradually context-free formulations are made to substitute for context-specific accounts. This is the work of producing a situation where the rules are stable and can be consistently applied to everyone. However, according to Garfinkel (1977) their efforts are unlikely to succeed for long: "But the world will fail to live up to such idealization. Such substitution is an enterprise that is an infinite task carried out without chance of success in the end." Nevertheless, players can and do use such idealization to structure their interaction. What is more likely to happen is that their attempts to turn their local interaction into an objective reality will succeed for a time, but gradually their affairs will again come unglued from their objectivations, although they may not notice what has happened, and they may not notice it deliberately. They may pretend that no change is occurring. They will bend the rules, alter the interpretations, and find newer ways to normalize each minor transformation, under the illusion that everything has remained the same. It is one way that society can be made to work.

There is no better illustration of this than the rituals performed by the traditionally oriented Aboriginal people of Central Australia, with whom I lived for two years. They steadfastly maintained that the religious rituals they practice have not experienced an iota of change since they originated in the Dreaming (*tjukurrpa*). In the case of these Central Australian Aboriginals there exists an extensive record of documentation of their rituals from the first explorers in the nineteenth century to the many anthropologists who studied their rituals during the twentieth century, and it is apparent that there have been a great many changes to their ritual observances. The record is clear: Aboriginal people today do not practice their sacred observances in the precisely the same way that was recorded by Spencer and Gillen (1899), Elkin (1933), and Stanner (1966), but they think that they do, and thinking that way lends force to compliance with what they believe is required, the "external coercion" mentioned by Durkheim.

This also is the natural attitude—the common sense, everyday presumption that confines itself to the immediate world and remains there, the natural attitude of people "who are born into this sociocultural world, have to find their bearings within it, and have come to terms with it. This world is pre-given to them and taken by them unquestionably for granted" (Schutz 1971, Vol. I: 145). It is a worldly attitude that misses the transcendental or "constitutive becoming of the world in the sense-performances of transcendental life" (Fink and Husserl 1995, 4). In the first line of his seminal work, *Ideas Pertaining to a Pure Phenomenology*, Husserl (1982, 5) writes, "Natural cognition begins with experience and remains *within* experience." Confined and "naively absorbed in ongoing life" (Husserl 1970b, 150), living within "the dogmatism of the natural attitude" (Fink and Husserl 1995, 4), I do not inquire into the being of the world and miss the role that I and my cohorts have in its development. I do not escape my own propaganda, and treat the constituted world as the only world there is. Similarly, rules are treated as externally existing facts whose meaning is static and knowable in certain terms. That two cohorts' play of the same game do not always correspond demonstrates the contingency of rules.

In contrast, ethnomethodologists sustain the transcendental insight that the social order is always our local achievement—"our" and not "my" since it is always the result of the concerted activity of a community of fellows. The theme of our investigations concerns how players work together to make the just-so story of governing rules that exist externally to the occasion come true. A game-with-rules would seem to be an excellent example of a well-planned activity—a game's actions are planned in advance according to the designers' rational designs, and everything they anticipate is orderly. A formal analysis that examines the rules for this sort of rationality will usually find what it is searching for. But we have learned that the rule-writers are unable to plan for everything, and the actual world of play quickly outstrips the planned provisions. And if they do not outstrip them, it is because the players are skillful at constructing a unified account of what the game consists of and learn to adapt the rules of their play to that newly furnished account. The two of them—the rules and the play the rules are inscribed in—evolve together; each determines the other. It may seem that rules preexist play; after all, they are there lying in the box before the cellophane is unwrapped. But they are without sense and reference until the players do their work. Players organize the play to which their attempts to "follow" rules have led them, they also regularize and stabilize that play, and finally they claim unashamedly that what they have organized is the correct meaning of the rules "all along."

It is not merely that the local interconcatenation of sense is contingent and does not produce an enduring totalization; it is that some locally efficacious, orderly, coherent social procedures are worked into the play and gradually become more routinized, though never perfectly so. Jeff Coulter (2009, 400) suggests that this situation comprises the usual conditions for effective rule use:

> The lack of a totality of defeasibility conditions on rules which might be consulted "objectively" to settle issues of sense or relevance, far from being subversive of rule-governance and rule-following, comprise conditions for their involvement. . . . The lack of logical *formalism* for incorporating constitutive rules in no sense undermines either their cogency or their applicability to human conduct.

Any study over time, especially under the gaze of a video recorder, will reveal the many ways that rules keep evolving, always remaining subject to the immanent contingencies of the play.

## *NON*-NEGOTIATION

Formal analytic theorists are also prone to locate all principles in a place that preexists the local occasion, in the hope of finding some metaphysical basis to society,[12] but they do so only by *ignoring* the intricate details of the *players' work* in organizing the intelligibility of their affairs. Some social analysts will grant that members of society "negotiate" some of the rules, but this too is one more unfounded belief in the hyper-rationality of social affairs. It is clear on these tapes that for the most part the players don't know what they're doing, and players rarely "negotiate" in the way that social theorists speak of it. In order to negotiate one has to have a clear, autonomous point of view, an individual perspective about which one has some certainty, which can then be negotiated with someone else who likewise holds a point of view. Certainly, on occasion this can be the case: there can be debate and compromise. But in the vast majority of instances the players are too confused to engage in such planful, rational negotiations, and for the most part they do not have much of what can be called an individual perspective—that is only a notion derived from individualist social mythology, which has emerged from the metaphysics of the European Enlightenment. As Schutz (1970, 134) comments, "We deliberately disregard the fact that only a very small part of our experiences or knowledge genuinely originates within the individual himself." Players are addressed to the massive presence of the public spectacle that is before them, and whose import and sense loom everywhere before them as a plenum of possibilities. More time is spent studying the game board and organizing the game's intelligibility by means of offering accounts about what they see than is spent reading the rules. Frequently, the rules are lying open on the table beside the players, but only occasionally does anyone look at them. The gaze at the game board is a corporate gaze, not a collection of individual or even intersubjective gazes,[13] and the best the players can do is work to tame the plenum they are observing together so that they can get the game played and still be home in time for dinner.

Let us further examine the *non*-negotiation that players of games-with-rules engage in. While many social scientists tend to idealize what takes place as "decision making," and follow in the long tradition of just-so stories set into motion by Thomas Hobbes and John Locke (among other founders of European social thought), ethnomethodologists draw their insights from observing worldly activities *in situ* or by repeated studies of video recordings of microinteractional detail and have learned that orderly methods for interacting in local settings are organized by parties in ways very different than the hyper-rational models that most social scientists impose upon their data. Players are not solely preoccupied with "an ideational realm" (Livingston 2008, 234). Only on rare occasions can one say that a "shared agreement" is made. Rational choice theorists, for example, place far more deliberateness and clarity into the minds of parties than is the case empirically. Instead, real-world processes are more chaotic, indeterminate, but in the end perfectly effective; moreover, these theorists miss the *actual* brilliance and ingenuity of the intellectual faculties of those they study. The rationality of rational choice modeling is an assumed rationality that is conceived within theorizing independently of, and prior to, what persons are actually doing; therefore, they are biased and ethnocentric accounts. They are "ethnocentric" because they naively recycle European Enlightenment social mythology and are not very amenable to being changed by actual events. Because rational choice discourse is a common theoretical language in academic cultures, political scientists and economists are able to readily communicate their ideas when they use this language. Their formal models receive further encouragement by the fact that theorizing that way may afford them opportunities for professional advancement and by the fact that statistical studies can be adapted more easily to these models. These techniques provide a veneer of scientism, but fail to make direct contact with any real, naturally occurring social occasions, and are grounded in nothing besides a technical language and some strategies for reducing persons' activities to rationalist portrayal.

In our own data it is commonplace to find players who offer to comply *before* they know with what they have agreed to comply! So what sort of "shared agreement" can it be? Speaking of "shared agreements" sounds like an intelligent way of describing something, except it *misses* what is most extraordinary about what the players of games are doing. Consider this attempt to understand some rules:

> Bill: [Reading rules] You may trade resources with other players for using maritime trade.
>
> Linda: Okay.
>
> Bill: Which we don't know what that is.
>
> Linda: 'Kay.
>
> Bill: [Summarizing rules.] You may build roads, settlements, or cities. And/or buy development cards. You may also play one development card anytime during your turn. After you're done, pass the dice to your left, who then continues the game by repeating what we just did.
>
> 10
>
> Linda: So I can like roll and get settlement cards or I mean like resource cards and then I can like do stuff?
>
> Bill: Yep.

It seems that Linda may not yet have a clear idea of what she is agreeing to in line 5 when she says, "Kay." For there to be rational negotiation, parties have to have some concept about which they are for the most part certain. Here neither player has much more than a clue. It is another case of reading and listening senselessly in anticipation of the appearance of something that can be fathomed, and when it appears it is not always the case that the players "construct it;" it just appears, authochthonously. This makes a hash of rational choice theorizing, especially since not knowing what the rules mean is more ubiquitous than is knowing what they mean! Since Bill (line 6) seems embarrassed by speaking senselessly, he abbreviates his reading by trying to summarize the main points. After he pauses, Linda (line 11) attempts an account for what was just said, even though her account is far from clear. She makes an attempt to *simplify* the rules that were read, and simplification like this is a very common feature of accounts; in the natural course of accounting, these simpler versions (which some students referred to as "dumbed-down" versions) can be reduced to *even shorter glosses* that stand indexically for the many intersubjective understandings that have accompanied the interaction that the accounts describe. But what it all really means *remains to be discovered*, despite Bill's reassuring "Yep." It is discovered not in spite of the "Yep," but with the aid and optimism that the "Yep" provides.

Does this game get played strictly according to the rules? One can say yes, but it would be a very strange notion of rules; it is certainly *not* the formal analyst's rules that are clear and distinct, and straightforwardly applied. Very little game-play is analytically straightforward. Well, then is the game being played according to the players' interpretation of the rules? While the word "interpretation" is a well-intended bone to throw in the direction of intersubjectivity, "interpretation" doesn't come close to describing the intricate detail of what the players are engaged in, intricacy that Garfkinel (1977) has described in this way: "One of the really incredible things that members do with collections of rules is to get really detailed and deep in making Games intelligible, analyzable, and detailed with respect to a Game's character as an organized arrangement of ordinary events of play." Wittgenstein (1953, 80, no. 198) offered a respecification of the notion of interpretation:

> "But how can a rule shew me what I have to do at *this* point? Whatever I do is, on some interpretation, in accord with the rule."—That is not what we ought to say, but rather: any interpretation still hangs in the air along with what it interprets, and cannot give it any support. Interpretations by themselves do not determine meaning.

The players may agree, but following the agreement they may be seen still gazing out wide-eyed at the plenum in order to learn together what it is they have agreed to. If that is negotiation it is a very funny kind of negotiation, and I would propose that the term "non-negotiation" is equally appropriate. Considering the same phenomenon, Wieder (1984, 36) wrote, "The resulting organization is a temporally unfolding gestalt-contexture, the appearance of which varies for each of the participants." This is accurate, but it still bears a level of generality that we are concerned to reduce. Similarly, to say that rules are "socially constructed" also provides little specification regarding the details of what players are *actually* doing. Most of the sense is necessarily underdetermined, and usually overdetermined at the same time in that there is usually more than one reason why a particular procedure or account gets adopted; hence, it is not very informative to declare that the meanings are constructed. These are the ways that social scientists speak in order to give the impression that much is understood when in fact the more serious social analytic work has yet to begin. Aware of the shortcomings of rationalists' descriptions of negotiations, interpretations, shared agreements, and social constructions, Erving Goffman once spoke of "a working consensus," which may be informal enough for tentative use; however, Larry Wieder (1984, 35) criticized Goffman's notion as being too static. Wieder argued, "There does not need to be any shared agreement at all in the sense that the participants have the same or even similar thoughts. What is required is that each respond to the other in a fashion that enables the performance of each."

The discourse that many of my students used for describing what they observed in the videos of their interaction is infected by some of this same social mythology: "We spent the first twenty minutes questioning, deliberating, and eventually deciding on our interpretation of the rules." The solutions that players find, and which can be viewed in the videos, are more passive than active, so why speak of any "deciding" at all? Even when they do deliberately decide something, it is usually an outcome taken by default; moreover, no "decision" is unavailable for revision. So why use the term? Another student wrote, "My primary goal in analyzing the tape is discovery of how meanings are negotiated and how they are combined." In order to speak of negotiating, there should be bits of information that are clear in the minds of each of the parties that somehow get shared, brick-like pieces that each party can contribute to the building of a system for social interaction; but in most of our cases *the sharing precedes knowledge*, and knowledge is its precipitate. Their activities are not deliberate or rational except in the most general way. Many of the conversations move along without either party really knowing what the other means to say, and perhaps the players who are speaking do not yet know what they themselves mean to say. A conversation is not constructed—most of the time a conversation moves itself. It is not negotiation, it is not shared agreement, and it is not a working consensus; it is not even a continuously updated intersubjectively concatenated understanding. It is something else. For the moment, I am collecting my thoughts and data about it in a file that is labeled, "non-negotiation."

The idea for the term comes from my reading of some phenomenologists who have addressed the matter in a theoretical way. Speaking of the intertwining of my life with other lives and the intersection of my perceptual field with that of others, Merleau-Ponty (1968, 49) speaks of "this non-knowing of the beginning which is not nothing, and which is not the reflective truth either," and he observes that this non-knowing takes place "in the world, among the others." Consequently, this non-knowing that inaugurates social life is not my individual possession. While explaining his existential category of attunement, Heidegger (1996, 127) claims that what is "disclosed [*Erschliessen*] does not, as such, mean to be known," and that what is disclosed to cognition falls far short of what is there to which we are paying close attention. Following both of these thinkers in his later writing, Derrida kept seeking ways to infect his inquiries with what he calls "non-knowledge," since there is so much going on that is not conceptual. An observation by the physicist David Bohm (1980, 56) is pertinent here: "A fixed distinction between thought and non-thought cannot be maintained, for one can see that thought is a real activity, which has to be grounded in a broader totality of real movement and action that overlaps and includes thought." We need to put more effort into studying this broader movement that overlaps and includes thought, i.e., the role of non-knowledge in our social affairs, if only because there is so much of it.

It is naïve to say that people are simply understanding rules whose cogency arrives already made, or to think that players are reading rules as some sort of literal text able to stand apart from the game-playing activities. Instead, the players steadily address their gazes to their collaborative displays, courses of action that embody rules and that are exhibitions that permit all players to be witness to the rule-governed play. Above all, players are engaged in taming the exhibitions they witness. These activities may be set into motion by a reading of the rules, but there is no direct cause-and-effect that is operating. Rather, the players reflexively appropriate the practices they witness and tame, and this becomes the game according to the rules. As Wieder (1974, 171) has observed, "Rules cannot be literally described because the clear sense that each achieves in its contexture is contingent upon the concrete, historical, and ongoing course of experience of some particular observer. . . . Thus, the requirement of literal description for deductive theory cannot be met." Although the game cannot be played without the rules, the game is not directly deducible from the written rules. Important corollary questions here would be, which aspects of a game-with-rules are rational, and just-what is rationality?

Garfinkel (1977) describes the complexity of what players are doing:

On any occasion in which a rule must be defined as something determined, clear and certain, everyone will look to something further that yet remains to be determined. And that something further inhabits the thing already determined to provide for its present, clear, definite, decided, and decidable character. It is "definite," yet it is never said in just so many words what it is. It is not that members do not know what they are talking about; rather, they know what they are talking about in just this way.

Players usually do not *decide* on matters, and not once in these 40 or more studies involving 150 players did any group of them take a vote. The process is more collaborative and emergent than it is planfully deliberate. Just as Husserl came to recognize that his phenomenological account of the constitution of meanings was too idealistic, and came to further describe what he called *passive* synthesis (which he opposed to the *active* synthesis of meanings), so we could say that the development of rules is mostly passive. Many accounts get confirmed out of politeness, or gratuitously, and are not well comprehended. As confused as such ways might seem to rational choice theorists, it is still effective for providing an orderliness to the game. As one player remarked, "We are all trying to agree on something, yet it almost seems as though we do not even know what it is we are trying to agree on." Their interest in agreeing *precedes* the identification of what there is to agree about.

The game "Settlers of Catan" involves trading resource cards, but the guidelines given for trading the cards are incomplete, at least to the extent that the players read through them. It happened that a local procedure evolved according to which whoever offered to trade first received what cards were being offered for trade. As the game play continued and players observed this procedure, the procedure became *naturally objectified* as the correct system of play. By the end of the game it had became a rule as absolute as any rule in the instructions, although at no time was a deliberate decision made nor was anything ever negotiated. Probably more of the game-play was provided by player-furnished practices than by the formal rules, but because there are not usually preexisting meanings that subsequently get negotiated, once a sense emerges autochthonously *it needs to be exhibited* so that all can witness it and get on the same page. This is *local work*. As players see what the practices are and repeat them, the game's practices become more stable. Some of the sense that is grasped can be formulated in an account, be objectivated by the players who act in concert, and the result can be implemented as a social fact with all the pedigree of exteriority that Durkheim has described.

Ethnomethodologists wish to sustain an emphasis upon investigating the *public* understanding of the rules, in contrast to an individual's understanding of the rules. Almost always, the collective gazing is leading the way, and any rationality is embodied in that gazing. To be sure, we occasionally witness an individual's understanding (constitutional phenomenologists take heart), but the majority of "thinking" proceeds collectively by means of public displays. Thought is able to know itself only to the extent that it objectivates itself, and such objectivation is a social event. Some people never read rules, do not listen to what rules are read, are even incapable of listening to rules that are read, but they are incredibly perceptive at observing and noting the consequences of actual game-play. Even when players try to elicit other players' individual understanding, the attempt can fall flat. The rules of one game required that a player playing a spell card must cast a spell, including "going off" on another player. What this "going off" amounted to was necessarily left to the creative work of the player (how many lines of rules would be required to make such an instruction explicit?). This player asked the group if it meant she was supposed to yell (possibly to inoculate herself against being castigated for any unsocial behavior that may follow), and the group gave her license to teach everyone what "going off" might consist of, although no one offered her any guidance about what the instruction meant.

Players *pick up and recycle* anything and everything in the displays that is relevant for organizing the game. Once a practice is witnessed in the game-play, it is there for anyone's use, as the structure for the game emerges. Both the basic rules of the game and effective strategies proceed via these displays, and the players discover together what order there is. Their *exhibitions* are their richest resource for learning game relevant expertise, and such expertise is not deducible directly from the rules. Mostly the players do not grasp what the rules are until they witness them in the exhibits, and so the players are continuously scrutinizing the spectacle in order to teach themselves, and each other, the game. When a player provides a summary account for a rule that has just been read, the rule-reader also is learning the meaning of what he has just read, and *instantaneously* appropriates that as if that is what he really meant all along. Once something (anything) happens, it gains some status. As one student remarked in her analysis, "It is not just that we are seeing what is going on, but that what we are seeing comes back through our perception as an absolute." This is a natural way to describe the reflexivity of the occasion.

When players only partially understand a rule, they are undeterred and proceed in a way that allows the consequences to be left open. So players speak like, "Let's just go on," "We'll keep going," etc. Another group describes the way they are addressed to the plenum out on the board, although this group has yet to find the game:

> After reading the rule, he looks to M to see if his interpretation offers a sensible understanding of the rule. But M returns his look with one of incomprehensibility and unintelligibility. After not comprehending the rule we look to the pieces to give the rule coherency. After looking at the pieces and even they don't offer understanding, we move on to relying or setting up the game board in hope of understanding the rule. By moving on we hope to shed light on this rule that we don't understand.

One group reported that although it was obvious that one member was unsure of what he was doing, he "complied" with an account. Sometimes what players know best about a rule is that they must comply with it. They may repeat the rule in order to get a better handle on it, even nodding when it remains incomprehensible, and they will do this *even when they do not know the meaning of what is being repeated*. Occasionally, when the players reach an aporia that they are unable to sort out, they pretend that nothing happened and that everything is proceeding smoothly. Not all rules get settled. After reading what to do when an answer is correct, one player in the game still harbors some confusion and announces that she is "confused about the grade thing;" but the subject is changed and the matter is left unsettled. Some rules are too complicated to sort out everything about them, and a great number of player-initiated queries go ignored. Even when they are not ignored, they are not necessarily resolved:

> Susan: So you can only put the cards down here on your turn, like as a discard?
>
> Bob: Just lay them down whenever?
>
> Susan: On your turn. Only on your turn.
>
> Bob: Only on your turn . . .

Bob seems to respond to Susan's query in the affirmative, though both of their utterances are in the interrogative case and Bob appears confused himself. Is knowing-while-being-confused rare, or could it be that much knowledge is like this?[14] Is there an indeterminacy that operates at the heart of understanding? Is it the professional task of formal analysts to reduce or even deny such indeterminacies? It might be said that Bob's reply is a kind of semi-affirmation, but what sort of negotiations leave room for these semi-affirmations that are everywhere? Perhaps all of them, but we need to set aside any idealizations that render negotiations more clear-cut than they really are.

As we saw in the case of the Doublets Penalty, the rule—which was read, listened to, and to which all players responded to the rule-reader's "Does everyone get that?" in the affirmative—is forgotten by most of the players. While reading rules and applying them, an account may be suggested or implied, and the response might be "Yeah" or "Okay." But these responses are more prayers than confirmations; nevertheless, in the structure of the play that is developing, such senseless confirmation served for ratifying the account. This is more non-negotiation. Not infrequently, players commence playing in a kind of simulation of competent play, and somehow this simulated play shifts gear and becomes competent play, even as everyone is looking to everyone else in order to learn what it is that they need to do. All this while, the players are addressed to the plenum out there on the game board. Somehow in the end the players end up with rule-governed game-play that, in the words of one player, has become an "of-course-we-know, of-course-this-is-how-it-is-played" matter, and at this point the game comes to have a massive presence. What they have achieved is not a rational certainty about rules, but some habitual expectations regarding certain practices of play, in just the manner David Sudnow describes a jazz pianist who reaches for the melody (or conversationalist reaching for the discourse): "For there's no melody (or talk) as an objective structure, existing in nature. There are practices of melody-ing (and talking), of sounded articulated reaching."[15] The real game does not exist in the rationalists' ideal models; it rides tenuously astride the interconcatenations of the players' practices. That is, its correctness is one not of ideas but of practices. Generally players find it advisable not to emphasize the formal conceptual facets of game-play, but to become engaged in playing activities that can then be regularized and ordered.

Strangely, that the general agreement can be tendered even when people do not grasp what is meant is one way that people come to grasp what is meant. The astonishing thing is that when an account is confirmed senselessly in this way, the dynamics of reflexive understanding work adequately for making the account cogent. Much as readers of horoscopes marvel at the cogency of an astrological forecast—a cogency whose real author is the reader of the horoscope him/herself—players can use the wording of an account to collect the account's grounds. If many players who offer accounts *are not sure themselves that what they are saying is valid*, they are encouraged and can gain some assurance from the gratuitous confirmation other players are willing to offer them. This is what the yearning that follows such confirmation—and is visible in a player's looks to other players—is about.

Much more than being considered a summary of what meaningfulness has transpired, accounts can be a device for collecting its meaning. Garfinkel (1977) has described how this works:

> The rules and their consequences are in a relationship of reflexive accountability. This is a hermeneutic circle: it is not even chicken and egg; it is 20 times worse than that. The aim is to see that circle not as something mysterious but as routine, to see that in fact you are using it all the time, that you *need* it in order to play a game.

An important way in which accounts are not negotiated is that accounts are reflexive and their consequences are apparent only after they have already been used to organize the game. The following circumstances are by no means unusual, no matter how extraordinary they seem: A player offers an account, unsure of just what he or she means to say and looking to the plenum to pick up what meaning it collects. Another player mishears the account or applies to it an understanding that was not the intention of the person giving the account; while this second party is not really happy with the account understood in this way, in the player's politeness the player is ready to go along with what he or she (wrongly) thinks is what the first player is advocating. A third player, hearing that understanding, and thinking that it is a confirmation of the first player's account—so that it appears that the first two players are in accord—offers a gratuitous concurrence, nodding in indication of his willingness to go along with the group. The first person, who may have almost been ready to explain that that was not at all the meaning intended, observes the third person's concurrence ("agreement" is too strong a term to use here) and decides that since this meaning of the utterance has been successfully communicated to the satisfaction of most of the players, it is better just to go along with the flow of things than it is to "rock the boat;" so that first player nods in agreement as well. *Voila:* the group has an orderliness in hand, although *it is an orderliness that no one ever advocated.* Everyone conforms to what they believe is a transcendental order, and they keep staring at the plenum to learn what future they have cast for themselves.

While few analysts seem capable of capturing real-world events like this in which parties wrongly grasp the intended purpose or meaning of a partner, novelists occasionally capture social interaction in its meticulous local details and make our nonsense into studies of irony. Joseph Heller and Thomas Pynchon have offered fabulous descriptions, but perhaps the writer most skilled at describing such events is Marcel Proust, who presents these sorts of details while preserving the looks of the world for each one of a dozen characters simultaneously immersed in their interactions with each other. As one of a great many illustrations, take Proust's description of the garden party at the palace of the Prince and Princesse de Germantes in Paris just after the turn of the last century.[16] The Baron de Charlus, a brother of the host, is a closet homosexual, and the narrator is among the very few who are aware of this. The mistress of the Duc de Germantes (who is another brother) is at the garden party with her sons, two young men of "resplendent beauty," and the narrator notices de Charlus' instant infatuation with the sons. Despite his enamoration, de Charlus pretends to be disinterested in them and ignores them; instead, he endeavors to strike up a long and obsequious conversation with the mother/mistress, who is flattered that the noble gentleman has taken such interest in her. Most of the guests at the garden party have lined up against de Charlus' brother the Duc and on the side of the Duc's wife, the Mme de Germantes, in this affair. As the party proceeds, the mistress introduces de Charlus to her sons, which was his intention, and he proceeds to flatter their intelligence (one of them is a simpleton), even arranging to visit them, while keeping most of his attention trained on the mother all the while. De Charlus' brother the Duc is deeply moved by "this great kindness on his brother's part" for his willingness to be one of the few to befriend the Duc's mistress, so the Duc goes up to his brother and embraces him affectionately and expresses his fondness for him, saying, "Well, well, young brother." The Baron de Charlus is touched by this, but he is not about to reveal his actual motives, which did not include fraternal fidelity, for showing such respect to his brother's mistress. In fact, Proust is so skillful that he sustains two possible motives for the Duc's embrace of his brother—one being a simple genuine expression of gratitude for de Charlus' taking his side, and the other being a more calculating self-interest in the form of rewarding good behavior, in hope of insuring that "the kind of action he had performed that evening had not gone unobserved by the eyes of a brother, just as, with the object of creating salutary associations of memories for the future, we give a lump of sugar to a dog that has sat up and begged." Moreover, these several events during this evening-long course of interaction get interrupted by many other conversations and incidents that are described with similar intricate social phenomenological detail. Proust knows that the basis upon which people act is much of the time the fantasy of their own imaginings with little basis in fact. Throughout the six volumes of *In Search of Lost Time*, Proust tended toward celebrating each time his characters' social interaction resembled two ships passing in the night.[17] However confused, there is much "intersubjectively interlinked experience" (Gurwitsch 1966, 432) in the world, although there is much less shared agreement. Sometimes the world works this way.

## AN ORDER OF PRACTICES

Unfortunately, theorists are not the only ones who tell just-so stories; since ethnomethodologists face their own narrative demands, they are also sometimes victims of their own storytelling. In the foregoing account, I have described how it is not that rules are first grasped in an abstract coherence and only then the game-play is deduced from them. On the contrary, the practices of game-play progressively reveal the rules by means of the rules' consequences. As these practices are exhibited, players can witness them, learn them, the sense can be objectivated, and a developing objective order can be tamed. The rules acquire their massive presence as a temporarily stabilized order, which is the local accomplishment of the players. Players engage in more doing than discussing, and they gradually accumulate some routine procedures of play. The unfortunate part for anyone hoping for a simple description is that no game is completely settled for good. Yes, the players routinize some play and temporarily stabilize a sense of the rules, but they are quick to ignore what they have accomplished, and they continually press the envelope of accepted practices as the more strategic aspects of their game-playing mature. Many of the rules are never settled, especially of games that no one has played before.

Above we described the cases of dice throwers who, having agreed that dice that roll off of the table should be re-rolled, are still tireless in their efforts to act upon favorable rolls of their dice that have left the table. Now let us take up a more extended transcript of game-play, during which each player serially attempts to bend a rule with which they had just finished insisting that another player maintain strict compliance:

> Diane: [Reading] "What's the name of a thick layer of hot rock found beneath the crust of the earth?" Lava! [Looks to others for confirmation, but they all dead-pan.] No.

Diane makes an effort to elicit the corroboration of her fellow players, without it being clear that she is making an official guess. The others' silence indicates that the answer may be incorrect, and she withdraws it. Then two of the players gang up against her:

> Pablo: I think you've got to write these things down [giggles].
>
> Mick: You gotta write them down!
>
> Diane: Oh, "What is the name of—"
>
> Mick: Did you mean to answer?

Diane: No.

Mick: [to Kaleb] That sounded like her answer [Kaleb laughs]. You can't just throw it out there!

Diane: The announcer usually asks, "Is that your answer?"

In defense of her deception, Diane offers the procedure adopted by a popular television show, "Who Wants To Be A Millionaire?" [their game included a feature called The Million Dollar Question"] whose announcer usually would ask the contestant, "Is that your final answer?" Since no one had asked for her final answer, she contends (successfully) that she has yet to give her official answer, even though she has already learned that her initial reply is incorrect.

Kaleb: More revisions to the rules.

[All laugh.]

Diane: [Rereads the question aloud.]

Despite having just lined up against such manipulation of the rules, when Mick gets his turn he attempts his own similar gambit:

Mick: This is the only sport I've never played! [reads] "In badminton what is the name of the object that is hit over the net?"

Pablo: [Laughs]

Mick: Oh I know this. (1.0) Bird. [Looks to Diane and Pablo for confirmation.]

[No one responds.]

Having publicly castigated a player for trying to elicit corroboration prior to an answer, the players begin to congeal about their procedure and create an intricate silence. Mick tries to probe that silence, when at line 22 Kaleb attempts to enforce the "rule" that is emerging. But at line 24 Mick seeks more play in the rule they are offering:

Mick: Birdie? Bird?

Kaleb: Which one?

Diane: Which one?

Mick: Is it this specific?

Kaleb: It could be.

Pablo: It depends.

Kaleb: It depends.

Pablo: It depends what the card says.

Mick: [In the tone of 'of course!'] It probably says "bird" or "birdie."

Mick's tone is exceedingly crafty—since it very gently solicits their cooperation, it forces them to become unpleasant in a public way if they are to retain strict enforcement of the emerging rule, a rule that Mick had a hand in setting into motion. The tone of Kaleb's voice in line 30 makes it plain to Mick that Kaleb is prepared to become unpleasant, and so Mick instantly breaks into Kaleb's reply, making it unnecessary for him to be hard-nosed:

30    Kaleb: Ac /tual—

    Mick:    / I'm going to go with "bird."//

    Kaleb:    // O.K.

    Mick: [Reads back of card] " 'Birdie,' or 'A Shuttle Cock'."

    Diane: You said "birdie"?

    Mick: I said "bird" (1.0 pause)

    Kaleb: Or "birdie."

    Mick: Or "birdie."

Mick's pleading look for mercy to Kaleb is precious. Not wanting to take the onus on himself, Kaleb puts the responsibility for proper game-play upon Mick, enjoying observing Mick contend with the moral dilemma. Mick declines to decide, not an unsuccessful way to engage in "non-negotiation," and Pablo weighs in on Mick's side, though Pablo also is ready to defer to the corporate will. Everyone addresses their queries to the group in its anonymity, rendering what is at stake a witnessably public affair:

    Kaleb: [laughs] Well, what are you going to do?

    Mick: What do you gotta do? [Looks to the others.]

40    Pablo: I'd let it slide [looks to Kaleb]. I don't care, it's up to you [gestures to the group].

    Kaleb: [laughs] O.K. We'll let it pass.

When the turn next comes to Kaleb, he is unashamed in his own recycling of Mick's unsuccessful strategic gambit. Having been treated more or less unsympathetically by Kaleb, Mick remains silent, thereby forcing Kaleb to face a similar moral dilemma. Realizing the inequity of what he is doing, Kaleb apologizes (line 48), and the others laugh:

> Kaleb: [Reading] "Name the group of people in Washington D.C. that make laws for our country." I don't even know. Is this a general question, or is it fairly specific
> 
> [looks to Mick]?
> 
> Mick: [Silent.]
> 
> Kaleb: 'Kay. Sorry.
> 
> Diane:    / (Laughs.)
> 
> 50   Mick:     / (Laughs.)

The game-play practice that emerges here has to do with more than the literal meaning of a rule; it is addressed to the moral universe of their interaction, to their interest in cultivating each other's friendship, and in exploring the depths of each other's characters. At each stage, each player (excepting Pablo, who had been already been required to drop out of the game) was ready to require strict compliance with an emerging rule that each one attempted to evade themselves. The deliberations were not narrowly conceptual but performative. If this is negotiation, which it probably is, then we have hardly begun to do the research. It seems that nothing really gets settled. Jurists often speak of "settled law," but it could be that even law like that is always open for reapplication, and any stability it has is temporary, contingent upon jurists' active efforts to maintain it. What is striking here is that there is a broad horizon of human activity to which the players' efforts are directed, *and they are hardly ever focused exclusively upon the rule itself*. Analysts may act as if all that the actors they study are concerned with is only what falls within the purview of the researchers' focus, i.e. rules, and they draw a narrow portrait of interaction that represents no actually existing world; in real life actors' concerns will always exceed such an interest. Instead of reducing the life of actors to conform to the researcher's modeling, it would be better for researchers to adapt their methods to the real world of the people being studied.

### STRATEGIC PLAYING

A great many of the player/analysts' descriptions of what a game-with-rules is about made reference to the interest the players had in having a "fun" game and in smoothly running play; they observed that the literal correctness of rules (whatever that might turn out to be) was willlingly sacrificed in the interests of a "good" game. So I spent a considerable amount of time searching the tapes for what this "good game" could be. In game after game, after the players achieve some success at stabilizing the rules and the game becomes orderly, the focus of the players began to shift toward employing strategic ways of playing.

Rules are necessary for a game; more importantly, they are natural. In games, as in life, people seek order, not only so that they can avoid chaos: rule-governed practices that are stabilized can make a game interesting. Players have a field of regularized options to engage their ingenuity and creative thinking. As their wits are challenged, the play becomes entertaining, and "The game is afoot." This is an important feature, one that *identifies a successful game-with-rules*.

The strategic interests of players certainly commence before all of the rule-governed playing is organized, but after some rule-governed aspects of play have been stabilized, the strategic elements of the game develop in earnest. Just as rule-governed play is displayed and witnessed, so also various strategic elements of play are exhibited in, and as, the game's practices. These strategic practices are then observed by the players, copied, expanded, and mastered. These practices are developed and learned *on the game board*; that is, game strategies only develop in connection with game play.[18] Players learn, cultivate, and employ various strategies that they use for successfully competing with the other players. The rules say little about such practices although these practices are the very heart of a game. A "good game" requires that the other players also demonstrate some skill in developing strategies of play, both those they have keenly observed and copied and those they innovate and which others copy. When players are able to confidently and intelligently engage in a strategic play of the game, it may be said that the game is well played and the players have done their work competently.

In most games, there is a point reached where the collaboration to understand the game and to develop reliable procedures for orderly game-play diverges into a preoccupation with cultivating procedures for strategically competitive game-play and to winning the game. This can have negative consequences for the players' hermeneutic work of understanding the game, for once it is recognized how an understanding of the game may entail strategic insight, players may become less collaborative. As one player remarked about this transformation: "The rules are no longer a way to make the game coherent; rather, they have become a way for each group member to attempt to win."

Rather than thinking this through only in the abstract, let us examine some transcript of strategic game-play. In the same game as the previous transcript, excerpted from "Are You Smarter Than A Fifth Grader," the players first try to produce the rule-governed play, and then to play the game strategically. Naturally, they do not read all of the rules, which cover moves in the game that are named "Peek," "Save," and "Copy," and which refer to officially warranted reliance upon other players' guesses at replies to questions one is unable to answer oneself. The players did not read the part of the rules about the climax of the game ("The Million Dollar Question") until they came close to reaching that point in the game, under the nearly universal policy of never reading any rule until it proves itself to be essential.

They do read the rules about how to play the "Peek pawn." The rules state that if one is unsure of one's answer to a question, one can use the single Peek pawn one has one time only by selecting another player for peeking at their written answer. Here the rule becomes complicated enough that not all of the players fully appreciated the potential consequences—if one peeks and accepts the answer, and the answer is correct, the person whose answer was adopted (let's call this player the peekee) receives $1,000. If one peeks but decides not to use the peekee's answer, and one's own answer is correct, the peekee receives nothing. If one peeks, does not use the peekee's answer, and one is *incorrect* while the peekee's answer was the correct one, then the player is forced to drop out of the game. Given the complexity of this set of rules, it is not surprising that the group declines to read rules of equal complexity that describe the use of "Save pawns" and the "Copy pawns." Recall that divorced from any game-play, rules sound mostly like nonsense.

In this case, the players' minimalist reading of the rules results in a narrowing down of the field of play that the players can make strategic, since they have only fully considered the rules surrounding the "Peek pawns;" however, this proved to be enough for the players to cultivate some effective strategic playing. During play it dawned upon one of the players (Kaleb) that since there was an incentive for a player to go along with a peekee's answer (incorrectly rejecting a peekee's reply requires dismissal from the game), it could become a strategic practice to deliberately write a reply that is incorrect; then, when someone peeks and uses that answer, they will be led astray. This strategic insight leads to a course of deceptions:

Pablo: Can I get to peek yet? What is that about? I get only one of those?

Pablo's questions publicly formulate various game-play relevant issues for the group to consider. Diane responds by offering an account of the object-of-the-game, but this is complicated by the fact that there are really two ways to win the game. The best way, and the way that most captivates Diane's imagination, is to qualify for and answer correctly The Million Dollar Question. Another way, if none of the players is able to qualify for The Million Dollar Question, is to end up with the most money at the end of the game.

> Diane: You only get one of each one. You've got to get to a million. Well you don't have to, you just have to try and get as much money / as possible.
>
> Mick: / Is there, is there a uhh penalty?
>
> Kaleb: Yes!
>
> Diane: For what?
>
> Mick: If you, if someone peeks at yours, but you intentionally answered it incorrectly, is there a penalty on the person who was peeked upon?
>
> 10 Diane: No.
>
> Pablo: No.

Here we have the cultivating of a strategic procedure:

> Mick: Great. That's, that's uhh interesting. Okay.
>
> Diane: That's not very nice, oh that's messed up! But if you get it right though, you get a thousand dollars, so you would want to answer it right.

Diane's account of the strategic play is relatively shallow, and the other players are unconvinced.

> Kaleb: But at the same time / if you //can eliminate everyone,
>
> Mick:                  / Right.//
>
> Kaleb: you / are going to win the game. You just aren't going to have a lot of money.
>
> 20 Mick:     / Right.

Kaleb's account of strategic play is more convincing and receives Mick's confirmation, which contributes towards making that strategy an official game strategy, something that Diane and Pablo find disturbing. Diane responds by offering a competing account, which Pablo confirms, and which sets up two competing accounts of strategic play that each has a pair of supporters:

Diane: The goal is to get to a million dollars people!

Pablo: Yeah that's winning.

Diane: To get as much money as you can.

Pablo: Not to knock everyone out.

Kaleb: But if you knock everyone out and you have a thousand dollars—

Diane: Oh my gosh, you guys are messed up.

As the game develops, Pablo is forced to drop out of the game, and Diane fails to qualify for The Million Dollar Question. Mick does very well on his turn and qualifies for The Million Dollar Question, giving him a chance to win the game outright. Unfortunately he does not know the answer to his question, which is about the century in which the Revolutionary War was fought (the title of the game is "Are You Smarter Than A Fifth Grader?"). When he "Peeks" at Kaleb, who has deliberately written the seventeenth century, Mick loses his chance to win the game.

The turn comes to Kaleb, who has earned two thousand dollars during his previous turns and who answers several questions right (it takes ten correct answers to qualify for The Million Dollar Question), but then he gets a question to which he doesn't know the answer. He considers using his Peek pawn, but he knows that by now every one of the other players is gunning for him, so he thinks their replies will be deceptions. So he asks a strategy related question:

Kaleb: How many thousands do you have?

Diane: Just one.

30  Kaleb: Sweet. I'm not going to answer it. I'm done. I win.

Diane: Ohhh!

Pablo: [Applauds.] Fucking dude. That is *awesome*!

Mick: [Laughs.]

Diane: That's messed up!

Kaleb: So I win.

In spite of Diane's exasperation, the competency of the players in learning not only (some) rule-governed play but also in cultivating (some) competent strategic practice leads to an entertaining and satisfying game, as evidenced in the laughter and excitement following Kaleb's display of wit. Hence, a competent game includes not only rule-governed play that is regularized and stabilized but also a set—even a minimalist subset, as in this case—of strategic practices that offer enough complexity to challenge the players' wits. Employing some originality within a context of some stabilized game-play is what can lead to playing a "good" game.

Rules are used by players as a resource for developing a game; however, they are almost never "followed" slavishly. Instead, rules are resources that are selectively applied, affording considerable scope for the players' creativity. And it is that creativity that is the basis for a satisfactory play of the game, and for the coherence that the rules come to have.

FOUR

## COMMUNICATING MEANINGS[1]

Words and texts do not possess their meanings unequivocally in themselves. Instead, an occasioned discourse taken as a whole carries the sense, or rather is made to carry the sense, by serving as the vehicle for the discussants' worldly work of communicating meanings. The sense that is emerging guides the distribution of the meanings to each of the components of the discourse. These meanings are necessarily equivocal since the sense of the discourse is always emerging. "Meaning" has to be something about the words, but one cannot find it in the words alone. The words institute *a shifting system* of signification, but they themselves are subject to the very matrix they establish, which provides for them new traces of possible sense they can take up.

Emile Benveniste (1971, 105) proposed, "The sentence is realized in words, but the words are not simply segments of it. A sentence constitutes a whole which is not reducible to the sum of its parts; the meaning inherent in this whole is distributed over the ensemble of the constituents. . . . In practice, the word is envisaged above all as a syntagmatic element, a constituent of empirical utterances." In fact, if the meaning is dependent upon the contingent constituents, whose sense is reflexively adopted from the whole, then one cannot speak of meaning as "inherent." What is vital is the signifying work that speakers and hearers are able to do with the syntagmatic elements whose material, iconic-like quality continuously offers them opportunities for making sense. These opportunities are not static but occur in the midst of the flow of affairs, a flux that parties attempt to tame even while they rely upon it for what significant achievements they are able to make.

Discourse is not usually a monologue; more commonly, a discursive event involves parties who are mutually and reciprocally orienting to each other. Despite this fact, on occasion the science of linguistics loses sight of the dialogical nature of language use. Michael Halliday (1992, 21) has commented, "We have often pointed out that it takes two to mean; but we still tend to refer to consciousness as if it was an individual phenomenon, with the social as an add-on feature." Paul Thibault (1997, xviii) attributes part of this tendency to a cultural proclivity to individualism: "The analytic focus in these recent developments has been on an asocial individual—usually an analytic projection of North American folk-theories of individual mind and behavior." Similarly, William Hanks (1996, 236) faults standard linguistic accounts for assuming that it is the subjective states and intentions of self-contained individuals that drive linguistic production. Linguistic theory needs to keep discourse located within its natural environment, i.e., a community of speakers and hearers. Even in cases of a lecture, there are always listeners, and these listeners collaborate in the production of a system of communication that establishes the significative forces of the discourse's component parts. Linguists tend to emphasize speakers while minimizing the role of hearers. Maurice Merleau-Ponty and Jacques Derrida have developed a synthesis of semiotic and phenomenological theories to explain how signification works in the actual world where there are both hearers and speakers. Their theoretical insights may be given practical direction as researchable problems in the real world by applying them in ethnomethodological inquiries.

Both Merleau-Ponty and Derrida were guided by the semiotic theories of Ferdinand de Saussure, who directed our attention to language not as a container of static elements, but as a diacritical, relative, and oppositional system of signs, and by Edmund Husserl, who led us to examine the acts of meaning fulfillment on the part of the person understanding a statement, and hence to the study of understanding itself. Merleau-Ponty's and Derrida's theories of communicating meaning is a synthesis of phenomenology and semiotics that has much pertinence for ethnomethodological research. Merleau-Ponty described with eloquence the inherent indeterminacy of language use, observing the reflexive character of understanding. Pulling these analytic resources together, I am attempting here to develop an appropriate technology for investigating the *dynamic* play of signs and the ingenious ways that we work locally with interconnectedly dependent signifying traces as we make meaning in our ordinary everyday lives.

## SAUSSURE'S SEMIOTICS

The bedrock of Saussure's semiotics is the discovery that within the integrated system of signs the value of each element is constituted by its relationship with the other elements, and not by anything intrinsic. *Each unit of the system participates in determining the others*, no sign is foundational, and all are derivative of the same matrix that they institute; moreover, their sense is continually shifting with the addition of new signs, new speakers, new understandings, and new contexts. Strictly speaking, the meaning is nothing positive that inheres in the sign, although there is a degree of natural positivity to lexicogrammatic patterns that people prioritize and to customary typifications and routine uses of signs. For Saussure meaning is distributed among the signifying elements—what he calls "syntagmata"—by the whole system; hence, meaning is contingent upon the workings of the system, which itself is not something static but is always evolving dynamically. This suggestion has helped to lead Derrida to the thesis, against Husserl, that there is no "origin" of meaning and that all meaning is derivative. Instead, terms acquire their meaning from the system of differences they establish with the other constituents: "In the syntagma a term acquires its value only because it stands in opposition to everything that precedes it or follows it or both" (Saussure 1959, 123); and "The value of each term results solely from the simultaneous presence of the other" (Saussure 1959, 114). Or as Merleau-Ponty 1973a, 96) has rephrased it, "Words do not carry meanings as much as they separate themselves out from others." The meaning of a word is inseparable from its capacity to integrate the other words. Each syntagm in a series defines the other, as it is defined by them. Meaning is an activity of differentiation.

The "syntagmata" are the lexical units that engage in the work, or play, of signification. A syntagm is what it is, *not* because of any inherent essence it bears but because of the system of negations that it participates in founding and which institutes a public matrix of sense-making possibilities and devices. "Public" here is the crux of the matter. Linguistic interaction is an objective event. It is basic to the notion of "semiotic" that the signifying work inheres in the syntagmata and not in the predicative intentions of the individual speaker. It is not that people are without agency; rather, agency becomes efficacious only when it is addressed to the field of significative possibilities provided by an emerging public matrix. Semiotics is addressed to an analysis of the means of making sense, where these means are recognized to *exceed* the control of individual speakers whose collaboration constructs the system. Therefore the sociosemiotics that is vital is one that is not amenable to analytic strategies that concentrate upon the individual, such as found in much contemporary psycholinguistic research. As Thibault (1997, 140) contends, "The [speech] circuit as a whole regulates activities. Individuals *per se* do not." The system establishes its own aesthetic, ethical, and hermeneutic prescriptions, which the participants discover as one might inherit an estate.

It overstates the situation even to assert that the participants' intentions are "mediated" by the public matrix of meaning-making resources, since it is much more the case that they are *led* to their intentions by the semiotic structures in the first place; and it is not necessarily the case that participants always have an intention.² Voluntarism is rarely to be seen, despite the favored place it has in North European and North American folk mythology; rather, the social matrix, to which participants are oriented, is steering the event. Against individualist reductionism, which is given to inventing overly rationalized accounts, we would want to retain at all times Durkheim's keen sighting of the "immortal" ordinary society. People live and speak in social contexts, which involve processes of mutual confirmation and thereby social obligations. As Adorno (1973, 18) has suggested, here mimesis is as vital as conceptual rationality.

A sign does not bear a kernel of meaning. Apart from a network of reciprocal determinations, where could a kernel of positivity abide? Alone, a syntagm is rudderless. As Hegel has taught us, every identity owes its existence to its difference. Although syntagmata can bear nothing on their own, inscribed within a social praxis from which certain systemic and grammatical features have evolved, they can elicit a routine semiosis. But the semiosis of this structured matrix is not invariable, and the capacity of the syntagmata to signify depends upon their openness to transformation. This may be more apparent during intercultural conversations. Take for instance the Tibetan word "trul," which can mean either "a mistaken object" or "snake." A hearer is able to decide which of the two the word means by its relation with the words that surround it. Let us say the spoken phrase in which it occurs is, "Tak dra trul." "Tak," however, can mean *either* "permanent" or "rope" (while "dra" can mean "like," "as," or "-ly"). Hence, two possible solutions for a hearer are "mistaken as permanent" or "rope-like snake," both reasonable topics in Tibetan philosophical discourse (a "rope-like snake" is a rope that is mistaken for a snake). The point here is that the play of the syntagmata helps to provide the very context that resolves their own signification. The hearer must *remain open* to both possibilities (and to any third, yet unconsidered, possibility that may present itself). Further, it may be necessary for this openness to be sustained through some ensuing explanatory talk, *which can transform the preceding syntagmata.*

The ancient Buddhist scholar Nagarjuna (2nd c.) investigated how concepts accrue signification only amidst their relations with other concepts. One concept is interconnectedly dependent upon another (mother and child, east and west, "The East" and "The West," etc.). If there were something permanent, inherent and unchanging in the sign—like an essence—it would be the end of any potential for the transformation of meaning. Semiosis would terminate! The argument Nagarjuna (1995) offers in his seminal text, *Fundamental Wisdom of the Middle Way*, is helpful to consider; here "middle way" evokes the admission that terms are not without the power to signify, but they are empty of any intrinsic or inherent meaning. As we have just said, if an inherent positivity was established there could be no play of signification, no transformation of meaning, and linguistic activity would cease. To an opponent who accused him of nihilism, suggesting that if entities were empty as he suggests, the world could not function and nothing could be signified. Nagarjuna (1995, 308–9 and 317) replied quite to the contrary: if entities had the positivity that his opponent asserts, the world would be frozen in stasis. Nagarjuna argues,

> If all were nonempty, as in your view,
> There could be no arising and ceasing . . .
> If something comes from its own essence,
> How could it arise anew?
> It follows that if one denies emptiness
> There can be no arising.
> . . . If there is essence, the whole world
> Will be unarising, unceasing,
> And static. The entire phenomenal world
> Would be immutable.

Language is always that pregnant openness for potential meaning that is never finished with the process of becoming. Though signs do not bear positive essences, the language system exploits co-arisen and interdependent signifying possibilities. Routines of signification become naturally objectified in the language, and speaker/hearers know how to use the routines for stabilizing a shared meaning. Hanks (1996, 265) has documented how routine communicative practices can be grammaticalized and how habitual practices can become embedded in the system of a language. So while objectified, positive routines can coordinate and constrain discursive interaction, they are ever subject to further subversion by mundane conversation.

Greimas (1990, 4) reminds us that the relations and semiotic oppositions set up by words are flexible. Indeterminacy of meaning, long seen to be a problem by sociolinguists who over-rationalize behavior, is necessary in order to permit speaker/hearers to remain open for any transformation of meaning and any significance that is new or unanticipated. The *equivocal character* of the meaning of words is *creative* and constructive. As Ricoeur (1974, 56) contends, "Ambiguity or equivocity appears to be the permanent counterpart of polysemy, or so to speak the price to pay for a polysemic language," but even this account retains a bias towards a static view of language that needs to be abandoned. With our eye to empirical occasions of speaking, we need to describe "how humans, isolated yet simultaneously in an odd communion, go about the business of constructing, maintaining, altering, validating, questioning, and defining an order together (Garfinkel 1952, 114). Social-cum-linguistic order is a dynamic process. Claiming more stasis than in fact exists may obscure the actual lived processes, although such claims are a regular strategy used by actors to institute or maintain order.

Garfinkel has held that whatever else a term may mean it also bears along with it an "etcetera" that leaves an opening to members of the speech community to supply whatever becomes necessary for facilitating the creation of sense and the maintenance of order. But he warns against the notion that the et cetera is a minor auxiliary feature (Garfinkel 1974); rather, it is the ghost that rules the house:

> Yes, there is an etcetera that is printed at the end of the list, but that is only by way of remarking that indeed there is an etcetera; however, that does not quite cover it, since the etcetera is found in, of and as every part of that list, as a feature of that list that works like this: Here are the rules of play. With respect to any rule you want to pick up, with respect to any fraction of a rule, with respect to any event, where it might arise that at some future time there could be an issue as to what it is that is being provided for—*then*, at that future time we will reconsider what it is that is specified here, and review what we have been doing that led us to a recognition that it must have provided for something entirely different, and to have provided for it all along, in the way we now see that it has to have been meant, and you will understand it *then* to have been holding before and to be holding indefinitely for the future, but of course subject to the same agreement.

There is a vital labile character to terms that is essential to the production of local order.

## CONTESTING IDEALISM

The indeterminacy or instability of meaning is not a defect, to be remedied by formal analytic fiat, but a vital *resource* for understanding and communicating, and above all a resource for speaker/hearers (though not for formal analysts, perhaps). One can begin to appreciate semiosis only when one captures the lived work of *parole*. Sociosemiotics and ethnomethodology are at one in their contention that "*parole* does not refer to the consciousness of the individual language user" (Thibault 1997, 105). Ethnomethodology subscribes to Heidegger's deconstruction of Husserl's version of the constitutive consciousness, and ethnomethodology prefers to find and describe thinking in the world, as a public activity. Most structuralist and poststructuralist models are rejected. "Structuralism remains a formal theory of abstract and decontextualized *systems* of signs" (Thibault 1997, 5). Any formal analytic method that fails to address speech activity in a concrete way is vulnerable to imposing arbitrary limits on the complexities and paradoxes that are natural to social semiosis.

American social science has always displayed a bias that is cognitivist and individualist (Moerman 1996). Linguists, psychologists, and sociologists preserve a cognitive perspective that is ideologically individualistic, and their methods are pre-given to miss the collaborations that are the heart of communicating sense. Even those sociologists, like Talcott Parsons, who affirm the importance of "subjective" meaning fail to capture the looks of the world of the subjects they study; and they provide that content themselves from ideal configurations borrowed from their social interaction theory, in the process treating people as little more than homunculi—puppets who are able to bear nothing beyond what the theorist has placed there. Schutz (Grathoff 1978, 36) deftly criticizes Parsons: "He replaces subjective events in the mind of the actor by a scheme of interpretation for such events, accessible only to the observer, thus confusing objective schemes for interpreting subjective phenomena with these subjective phenomena themselves." Following Schutz's lead, Garfinkel castigates Parsons (who was also his teacher) and other researchers for treating persons like "judgmental dopes."

Toward the end of his career Schutz became increasingly appreciative of the fact that the natural organization of sense operates at *more than a strictly conceptual level*. Garfinkel took up the point even more vociferously, ridiculing as overly rationalist various notions of "social construction," "social production," and similar tropes of conceptual "negotiation"—some of which had their origins in the early Schutz. These tropes were an integral part of what Derrida has considered paternalist European mythology, and while he always affirmed his debt to Husserl, Derrida (1973, 84) was direct about the need for respecifying Husserlian phenomenology: "There is no constituting subjectivity." Derrida's student Francoise Dastur (2010, 9) has added, "The transcendental is understood in terms of facticity and existence, and no longer in terms of activity and subjectivity." Communication is more of an event than it is a theory.

The activities that compose this event revolve around the signifying work of expressions, work that belongs equally to hearers and speakers, a fact that is mostly unrecognized by generations of linguistic researchers. Meaning is not something that gets coded and then decoded, it consists of a wanting to be understood; *it is social*, and parties collaborate in exploiting whatever intelligibilities the words they are using come to produce. People use whatever means are at hand—means that are as serendipitous as they are planned—for cornering a partner into the confines of any intended understanding, and more often than not the events on the ground carry all parties into domains of sense that none of them had fully anticipated. Merleau-Ponty (1973c, 46) commented, "One does not know what one is saying, one only knows after one has said it." Meaning is worldly. One grasps the sense of an occasion in a gestalt, and that "whole" is used to set each signifying element into its proper place, and until then the word has no proper place. These "places" in no way inhere in the word itself.

Strategies for language learning that rely upon learning a language word-by-word and grammatical rule-by-rule fail until the learner can witness what the words actually *do* in the world, Chomsky notwithstanding. On occasion I have learned languages (Tibetan for one) that required more than a decade of study because my potential listeners were less than eager to carry on our conversations in any language but English, and at any rate seemed unable to clearly "hear" my Tibetan. I have learned other languages (Australian Aboriginal Ngaanyatjarra, for instance) in only a couple of years because of the marvelous skills at listening possessed by Aboriginal people. Although I applied myself assiduously in both instances, progress was swift in one case and hard-won in the other because of the interest and work of the people listening to me. For at least two decades, linguistic research has proceeded by means of protocols administered on computer consoles, a method that offers no scope for witnessing the free serendipity of the work of collaborative listening and one that structurally fails to capture the social context of the event of conversing. And this is so even when the research is given the label "sociolinguistics."

## THE PRAXIS OF MAKING MEANING

One never does finish with understanding anything. Take a poem for example, especially if it is a good one. The moment one fully comprehends a poem one renders oneself incapable of learning anything more from it. There is always this "more" to understanding, and one is never "finished" with it. The capacity to learn "more" is related to one's openness to the transformation of meaning, which is the counterpoint to authoritatively establishing definitions and then policing them. Similarly, in intercultural communication the semantic content of the words slips and slides like oil on grease, and fresh solutions to what is being said appear everywhere at hand. The hermeneutics of understanding a poem (or an Eskimo) rides upon *the materiality* of the signs. That is, words come to mean things—and *this is a local accomplishment* (Garfinkel 1991), which in turn is dependent upon the routinized practices that compose any local system, or what Saussure would call language (*langue*). The words produce the very semiotic matrix *to which they are then beholden*, but the matrix is not so much a structure that runs itself as it is "an open and dynamic system of structured relations and conventions which its users adapt to ever-changing material semiotic contingencies. *Langue* is both enabling and constraining" (Thibault 1997, 282). The ideal element is entirely projected and gains its articulations from the material differences among the signs, from which it learns what it has become. In this sense thinking is not an individual activity so much as it is a collective one. Each syntagm bears an assigned portion of the ideal projection with nothing positive residing within any one of them. There are no kernels.

I observed above that the meaning of a word is inseparable from its capacity to integrate the remainder of the terms in a verbal chain. The possible sense of each member of the chain (*unités significatives*, in Saussure's terminology) limits the possibilities of each of the others, as it is limited by them. This is part of what Derrida means when he says (1974) that the sign is always already inhabited by the trace of other signs. The significative possibilities exceed the actual indexical signification that a phrase collects. While further possibilities remain available for use by any local cohort of speakers, the actual signification of a phrase is fixed by the local sense and concrete social uses to which the phrase is put. Hence, it is by witnessing a verbal chain and how it is used, and witnessing the work it accomplishes, that members of a speech community come to know how to resolve the semiotic play of the words in a definite way, at least "definite" for the practical purposes at hand. Here the vital social phenomenon rests in *the display* of how a verbal chain can be employed to get the local work accomplished, so that the rest of the cohort present can *witness* how the production of meaning with that particular phrase, in that specific context, is achieved, and so repeat those semiotic devices oneself. If one is uncertain about a word or term, as in much intercultural conversation, one can blindly repeat the word to keep it in play. Or one can ask a question that uses the term, and so invite one's partner to once more display the signifying capacity of the term.

Each word bears certain possibilities for signifying. By replacing one word with a synonym, a different constellation of possible meanings will be present; and one can transform the meaning of all the other words of an utterance by doing so. The addition of a new word will likewise alter, constrain, and enhance the significance of the rest. Each syntagm's constellation will interfere or become cooperative with the others in new ways. Some of these transformations of meaning may be deliberate, as when a poet rewrites a poem; but most of the changes occur as surprises, even to the poet who knows the craft well. We are opportunists more than we are master planners.

A verbal chain does not unidirectionally produce meaning; rather, the consequences prompt members of the speech community to interrogate the chain in light of the sense they grasp. In this way, the *unités significatives* are clarified reflexively, by the very context they help to establish. Affairs are an open and boundless ensemble of particulars (Garfinkel 1996), and it is the practical work of the parties who staff any affair to keep drawing those particulars into a local system of signification, however contingent and ongoing it will always be. The material aspect of the work the parties do is central, but the sense of reference of these material particulars is subject to continuous recontextualization. In Thibault's words (1997, 125), "The syntagm specifies the respective values of the terms which are contrasted with each other by virtue of their being contextualized by a given combination, or enchainment, of units." It is important to note also that the context is both internal (to the language system and its indigenous logic) and external (indexical to the situation). Persons are not only interlocutors but interactants in a social occasion that may outstrip their strictly conceptual interests. Any cohort of actors is addressed not only to the meaning, so that mutual understanding can be enhanced, but also to the orderliness that can be provided for the situated activity. On many occasions, the adequacy of communication may be sacrificed in order to preserve the orderliness of the interaction, and this is especially true for much intercultural communication.[3] Members are oriented to the social purposes of a scene, of which meaning is only one factor, and the meanings of individual words may never be grasped in a definite way; much competent social interaction takes place when all of the words are not even heard.

## AN ETHNOMETHODOLOGICAL MODEL

What ethnomethodology has located is not, strictly speaking, a subjective point of view since the intelligibility of the scenes examined usually has an objectivity that *precedes* its meaning. The intelligibilities reside in the displays that parties use to demonstrate—to themselves—what they are doing. It is *the public display*, which operates in the realm of objective affairs, that retains the lead (see Liberman 2007, 85–118). Moreover, the technical practices that compose the practitioner's expertise are inevitably cohort-independent, and so they are not subjective. Ethnomethodology avoids a subjectivist hermeneutics by recognizing that it is the objective character of the practices that are emerging that provide interlocutors with their communicative possibilities.

In conversation, the auditors display their understanding of the sense of an utterance, and that becomes available for being the common possession of all. The just-how of words' work lies in something that is not provided in the words themselves. There is something less than a preordained order of stable meanings, and whatever such order there might be always defers to the actual local work that the words perform, work that is made possible by means of the public displays. Signification is always in movement— "the untiring way in which the train of words crosses and recrosses itself"

(Merleau-Ponty 1964, 40)—and one of the tasks of collaborating parties is to tame that movement. The meaningful signs produced by a local cohort concerned to concert their interaction in an orderly manner provide the mechanisms with which the intelligibility is displayed publicly, and thereby coordinated and "actively understood" contemporaneously. Husserl is wrong when he tells us that intersubjectivity is just like recollection, because the activity is social and not individual.

The *circumstantial details* provide parties with the semiotic resources for what can be accomplished. As Ricoeur (1978, 126) has observed, "The vague character of the word, the indecision about its frontiers, the combined action of polysemy, disseminates the meaning of the word." The work of exploiting the semiotic opportunities is delicate work, and the signs *just as they are displayed* offer infinite resources for parties. "The idea of complete expression is nonsensical, and all language is indirect" (Merleau-Ponty 1964, 43). The semiotic possibilities are not predictable, and the situation provides the parties with what can be accomplished:

> A discussion is not an exchange or a confrontation of ideas, as if each formed his own, showed them to the others, looked at theirs and returned to correct them with his own. . . . Someone speaks, and immediately the others are now but certain divergencies by relation to his words, and he himself specifies his divergence in relation to them. . . . Each is caught up in the vortex in which he first committed only measured stakes, each is led on by what he said and the response he received, led on by his own thought of which he is no longer the sole thinker. (Merleau-Ponty 1968, 119)

The meanings emerge not by any "negotiation" of ideas but by the parties' reflexive use of the semiotic resources that are at hand.

A common model of linguistic communication speaks of meanings being encoded in words by speakers, which are then decoded by listeners. This "conduit" model of communication may be represented pictorially in this way:

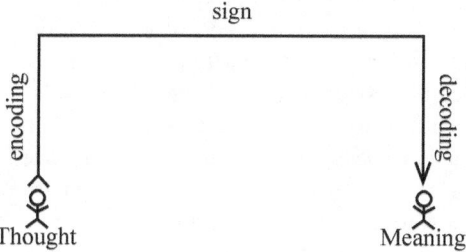

Figure 4.1

This model, all too common in linguistic science, suffers from a notion of speaking that is too rationalist—i.e., it is presumed that a speaker knows what one is going to say and that a listener is going to hear it more or less just that way. In the actual everyday world, which is the only world there is, *neither* is the case; both of them know what is being said only when the semiotic work of the utterance is displayed and witnessed. The knowledge of which one knows what one is saying only after one has said it speaks to the importance of *the interpretive accomplishments of listeners*. That is to say, meaning is a collaboration, and therefore the ethnomethods that make up this collaborative activity must be made a central part of linguistic investigation. Words collect their meanings according to their collaboratively established usages. What an expression has come to mean, at a given time and at a given place, informs the speakers about what expressive possibilities are available—and only those possibilities, in precisely the way the listeners and speakers provide for them, and no more. Or if there is "more," then there has to be the local work of the listeners and speakers providing for that, too.

According to Michael Silverstein (1992), participants work to achieve an "interactional text," a local register that can be used to coordinate the discourse. In doing so, participants mutually orient themselves to the sense of one another's activities. Accomplishing this sharedness of orientation and perspective requires skillful collaborative work, and public accounts may be offered to facilitate this formulation of the sense. What matters is what is made publicly available, via displays and witnessings, such as accounts. The mechanism by which collaboratively produced usages can be shared is the public display in the talk: *these displays instruct participants about what can be done and how to do it*. These displays and accounts play the role of a sort of serial auctioneer and permit the emerging social praxis to be continuously and collaboratively witnessed, monitored, and objectified. Thibault writes (1997, 131), "Meanings are *not* transmitted and, hence, communicated by Sender to Receiver; rather, they are jointly made or constructed by the ways in which interactants co-deploy the available social-semiological resources on a given social occasion of discourse."

Like other sociolinguists, Thibault (1997, 117) is quick to speak generally: "*Langue* . . . is a systemic resource which social agents draw on in the joint social construction of linguistic and other semiotic activities." While this is a suggestive description of the matter, we need more specification than a reference to "social construction" is able to provide. Lynch (1993, 266ff.) critically engages the notion of "social construction," the use of which is prevalent in Schutzian social phenomenology: "The word *construction* can sometimes imply a deliberate manufacture or manipulation of an object in accordance with a plan of action. Commonly, constructivist theories treat socially organized actions as though they actually or potentially pursued tangible objectives, were based on clear-cut interests, and involved deliberate choices of means to facilitate those interests and objectives." The choices of meanings are more ad hoc than deliberate, and agency involves more *bricolage* than predetermined courses of action. The "jointly made" character of making meaning is an always already ongoing and mutually adaptive "co-deployment" that is more jerry-built than it is a rational plan of action.

Linguistic analysis must retain the *haecceity*[4] of the events it studies, that is, the just-here, just-now, communicated-and-made-communicable-in-just-this-way character of any actual embodied social event. Another way to say this is that "the context" for any speech act must be retained; however, speaking of "context" is usually too general a way to speak about it and may only obscure the radical reflexivity that is in play. To be sure, there are "contextual processes," but "contextualize" serves as a gloss for immensely detailed practical activities of speakers that remain to be identified. Much of the practical work of speaker/hearers involves finding their way to an orderliness in the world just-here and just-now, an order in which the sign has found its efficacy, at least for here and now. For example, in the following dialogue (translated from the Tibetan) three Tibetan Buddhist monks are discussing what about an entity might exist after one has excluded all projections by mental activity. Their discussion centers, first, around entities that exist from their own side but are presented only through mental apprehension and, second, around phenomena that are exclusively mental positings. The precise meaning of "presented" and "posited" becomes slippery, and very local. Here the monks are considering whether the terms are different or the same:

> T: "Presented through the force of appearing to the mind," and the mind spoken of when we say, "posited by the mind" are two different notions aren't they?
>
> L': There is a difference between the two—"presented through the force of appearing to the mind" and "posited by the mind." There is, isn't there?
>
> T: Here they are the same.
>
> L": Are they the same?
>
> T: Yes.

When one accepts a collaborated decision that the terms "presented" and "posited" are the same, one is led to *a certain sort of understanding of their meaning*. However, if one comes to the decision that the terms are different, one is led along another avenue of reflection about their sense. T and

L' collaborate to produce one possible order, and T and L" collaborate to produce another. The order that is construed will set the context for the meaning of the terms, and yet the terms are what motivate the reflections of the parties about the context.

According to Garfinkel, the sign and the order are *mutually elaborative*. Herein lies the most profound work of sense-making that people do. As Garfinkel describes the reflexive use of rules, any formal procedure creates the very context that provides that same procedure with its own sensibility and definiteness of reference.[5] In innovative ways talk is able to institute a context that makes possible its own comprehensibility. But as Garfinkel and Sacks (1970, 344–45) describe, such mastery of natural language is a very peculiar genius:

> We understand the mastery of natural language to consist in this. In the particulars of one's speech a speaker, in concert with others, is able to gloss those particulars and is thereby meaning something different than he can say in so many words; and he is doing so over unknown contingencies in the actual occasions of interaction. . . .
>
> The idea of "meaning differently than he can say in so many words" requires comment. It is not so much "differently than what he says" as that *whatever* he says provides the very materials to be used in *making out* what he says. . . . The talk itself, in that it becomes a part of the self-same occasion of interaction, becomes another contingency of that interaction. It extends and elaborates indefinitely the circumstances it glosses.

While context is not strictly extrinsic to the language system, neither are the contextualizing practices exclusively internal to the system. What comes to be consequential is whatever people do with the possibilities that the system provides to them.

There is not a private language or even a collision of private languages, but there is the local establishment of the conventions of a language game whose rules never get fully written. "In dialogue a personal and interpersonal tradition is always founded" (Merleau-Ponty 1964, 92). But "tradition" is another too general a gloss, since the interactive work to which it refers is very specific in its details. Particular words and meanings are displayed by speakers, and in turn by listeners whose interpretations are redisplayed, again and again if necessary, and once displayed become available for copy, further invention and elaboration, or adoption as what was meant "all along." As the components of an emerging system are displayed and these usages are ratified, a competent system of linguistic communication becomes ready at hand for the participants. And the system will bear—as gifts—the communicative possibilities that are present.

Although speakers and listeners collaborate in the production of the system, it is that emerging system that provides them with what they are able to accomplish. The system is public and exterior, always unfinished and open to transformation, but in the end beyond their control. Moreover, the syntagmata inscribed within it are always available for reinterpretation. Expression is not definitive and interior but indeterminate and exterior. I am speaking here of the real exterior life of hearable words.

Having spoken, and been heard in just the way one is heard, the possibilities available for communication become apparent. And this system of possibilities is publicly available to one and all, and is continually being transformed. In the end speakers witness the meaning of what they have said as if it was the public spectacle that it is. This is the import of the observations of Saussure, who emphasized that, "the language system . . . is the product which the individual registers passively; it never presupposes premeditation" (in Thibault 1997, 22).

The spectacle is *independent* from participants in the way that Durkheim has described, although in each instance it is *their own production*, and participants must "revivify" (Durkheim 1915, 240 and 391) any systemic features if they are to have vitality on any actual occasion. The emerging system also bears its unique aesthetic order, which perpetuates its own sensibilities and can be a force for conservatism. Even the rhythmic contours of the speech can enhance the ease with which the work of the system may be recognized and so reproduced. The validation that such recognition and reproduction provides lends a moral dimension to the system, and the social responsibilities that proliferate in this way require that one conform to the communicative system. Because face-to-face linguistic praxis is dialogic, participants are oriented to others. This entails a responsibility that compels parties to become committed to the specific practices of signifying that have emerged. These are shared commitments, and as shared they bear the moral force that Durkheim (1915, 263 and 387) says is derived from their collective experience and the social solidarity that adheres to their symbolic productions.

## THE "MORE THAN" RATIONAL

Understanding is always *more than* can be put into words. The "more than" here is not a fuzzy excess or a fleeting moment (Gendlin 1992, 35 and 47–51). As Eugene Gendlin describes it, it is an order more intricate than what formal analytic accounts of order know about. There are understandings that are at once vague and precise, *intricate* while not yet explicit. There is always work that words have yet to do but which are already experiencable within the field that the words make possible and from which they discover their efficacy. The phenomenon here is something less than premeditation.

The possibilities for meaning always exceed what a sign signifies explicitly; however, a significance may be there implicitly, so that when it first becomes articulated it may be already familiar to us. On other occasions, an understanding may arrive unexpectedly, even for the speaker. A rationalist model would want meaning always to be provided for in advance, and then limited to only what is authorized; but meaning is something that can always be collected later on, when we are able to reflexively put those new acquisitions to work in reordering the meanings of the system. An intricate order is at work, and it is one that is always superseding itself.

Merleau-Ponty (1962, 180) has written, "The orator does not think before speaking, nor even while speaking; his speech is his thought." Thought does not always emerge under the strict code of logical intention but is beholden to the public spectacle that it becomes. And as Derrida (1973, 84) has affirmed, "There is not constituting subjectivity" that could be the origin of all order and serve as the basis for a rational regime. Rather, the order keeps outstripping all efforts to contain it.

In Figure 4.1, the act of encoding and decoding thought as rendered by rationalist theories conceives the relation between thinking and expression as something like Figure 4.2.

**thought → expression → meaning**

Figure 4.2

*This needs to be rewritten* in order to bear the wisdom that recognizes that speech does not know what it means until the spectacle of whatever gets expressed publicly provides for it. Accordingly, thought → expression must become thought ←→ expression. Further, appreciation of the indeterminacy or openness of meaning requires that expression → meaning be reconfigured as expression ←→ meaning . . . , with an ellipsis accompanying the meaning (the "etcetera principle"). Finally, the reflexive character of all understanding, according to which the achievements of understanding are put to work in providing the justification for their own cogency, demands that the formula be redrawn:

**thought ←→ expression ←→ meaning ...**

Figure 4.3

In this formula *there is no point of origin in consciousness*, as a rationalist theory would have it; it is a hermeneutic circle, in which no sovereign subject is in control of affairs. All subjects are subject to the emerging semiotic system, which is itself unstable. But, in this instability lie all of the openings through which ideas can be communicated. There is no realism here, but no idealism either. A middle way, the activities of semiosis *at once material and ideal*, renders all of the possibilities that are visible, hearable, and sayable. Meanings that are not rendered hearable do not exist, even in dictionaries. Meanings are tied to the material expressions, which as a system of signification dictate the communicative possibilities. But this materiality does not found language, or reason or order, in any logocentric sense, and speaker/hearers do not lose their agency. It is the emerging public matrix in its specific material details that offers to speaker/hearers what agency they have. It facilitates a social praxis for communicating meanings.

FIVE

# SOME LOCAL STRATEGIES FOR SURVIVING INTERCULTURAL CONVERSATIONS[1]

> This anguish is... the necessarily restricted pathway of speech against which all possible meanings push each other, preventing each other's emergence.
>
> —Jacques Derrida (1978, 9)

The materials on which this investigation was based were collected during my first six months of study in a traditional Tibetan Monastic University. I had previously studied with Tibetans for 16 months, living with Tibetan groups in other localities, including two monastic universities, but these were places where most of the Tibetans' English was better than my Tibetan. Moreover, many Tibetans in India insist upon conversing in English, in part so that they can practice their own language skills, so my oral capabilities were still primitive. I had been reading Tibetan texts, and many more texts in English translations, but my study these first months in the monastery (of nearly three years of residence over two decades) was my initial attempt at receiving sophisticated philosophical teachings one-on-one from teachers who could only speak Tibetan and where no translator was present to assist me. The one-on-one format placed terrific pressure upon me to perform in a competent manner; however, discovering what competence might possibly consist of at each pedagogic moment was a local and collaborative affair. These transcripts capture my naturally occurring efforts to struggle with understanding complex notions in a new and very different language.

During this time I audiotaped each session, and then reviewed the tape in order to catch whatever I had missed in real time; while I was reviewing the tape for the purpose of learning the subject matter, I made some transcripts of hermeneutic incidents that I had recognized at once had import for the ethnomethodology of intercultural conversation, and some of these transcripts are included here. These intercultural colloquies took place on alternate days and were devoted to a close explication of two texts about the Middle Way (*Madhyamika*) philosophy that utilized a pre-modern, literary Tibetan, and some of those texts and quotations conformed to metrical constraints that occasionally reduce their language to a haiku-like philosophy. Consequently, I had difficulties with comprehension. The first session, held three times each week, was intended to be 90-minutes long and was offered by the Abbot of the monastery, a brilliant scholar aged 68 at the time; however, he frequently liked to continue for two and occasionally three hours. I would generally stop the session when I ran out of blank tapes. The second one-on-one session, held three times a week also (on the alternate days), more strictly adhered to a one-hour length and was given by a senior professor (or Geshe) at the monastic university, who subsequently became the Abbot of the same monastic university.

The basic structure of the texts involved in these sessions consisted largely of reviewing and summarizing the philosophical arguments of Tsong Khapa (14th c.), who relied heavily on the interpretations of Chandrakirti (7th c.), who was refuting Bhavaviveka (5th c.), who was commenting on the founder of the Middle Way School, Nagarjuna (2nd c.), who himself was engaged in refuting the philosophical tenets of the Hindu Samkhya School. Keeping the players straight without a scorecard was not a simple task. The text in the second tutorial, although not as dense as the first, employed many citations, including quotes within quotes and debates within debates, and it was easy to lose track of who was speaking there as well. Although with proper preparation I was usually able to keep track by myself, I was frequently forced to call for clarification from the Abbot or Geshe, which led me straightaway to the hermeneutic tasks of communicating in an intercultural setting.

My Tibetan teachers and I were sincerely committed to learn philosophy and teach philosophy, and we were further motivated by an analogy of the contemporary transmission of Mahayana Buddhism from Tibetans to the West with the transmission that originally brought Buddhism from India to Tibet. So we accepted our task seriously; even so, *the attention we paid to local organizational matters and obligations exceeded the attention we were able to give the substantive philosophical issues that brought us together*. My inquiry in this chapter was motivated by my surprise with how many critical communicative issues arose that had nothing at all to do with philosophy but were about the structure and dynamics of formatting mundane human interaction.

Analyses of intercultural communication too frequently read as if they consider such communication to be rule-governed events; however, participants rarely perceive them that way. Parties to a conversation are deeply embedded in a world of particulars, always still emerging, the rules for which do not yet exist; nevertheless, participants are engaged in their own local analyses, but these are not the analyses of professionals. Unlike disciplinary theorists, members' analyses commence with local events that are not fully organized *and whose organization is their immediate immanent task*. They are ever attentive to what Edmund Husserl (1982, 51–52) has termed "horizonal" events, in which vital but indeterminate details at the horizons of perception are attended to polythetically, and they can never be certain about which of these details will prove to be decisive for their organization or understanding.

When doing studies of intercultural communication it is important to present to the reader the looks of the world for the participants, for that only is what the participants are attending to and hence are the pertinent facts. A faithful recording—faithful not to disciplinary principles but to the looks of the world for the participants themselves—necessitates laying out the contingent details of interactional events to a precision that readers may find tiresome. Throughout I refer to the "collaboration" rather than to the "conversation" or the "communication;" this is in order to keep emphasizing that communication is always a collaborative activity. As discussed, linguistic analysis commonly emphasizes the work of speakers over the work of hearers, but spoken communication *always* involves an ensemble of speakers and hearers. At the Tibetan monastery I found that my ability to express myself varied greatly from listener to listener. This was because listeners had varying capacities to hear and varying skills for engaging in intercultural dialogue. For successful communication to occur there must be not only competence but motivation and effort, and these two factors steer us to the interpersonal relationship with which this study is preoccupied.

The reader may possibly conclude that as a participant in these collaborations, I was either ignorant or dishonest, and on occasion both, but such an assessment is only partly true. The topics at hand are topics that the vast majority of Tibetans themselves would be incapable of comprehending. The level of discussion would be roughly equivalent to that of a graduate seminar in philosophy at any Western university. My lessons took place in the early morning, following which I would spend an additional six to eight hours each day reviewing the tape of the previous lesson for the next morning's tutorial (the Abbot referred to the tape-recorder as my "translator," and he came to respect it). Despite my preparation, the Abbot was free to select a different section of text to elaborate, or he might repeat a previous portion to test my understanding; in these cases I could be caught less than fully prepared. Each section of the text involved vocabulary and discourse routines that had to be learned anew, like the labors of Sisyphus, and my ignorance at these times was apparent.

Given the natural limits on asking questions and requesting clarifications, as a practical matter I developed the practice of not asking questions about issues I was reasonably sure I would be able to resolve myself during my careful study and replays of the tape. On this basis I would frequently let confusing matters pass, especially if they did not seem pertinent to the day's tasks. Far from being dishonest, this practice was a sound one, for it maximized the opportunities for learning. More frequently than not I was able to resolve such problems when I listened to the tapes. By progressing in this fashion I reached the point at the end of the year where I could follow most discussions first-time-through. If at the outset I had called for clarification of everything I did not understand, it is possible that the instruction itself would not have been able to proceed, and I would never have developed the competence that I eventually gained.

The lack of frank feedback presented many difficulties, however, which became topics for this study. But the first rule of intercultural interaction is survival, and understanding meanings takes second place. Given a choice between honesty and survival, the practical exigencies of conversation that ensure survival will prevail. The irony is that over the long run it may well be the only way to achieve adequate communication.

## NORMALIZING A CONVERSATION

The collaborative work involved in any conversation requires that the participants build local vocabularies and discourse routines. To speak of "normalizing a conversation" is only a way of talking. Specifically, a local and particular scheme of communication must be worked out among the participants. Not only are glosses and indexical expressions involved, the mode of turn-taking and the pacing for the talk needs to be displayed and established, along with analytic strategies that are indigenous to one or more of the parties and which they learn how to share. Another way to talk about it is to say that a praxis for communication must be developed. That may sound better, but without further specification it too is only another way of talking generally.

The establishment of a shared sense of any indexical expression requires local work, but philosophical access to the question of indexicality will not provide a researcher with the radical nature of this work—radical in the sense of the then-and-there roots of the genesis of meaning. Indexicality must be understood not only philosophically but practically, by witnessing the interactive work that attends to it. Until the uses of words *have been displayed publicly*, until that practical work has been undertaken, actual communication cannot take place. A cohort of conversationalists learn only by observing how the work of these indexical expressions is done, and then doing it.

In addition to establishing a vocabulary and ways of formatting the conversation, interlocutors must also develop and train in a metadiscourse for monitoring the adequacy of the communication. This monitoring constitutes a channel additional to the semantic channels[2] that are in operation, and this monitoring channel performs a great deal of work that enables a conversation to survive. Collaborators naturally develop routines for monitoring the adequacy of the communication, and this monitoring performs much work that is essential for a conversation to survive. Collaborators *naturally* develop forms for monitoring the adequacy of the communication. At the same time, intercultural communication involves a great deal of gratuitous concurrence (Liberman 1985, 197–202), that is, *facile agreement with utterances that are not comprehended*. Gratuitous concurrence is the grease that lessens the potential friction of an intercultural interaction, and it is a facility that can run almost on autopilot, without the parties being even aware of it. There are occasions, however, when one needs to really communicate and be certain that the communication has arrived home, and on these occasions one needs to monitor the "arrival." Transcript 1 illustrates well the successful operation of the competence monitoring channel, as well as a successful communication.[3]

Transcript 1

Abbot: Except for asserting that one only refutes the true establishment, the term "non-inherent existence" itself is not established. We say that the true existence of non-inherent existence is not established. Understand?

5   KL: I understand.

Abbot: You don't understand at all. A little mistaken—

KL: I understand. I understand it well.

Abbot: So then, this is the meaning of these words.

In collaboration with me, the Abbot had produced a device for his signaling when he accepted that I truly understood and that the results of the immediately preceding talk had become an achievement-in-hand. He would say (literally) "It's said like that,"[4] implying, "So, that's the way it is" (a related device operates in Transcript 1, line 8). When exchanges so anointed end up exposed as just another gratuitous concurrence, they constituted plain fraud in the Abbot's eyes, and so this device became a useful tool for us to employ when we wished to monitor seriously the adequacy of our communication. I developed my own parallel device. When I was very serious about my having comprehended a point, I would read the succeeding line of the text, as if to say, "I understand, now let's continue." This was a performative that I used effectively throughout our time together.

Nodding can become an intricate tool for communicating comprehension, and the orderliness of its use kept evolving over the course of our year-long tutorials. At one point, the Abbot naturally developed a way to normalize the orderliness of my nodding. After a period of satirizing the baselessness of some of my nodding, he came to divide my nodding into two varieties: "accomplished nodding" (*mgo grub pa*), by which he meant (with a note of irony) a nod that indicated that I really understood a passage, and a "less than accomplished nodding" (*mgo ma grub pa*), by which he meant that he was not buying my nod as a case of genuine understanding. On occasion, this stratagem would force me to justify some of my nodding or admit my ignorance. However, I was then able to use a simulation of that more accomplished practice to effectively offer a gratuitous concurrence. The Abbot retained the opportunity to offer his skepticism by playing upon the irony of his term "accomplished," which implies that there is much scope for performance. Although the organization of the nodding and its reception kept evolving through our sessions, at nearly every point we were able to use it to shepherd the conversation through whatever difficult patches we found ourselves in. On occasion, he was complicit in accepting a less than accomplished nodding as adequate, for the purpose of maintaining the local integrity of our conversation. The intricacy of it all is astonishing.

The Abbot was skeptical about people who just say, "Yes, Yes," "Oh right!" and so on. And more than once he impressed upon me the fact that such people were to be considered dull. He would advise, "It's not sufficient to say 'I understand' without listening. In such a fashion one can't begin to understand." This made me cautious about concurring gratuitously, and possibly reduced such occasions from hundreds each session to dozens. Two strangers can pull off gratuitous concurrences readily with little fear of detection, and so the first weeks went along with relatively ease. But after interlocutors have collaborated in "normalizing" a conversational praxis, especially after some months, each partner is better able to recognize which concurrences are suspect. The concurrences come to be used and recognized as indicators of varying degrees of comprehension, part of the indexical language that is being established. It is then that the work of competently comprehending the discussion increases, along with the work required to conceal incompetence.

## WHAT IS COMPETENCE?

Competence is not something static but refers to processes that are always emerging. And many types of competence are involved. Just what is it to claim competence, when it is always in progress, always a dynamically developing complex of abilities? Further, these abilities are always interactional; without the interactional competencies philosophical expertise cannot be displayed. When another asks me, "Do you understand?," whether I understand every single point that could be made regarding a topic is *not* the question that is being asked. Rather, what is meant is something more like,

"For the practical matters that appear to be central to our communication, and given the limits on our time and the need to use our energies in the most efficacious way, do you understand well enough for us to continue?" To have grasped something useful about a topic, to have developed some degree of comprehension about the matters that *seem* to be central is enough grounds for claiming competence, as in "Yes, I understand."

Complete understanding is impossible, for there is always the potential for further significance. This is especially true when one is dealing with Tibetan philosophy. No one will claim, "I understand well the profound view of the Buddha," for that would be to claim enlightenment; it is accepted that The Profound View is always deeper than one can imagine, and it is not always deceptive to claim to understand when that understanding is merely partial.

Take two illustrations, for example. In the first I understand an extended explanation (five minutes or more) of an important philosophical point but do not understand the last three words only, which I had not heard before. If I am asked, "Do you understand?" do I reply in the affirmative or negative? In the second instance, I do not understand very much of the explanation but I do grasp well the meaning of the final two complete sentences. What am I entitled to claim about my competence then, if I am asked? Transcript 2a illustrates this latter case well.

Transcript 2a

Abbot: According to the Svatantrika School of philosophical tenets, you need both the object's true existence and an appearance to awareness before a real perception can arise. The Prasangika School does not need this.

5   KL: Yes.

Abbot: According to the Prasangika, objects appear merely through the projections of conceptual conventions.

KL: Yes.

Abbot: Through the force of the mind's projections.

10  KL: Yes.

Abbot: Phenomena whose existence cannot be harmed by withdrawing conceptual conventions are not accepted by the Prasangika.

KL: Yes, yes. I understand.

Abbot Do you understand?

15  KL: [Nods.]

160    MORE STUDIES IN ETHNOMETHODOLOGY

Abbot: What?

KL: I understand. [transcript 2a continues as 2b later in the chapter]

The Abbot had been explaining the details of the Svatantrika (Autonomous Syllogism) School, a school of Buddhist philosophy that is not studied extensively by Western scholars, and I had not grasped everything he had to say about it. His comments on lines 11–12 about the Prasangika (Dialectical) School referred to a topic I have studied well, and so I could with impunity claim competence about it (line 13). When the Abbot repeated his call for confirmation of my adequate comprehension (line 14), it seemed to apply to the entire discourse, and so my reply was more ambiguous (line 15), but I was still ready to make a claim to competence based on my comprehension of the topic of lines 11–12.

Transcript 3 illustrates a similar phenomenon; however, under more severe scrutiny by the Geshe, I moderated my initial claim to competence:

Transcript 3

Geshe: If one has the mind that seeks enlightenment, one cannot put aside (*par phyogs*) the generation of the altruistic mind of the Mahayana practitioner who wishes to attain enlightenment for the sake of others.

KL: *Par phyogs?*

Geshe: The "mind of enlightenment" is not the same as the Mahayana generation of the altruistic mind.

KL: Ah!

10   Geshe: However, all generations of the altruistic mind of enlightenment are instances of the mind of enlightenment.

KL: I see.

Geshe: Do you understand?

KL: Uhuh, uh-m.

Geshe: Do you understand it?

KL: I understand some of it.

Geshe: You understand some of it. All cases of generating the altruistic mind of enlightenment are also cases of the mind of enlightenment. Is that so?

KL: Uh-huh.

20  Geshe: Understand?

KL: Mm-hmm.

Geshe: Understand?

KL: The mind of enlightenment— (0.3)

Geshe: is different from the generation of the altruistic mind of enlightenment.

KL: Yes, yes.

Geshe: Understand?

KL: [Stutters.] I understand. I understand some. I don't fully understand "the Mahayana generation of the altruistic mind of
30  enlightenment."

Geshe: The generation of the altruistic mind of enlightenment means, now [sighs], this. Uhh. A bodhisattva . . .

I had comprehended *that* there was a difference between the two minds of enlightenment but not *what* the difference was; that is, I had understood some but not all aspects of the Geshe's remarks about the Mahayana's altruistic mind. But at lines 1–6 my attention was drawn more narrowly—I had not at first caught the meaning of the word *par phyogs*, and so I directed my query to that (line 5). After hearing a brief explication of his point, I correctly comprehended that *par phyogs* meant "to put aside, discard, ignore," and so I confirmed my understanding of that at line 11; however, I could not confirm that I understood *everything*, and when being pressed on the matter (especially lines 12 and 28) I confessed that I did not fully understand the point, leading to some exasperation on the Geshe's part. It is to avoid exasperation like this that one concurs gratuitously in the first place, and my equivocal response at line 13 was meant to spare the Geshe the trouble of his sigh, which comes at line 32. In Transcript 3 a claim to competence *or* incompetence would be equivocal, but the important point is that it is the competence-monitoring channel that dictates what happens here and not the adequacy of meaning. That is, it is not the merits of my competence but the Geshe's uncharacteristic *full-court press* (lines 12, 14, 18, 20, 22, and 26) that throws me from my claim to competence (line 11) to a moderation of that claim (line 28).

Transcript 4 offers an illustration of an explanation that I followed fully, except for the final four syllables of line 8, for which I called (line 9) for a clearer pronunciation.

## Transcript 4

Abbot: Results are produced, are they not?

KL: Yes.

Abbot: There are two possibilities for such production: production in dependence upon a cause and production that does not depend
5   upon a cause. There is no other way to theorize about production. Generally one does not speak of production without a cause; however, theoretically a result is produced either in dependence or not in dependence upon a cause. There are two modes of "ka-su che-pa."

KL: Two "ka-su che-pa."

10  Abbot: If one says "ka-su che-pa" it "ne-pa" [abides].

KL: "Ne-pa."

Abbot: If it arises, it must be produced by a cause or produced without a cause. Do you understand?

KL: Umm, umm, I half-understand; otherwise, I don't understand.

Abbot: You don't understand.

The Abbot recognized my call for a repeat of the term and complied (line 10), also providing a brief exposition of its sense, which involved another word I was unsure of and that I merely repeated (line 11), repeating being another way to concur gratuitously. Although I comprehended *the lesson*, the syntax of the interaction's adequacy-monitoring efforts forced me to give more priority to the more local incompetence than it merited, with the unhappy fallout that the Abbot (wrongly) concluded I didn't understand a thing and so launched into an unnecessary repetition of that entire portion of the lesson. In this way the monitoring facility we had developed was too crude an instrument to perform all of the tasks of organizing our dialogue that we required.

There are different types of communication troubles. Sometimes there are problems with diction or with simply hearing the word clearly (an external noise, such as a gate slamming or the sound of a very large gong, kept interfering). On other occasions one hears clearly but does not recognize the meaning of what is being said. On yet other occasions one knows the meanings of each word that is spoken but still is unable to put them together and grasp their sense; the problem may have to do with the grammar or with the identification of the proper context. Competence can refer to knowing the formal or "inertial meaning" (Khubchandani 1990, 291) of a sentence and does not necessarily require a full application of the meaning in its correct context. Also, there can be problems with one's partner conflating one's not having heard the sounds clearly with not having understood their meaning.

The case of having a grammatical difficulty is similar. The solution to a problem with grammar is different than the solution to a problem of philosophy. In such a situation to say, "I don't understand" is vague and can prompt a long repetition of an explanation already well in hand. On such occasions it might be better—for the purpose of good communication—to let a small difficulty with grammar pass unresolved and claim competence; but that implicates one in a minor deception, and one can be caught in such a deception and be forced to look around desperately for the quickest way out of the room. Too frequently, the Abbot attributed difficulties I had with grammar to difficulties with the profundity of the Middle Way view itself, which I do find profound but not usually confounding. I did not dispute such assessments, however; instead, I allowed this to permit him to think that my grammatical competence was greater than it was, so that he would retain some confidence that I was qualified to continue our discussions.

The distinction between word-sound and its meaning does not run as purely as one might imagine. As Ferdinand de Saussure (1959) wrote, a signifier and a signified arise simultaneously. That is to say, an understanding of the sense of an utterance helps to implicate which signifiers are involved. Signifiers and signifieds are mutually constitutive. Each comprehended meaning situates a set of signifiers within an arrangement, even if it be an erroneous one; any new meaning will resituate the entire set of signifiers, and there are no limitations on the number of incorrect solutions that can be serially applied. What is certain is that every semantic solution is accompanied by an arrangement in which all the signifiers fall into some place (Liberman 1982). Attending to this highly reflexive semantic activity involves a great deal of mental concentration, which can quickly exhaust even the most diligent interlocutor; but it is a vital part of the labor of intercultural collaboration.

There are also those occasions when a fuller understanding may not be desirable. For example, at one point the text we were studying included several pages about the sufferings in the realms of hell, a sort of Buddhist equivalent to hellfire and damnation. I have little interest in this aspect of Buddhist metaphysics (insufficient interest, in the thinking of the Abbot), and so I felt I had a warrant to claim competence about matters upon which I did not consider it fruitful to dwell. On such occasions one needs to move skillfully *and quickly* through the exegesis without allowing the integrity of the educational relationship to be offended. *The skills here do not involve the comprehension of meanings*; they involve competence regarding how the conversation is being formatted. A technique that I came across as a "discoverable" (Garfinkel 1975) and that I employed from time to time was to ride on one of my partner's (incorrect) presumptions about my competence and let that carry us through a portion of text. Once one slows down this swift passage through the text for any reason (to make an issue out of diction, spelling, vocabulary, semantics, or anything else), the pace of one's partner's gallop through the text will be slowed and one may be called on to display and not merely to claim competence; in this case, failure at such a display would have been followed by a tedious stroll through the gory details of each of the hell realms. My strategy relied on allowing my partner to develop his intentional projects and to try to stay out of their way, allowing their momentum to carry him past the section that I wished to skip. Again, it is important to note that the skills here are technical ones and did not require very much semantic competence.

## DISPLAYING COMPETENCE

The concern a partner has about one's competence may require that competence be displayed from time to time, that one's understanding be made available and ratified as accurate and sound. This compels one to prepare an account of one's understanding for public examination. But *understanding the meaning and displaying this competence require different competencies*. Having a correct (adequate) understanding and producing grammatically and semiotically correct speech are *not* coincidental; hence, *one's communicated understanding may be reduced to fit in with what one's oral capabilities are capable of displaying*, an experience not unlike those to which Derrida referred in the epigraph to this chapter. One may grasp a matter well, but what one's partner is able to ascertain regarding what one has understood is limited exclusively to what is provided by one's account of what one has understood. That is, there is one's understanding and there is the discourse about that understanding, and one's partner's examination is directed to the latter. The success of one's display of competence depends not as much on the competence of one's understanding as on one's competence at constructing an effective account of that understanding: it is not what one knows that counts but what can be conveyed about what one knows.

Accounts are highly collaborative events, and the structure of any semiotic system forces the intelligent analyst out of a voluntaristic model (such as transcendental phenomenologists may offer) into the passive tense: not "what one conveys" but "what is conveyed." Every new articulation finds a location in the emerging scheme of detail whose material organization lends itself to strategic manipulation. What can be achieved is limited by the entire semiotic scheme that is emerging. Derrida (1976) acknowledged the near *autonomy* of this scheme of detail when he discussed *writing*, that is, that these semiotic possibilities are provided by "the text." The collaborators are tied to the scheme of detail they have developed or that has developed, and the success of any display of competence is tied to the opportunities that the scheme of detail provides.

A recurring problem that I experienced during our sessions was that although I was able to comprehend the underlying philosophical import of most topics, I frequently became entangled in the syntax of my display of that competence. Alternatively, there were occasions when I succeeded in developing an effective, impressive display of competence when I had not really mastered the material (students will recognize this phenomenon). It was as if philosophical competence and displaying that competence were located on different channels. Here again, what is decisive is the meta-discourse that formats the interaction; the philosophical discourse itself was less consequential for the survival of the interaction.

Yet our philosophical interests motivated the event! Therefore, on occasion it became important for me to secure some clarification from the Abbot or the Geshe, and this required that I advise him about what I did and did not understand. Clarifying what one does not understand is more difficult than clarifying what one does understand. It also involves a display of competence because one needs to know something about a topic before one can claim to have a problem with it. Students are expected to have intelligent questions that demonstrate to the teacher that they are working at pertinent intellectual tasks, failing which one's teacher will consider one to be dull.

Clarifying what one does not understand can become an ironic exercise. I would find that I had questions, even intelligent ones, but my mastery of the semiotic "surface" of the discourse was not so fine that I could communicate important distinctions and confusions without embroiling myself in new and irrelevant confusions. This made me gun-shy. I sometimes chose to retreat behind a screen of gratuitous concurrence even when my comprehension was fair. At times this caused the Abbot to become skeptical about my claim to competence, a skepticism that occasionally spilled over to those occasions when I understood the matter very well. I coped with this organizational problem by discovering new ways to convey to the Abbot or Geshe that I understood well (e.g., "*This* one, I understand!"). But in the end all this did was to provide the apparatus for formatting the interaction with new devices *that in their turn became available for me to exploit later on occasions when I might be desperate for gratuitous concurrence that would really work*. Ethnomethods can keep getting recycled and subtly transformed in this way.

Each communicative event takes its place in the corpus of interactional devices and remedies. Although it may have its origin as a spontaneous and genuine display of understanding, once generated as an event, its very objective corporeality destines it to become a component of the system of meta-discourse that is organizing the orderliness of the interaction. For example, my reading a next line of text in order to indicate that I understood the topic quite well and that we could get on with the next part of the discussion could, in its materiality—i.e., in just how it gets done, along with my expertise in the doing of it—become available for any strategic work in the interaction for which I might later choose to employ it. Once performed, it sits there as part of the toolbox of organizational details, as one tool among an ensemble of tools.

Any interaction will have its unique scheme of details arising from the local history of its communicative events, and the organizational capacity of these interactional details is always evolving and *is never a reified "normative order."* After all, that is what the asterisk in "order*" (Garfinkel 1991, 10) intends to convey. In this case a set of organizational devices that permit gratuitous concurrence (g.c.) provides the setting also for "serious" devices that convey competence really. As the interaction evolves, a *routinization* of these "serious" organizational items occurs, leaving them available for strategic use; we can call these "g.c.$^2$." Just as in semantic domains, the organizational items are not static but are vulnerable to continuous slippage, what Derrida (1986, 91 and 92) has called "gliding" (*glissement*). Indigenous collaborators are well tuned to this slippage, even if some analysts are not.

Discourse about understanding has its own exigencies; and it operates semi-independently of the understanding itself. For example, I may appreciate that something is funny, but may not consider it funny enough to laugh about; however, I may be required to display a laugh in order to indicate in the competence-monitoring channel that I do indeed understand. This is not a flaw with the interaction nor anything inauthentic (e.g., a fake laugh) but a vital part of the interactional competence that leads parties to successful communication.

In my sessions on the Middle Way philosophy, there was this recurring phenomenon: there were a number of well-known answers to philosophical questions that one could (and was at times *expected* to) parrot when being quizzed. One need not have philosophical mastery in order to parrot these replies. So routinized has certain elementary Tibetan philosophical instruction become over the centuries, these replies have become well known, written down in one or more of the debate manuals, etc., and the replies can be learned even before their meanings are appreciated (in fact, they are memorized as a means for appreciating them). It was my preference to answer to a philosophical query not with a routine reply but with something more original that bore evidence of a more personal understanding (this may reflect a typically American, individualistic orientation). But I would find that striking out on my own like this with an original philosophical formulation would inevitably lead me into troubles that were extraneous to the topic and so were best avoided. Although there are benefits to putting into words the itinerary of one's understanding, as it can improve the level of discourse, I found myself retreating into the safety of the routine replies. For example, to the question, "If emptiness is ultimate, why does it not truly exist?" I was capable of delivering a short dissertation on the topic. But I chose instead to parrot the standard reply: "Because it exists merely in dependence upon the imputed existence of something else." An attempt to offer an extensive reply would be more likely to lead to the Abbot's downscaling of his assessment of my understanding than it would impress him, even though the incompetencies that might arise would be at worst grammatical ones or some slight terminological aberration.

The lesson in this is that there are many contingencies of the interaction that force the attention and concern of the participants away from the comprehension of philosophical matters into a more narrow and technical range, *which a phenomenology of meanings alone is incapable of revealing.* This narrow range or field is the obsession of interlocutors, yet it is a phenomenon that is frequently missed by analysts.

A concern to develop a deeper appreciation of a topic can lead one to want to confess one's ignorance, but the difficulty of expressing what one does not understand in a form that permits one's partner some access to that understanding may be so great as to convince one to abandon the attempt. For example, one might understand the words, grasp "the" (or "a") meaning of an explanation, and even appreciate some of the implications of the meaning for the philosophical perspective as a whole, but on occasion one can sense that there is a further significance that one has yet to appreciate. *How does one push the inquiry deeper, when one does not know toward what to push?* The act of calling for further explication operates by means of the apparatus that organizes the interaction, and this can be a very crude instrument that fails to fulfill the hermeneutic needs of the moment. One can say, for example, "I don't understand," or "Say more," but these interactive devices might only lead one's partner to review the word meanings term-by-term, which can be a less than efficacious endeavor, while the larger context that one wishes to explore will be left unexplicated. How does one develop sophisticated tools within the meta-discourse channel that would be effective for directing the interaction—local methods that can competently manage the agenda of the conversation? This is the part of the art of conversation; however, in intercultural situations all too frequently the interactive work can become so complicated that *parties become lost in its fine details,* distracting them and making a mess of what had been previously a useful collaboration (Liberman 1985, 171–215).

## THE INTENTIONALITY OF ATTENTION

When one converses, one easily tends to lose sight of the fact that frequently one's partner does not see things the same way as one does oneself. The meaning one's partner gives to individual words can vary. Further, one's partner does not passively receive one's messages one at a time and then deduce a meaning from them; rather, the partner is relating those messages to an active and lively organization of the talk's emerging sense. The sense being organized by one's partner gets projected upon the communicative events so that any given event is interpreted to be consistent with the projected significance. The understanding that emerges for one's partner is related to this intentional project (Husserl 1982, 199–201) that is a person's preoccupation, and so one needs to orient one's contributions to that project, for that is the only game being played. When one ignores this intentional project, one will work at cross-purposes, and usually the communication will fail.

Each meaningful contribution is related by one's partner to a whole. This whole—the emerging sense—gives life to the parts, even though it is composed of those parts. It is not as if each part has an equivalent value in an additive process; rather, a hermeneutic circle is at work. One is dealing with a praxis of interpretation that is actively engaged, and one—as well as one's partner—is able to attend to what one's interpretation can provide and little else. There will be times when one's partner simply cannot hear because of preoccupation with a different intentional project. When one attends more persistently to the intentional character of one's partner's comprehension, many misunderstandings can be avoided.

On one occasion the Abbot was explaining to me the difficulty with removing ego-grasping and described several techniques for learning to recognize that one's "self" was a conventional artifact to which one became attached but which did not truly exist. I asked him whether a recognition of the nonexistence of this ego, once fully appreciated, endures or whether one alternates between insights into its false nature and the habits of ego-attachment. The Abbot replied with an extensive and original exegesis of what is capable of being carried forth into a subsequent lifetime, and he concluded that when one recognizes one's lack of having a truly existing self, the wisdom established by this recognition will transmigrate. However, my question was not concerned with the metaphysics of rebirth but was more practical and immediate. I reformulated it several times, but so occupied was he with the extant debates about the nature of rebirth that he never took up my question in the way I had intended. In such situations there is nothing to do but let it pass. Transcript 5 offers a case where I had tried to share an observation (line 5) about there being a hiatus in the flow of the grammar, but the word I used was too close to a word that was in the text, and so the Abbot kept reading my observation as a mishearing on my part.

## Transcript 5

KL: If one says, "It's contradictory" [*'gal*, pronounced "ge"]; it is mistaken isn't it?

Abbot This is contradictory [*'gal*]; existence and production are not contradictory.

5   KL: Oh. One has to stop or pause [*bkag*, pronounced "ga'"]. A pause [*bkag*].

Abbot: Contradiction [*'gal*], contradiction [*'gal*].

KL: One needs a pause [*bkag*] here.

Abbot: Not "pause" [*bkag*], not "pause" [*bkag*]; contradiction [*'gal*],
10   contradiction [*'gal*].

KL: Contradiction [*'gal*].

Abbot: Here it's contradiction; we're saying "contradiction." The genitive [equivalent to an apostrophe] here is a sign of relationship.

KL: Oh yes.

Replacing an intentional project that is underway is usually too burdensome a task to attempt. Instead of interfering with the intentional project, it is better to wait until its work has been completed and a natural hiatus in the conversation occurs; then one can more easily commence a fresh line of discussion.

When one is incapable of using other means to display competence, *one can use the intentionality of one's partner's attention to help avoid embarrassment*. For example, in Transcript 2b (a continuation of Transcript 2a), I did not grasp very well the points being made about the Svatantrika School, but I was able to provide enough of a statement (lines 25 and 27) to provide a substantial enough push-start for the Abbot to recommence his own intentional project. It required less than a sentence from me to get me past the threat to my competence.

## Transcript 2b

KL: Yes, yes. I understand.

Abbot: Do you understand?

20   KL: [Nods].

Abbot: What?

KL: I understand.

Abbot: Positively do you understand? If you don't understand this well, you'll have plenty of difficulty later. Saying, "Yes, yes, that's right," when you don't understand is not alright. Theses are the principal views of the Middle Way School.

KL: According to the Svatantrika School, um, um, true existence /

Abbot:   / That's right.

30   KL: And, um, um, existence under its own power—

Abbot: They say it like this. The Svatantrika say that an object such as this coaster . . .

In this fashion an awkward moment can be surpassed.

One's own understanding has its intentional interests and priorities, a direction that one's attention is already taking. In intercultural communication there is a tendency to make much out of what one does know (one seeks any consolation); however, preoccupation with one's own formulations can lead to one missing critical communicative events that offer new insights. An essential skill in listening is learning how to *give up one's interpretation* and so *remain open* for fresh possibilities of signification (Heidegger 1962, 191 and 204–206) that one may have missed. If one can sustain the projection of multiple possibilities, the likelihood of successful communication will be enhanced.

To illustrate, on one occasion there was a reference to a portion of a textual citation. The portion, literally, was "foot – first – two,"[5] but I was uncertain whether this meant the first two lines, the second line of the first stanza, the first line of the second stanza, the first two stanzas, etc. I kept myself attentive to the ensuing sense in order to identify which of these possibilities would become apparent as the correct one, and I had to *simultaneously sustain* the projection of each one of these possibilities until some additional information permitted me to rule out the incorrect ones. Although this written account may not make it evident, the *practical* genius involved in *remaining open to* and *sustaining* multiple projections of possible interpretations over the course of an unfolding discussion is as awesome as it is exhausting. It is otherwise called listening.

## GETTING BY

If the truth be told, words keep doing strange things. They are capable of acquiring a significance that is totally unaccountable, and such marvels can become discouraging for a new second-language speaker. As remarked earlier, a single signifier can be made to fit with a number of different signifieds. Each understanding of an utterance organizes a specific syntagmatic system of signification, and a new reading will create a *shift* throughout the entire system. Over the course of a conversation, the meaning of a collection of signifiers that operate together as a system can shift several times (for many detailed illustrations of this phenomenon, see Liberman, "Semantic Drift in Conversation," 2012), and there are times when despite the vertigo, one's partner will call for some confirmation that one has understood. It is then that one must find a cogent reply, and any reply that will work will be cogent enough. Sometimes one's partner will ask a question in order to test one's knowledge, putting one on the spot (see Transcript 6a, lines 3–4). Even though I did not really grasp just what was the purpose of the Geshe's interrogation here and simply repeated his words (line 5), I did at last find an utterance (line 14) that was complex enough to satisfy him. The answer was not for the purpose of learning anything new but for merely surviving the dialogue with my reputation as a worthy scholar intact. The topic concerns how one invents the notions of "I" and "mine" based upon what Buddhists call "a transitory collection," which is the mortal combination of a body with a mind in which no "I" or mine" can be found.

## Transcript 6a

Geshe: The sense of "mine"-ness spontaneously arises when I apprehend a transitory collection [of mind and body, which is interpreted as a mundane ego]. What sort of object of perception does this view of a transitory collection witness?

KL: Object of perception.

Geshe: Yes.

KL: "Me."

Geshe: Right. The object of perception is myself. This spontaneously arising "mine"-ness has the aspect of appearing to be established
10   on its own, according to its self-characteristics.

KL: Right.

Geshe: Phenomena other than this object of perception also appear to exist according to their self-characteristics.

KL: But they are not views of transitory collections.

Geshe: They don't need to be views of transitory collections.

At such times one's priority is to give a competent response in order to preserve the integrity of the interaction; *one's concern has a very local range* and may not include an interest in comprehending the topic. Nevertheless, the interactive skill involved in surveying the immediate horizon of events for a way to "get by" the call for a demonstration of competence is a skill equivalent in importance and sophistication to any semantic aptitude. In the early stages of an intercultural relationship, it is easy to get by through employing a gratuitous concurrence along with a sincere expression on one's face. The sincere look forces one's partner out of objectifications about oneself and opens the partner up to one's "subjective" life (cf. Sartre 1956, 252–302), which makes the partner more vulnerable and more flexible. On many occasions one can get by on politeness alone and on one's partner's desire not to make one feel uncomfortable.

Not all trouble is dispelled so easily; as early as lines 16–17 (see Transcript 6b) I had difficulty with how a term was to be understood and attempted to resolve it, only to find myself in deep water (line 18) before I could find a way to work out a meaningful reply. A silence as long as 2.5 seconds (line 18) portends problems. Although my strategy was to uncover an unknown phrase's meaning by working out its relationship with other semantic components of our discussion, the Geshe took my query to be a wrong question. I beat a quick retreat in the direction of a near platitude (line 22), but that did not satisfy my interest. It did satisfy the demands of the interaction, however, *which are paramount*. I continued my retreat by offering the Geshe a facile reformulation (lines 24–25) of the information he had just stated to me. This solved the "trouble" but left the meaning of the phrase I did not comprehend unexplicated.

### Transcript 6b

15   KL: If something is "[a fixated cognition],"[6] it is not necessarily a view of a transitory collection.

Geshe: What do you mean?

(2.5)

Geshe: For that the object does not need to be a transitory collec-
20   tion. If it's a transitory collection it is a consciousness.

KL: "[The fixated cognition]" is also a consciousness?

Geshe: Oh, it's a consciousness.

KL: But if "[the fixated cognition]" is also a consciousness it does not need to be a view of a transitory collection.

There are also those occasions when one's partner's call for confirmation is more a matter of form than a serious interrogation. As the partners become accustomed to the apparatus for monitoring competence, its use becomes routine, and it runs almost on autopilot. One's partner might even insist that one concur gratuitously in order not to have to belabor a minor point and delay a more vital part of an explanation. Transcript 7 offers an illustration of a forced gratuitous concurrence.

## Transcript 7

Abbot: An illustration was indeed formulated, but not the example of a cause and effect that exist simultaneously. The opponent claimed that the illustration of a simultaneously existing cause and effect was formulated. Do you understand?

KL: [No response.]

Abbot: Isn't it?

KL: Yes.

Abbot: So, it's like that. Isn't it?

The silence at line 5 is surrounded and overwhelmed by devices for compelling a concurrence.

In Transcript 8, the Geshe was wiling to entertain some clarifying inquiries.

## Transcript 8

Geshe: When one says "trainee," there are [SHEE] grounds for which one can say there are trainees.

KL: Four [SHEE].

Geshe: [TREE], We speak of [TREE], do we not?

5   KL: We speak of [TREE].

Geshe: Right. We often speak of them.

KL: Hm-mm.

Geshe: We say "trainee."

KL: I see.

10   Geshe: Trainee.

KL: I see.

Geshe: Do you understand?

KL: I understand.

The repeat at line 3 was an effort to have the Geshe pronounce the word once more, which he had spoken using his strong Eastern Tibetan accent, and he understood that and so re-pronounced it using the Central Tibetan accent that was more familiar to me; unfortunately, I still did not know what the word meant. Despite that, since I had already interrupted our conversation with one query I did not dare to probe any further and instead retreated behind a gratuitous occurrence (the repeat at line 5). One cannot dwell upon every single difficulty, for if one did a conversation would never be able to make progress; and there is a tendency to comply with a collaborator's wish to keep the conversation moving along. The organizational interest of the interaction more or less forces the issue, and only by being stubborn could one convince one's partner that further clarification is really needed. Such interactional pressures account for a great deal of communicative work.

## LOOKING FOR THE NEAREST EXIT

Given these constant pressures, a very local concern with interactional organization predominates. That is, *local interactional concerns* and obligations can, and usually do, overshadow the semantic issues. Never is this more the case than during occasions when one's lack of competence is just about to be laid bare. Facing a demand for a display of competence that cannot be fulfilled, one may examine the surrounding talk for a way to make it comprehensible; is it not uncommon that the increased energy devoted to the task will result in a semantic breakthrough? But if this fails, one will have to turn one's examination of the local talk into a search for the nearest interactional tool that can bring the interrogation to a swift but happy closure. The feeling of desperation is not to be underestimated (I speak here as informant as well as analyst): the search-for-the-nearest-exit will overwhelm all other interests.

And any exit will do. These include responding by asking a question, directing another's attention to a portion of the discussion for which one is able to generate intelligible talk, or stalls (repeats, blowing one's nose, lighting a cigarette, etc.). Asking a question is also an excellent strategy, especially when one is a student. The question can be about the meaning of a word, about which chapter of a text an author is citing, and so forth; even a stupid question is preferable to a wholesale confession of incompetence. For example, the Abbot once asked me, "By another, consciousness does not have formal existence; do you understand?" I replied, "What other?" to which he commented, "The author doesn't specify here," and proceeded with the explanation. It is commonplace that questions are taken as more intelligent than they really are.

On another occasion the Abbot had given an informative but intricate explanation of the point at which an understanding of emptiness that is based on analytic reason becomes a direct understanding of emptiness (i.e., an awareness that is without any conceptualization), and I had followed most but not all of his explanation (in the end, for a fuller understanding I had to rely on my review of the tape). When the Abbot asked if I understood, I didn't know whether to say yes or no; instead, I asked him which chapter of the *Autocommentary* to Chandrakirti's *Madhyamikavatara* the author was citing. This worked for a time, as the Abbot reviewed the possibilities, but at its end I was caught-out when the Abbot reminded me, "Do you understand the meaning? Forget your interest in the *Autocommentary*!"

By directing one's reply to any portion of the talk that one can make something of, it is possible to provide the appearance of being a full participant even when one is not. One can *read a few words from the text* and hope that one or another of one's collaborator's own intentional projects will lead the collaborator to carry on from that point. The turn-taking structure of the talk requires that any call for a display of competence be responded to by speaking; so once one has spoken, no matter how inconsequential the contribution might be, it is then appropriate for one's partner to take up the next turn and carry the conversation along. When the Abbot offered a lengthy exegesis and explained, "When he is speaking like this he is principally speaking to the Svatantrikas I think," and I repeated, "the Svatantrikas." The implication of my repeat was, "This perspective that I understand well is attributable to the refutation of the Svatantrika position"; however, in truth, everything about the refutation except the term "Svatantrika" was a blank for me, and I was going to have to rely upon my review of the tape that evening. Fortunately, I was assisted by the capacity a collaborator has for reading any contribution favorably.

During one of my very first sessions with the Abbot, the duplicitous quality of the situation was affecting me badly. The Abbot had been telling me his biography, which included much nonphilosophical vocabulary that I had not studied, and I was so preoccupied with the task of finding any miniscule topic within his talk about which I could display some sort of competence that I was distracted from the actual task of understanding what he was saying. During the first weeks, my paramount commitment was to maintain a facsimile of the integrity of our conversation. The two agendas here are different and can interfere with each other. The more desperate strategic work like this becomes, the more one's horizon of concern narrows to only some strategic aspects of the interaction's organization. Only afterward was I able to take my tape and pay close attention to the meaning of the extraordinary story he was telling.[7]

When one is pressed by one's partner and about to be discovered as lacking competence or having taken refuge behind a smokescreen of gratuitous concurrence, one's exclusive preoccupation is with how one is going to extract oneself from the "rotten" predicament of letting events expose one's not-really-understanding-while-claiming-to-be-a-competent-partner. At such times the prerequisite skills for escaping through the nearest exit are *no less impressive* than those necessary for adequate comprehension, but they are different skills. Understanding a difficult philosophical exegesis can be a challenging matter, but *real trouble* is when the interaction itself threatens to break down. Without some skill in handling the organization of the conversation itself, one may even comprehend the main points and still not "get by." The matters on which pivot the success or failure of communication *are more narrowly fixated on the immediate local details* of the interaction's organization than analysts who are preoccupied more strictly with meaning usually appreciate; and the events there may not conform to the concept-centered interests of these researchers. Ethnomethodology can offer a propaedeutic to some phenomenologists and symbolic interactionists and by recovering the lived looks of events, to which persons are addressed as a matter of survival.

## COMMUNICATING

Although it sounds less than noteworthy to say it, the most effective means of preserving the integrity of an interaction is to really communicate, and this can involve providing one's partner with a display of correct understanding. Offering *a full-line formulation* of the topic is a proper means of displaying one's competence as an interlocutor (e.g., Transcript 6a, line 13). Offering a provisional but still competent formulation of what one has understood is also an excellent method for improving communication, since it enables one's partner to suggest slight adjustments that can lead to a more correct understanding. In offering candidate formulations there is a tendency to shy away from specificity and to generalize one's assertions by adding an *et cetera* or by qualifying a noun with a modifier such as *like* or *sort of*. Here again, a correct interpretation can be betrayed by a poor account of it, and one's collaborator's intentional projects play an important role. Moreover, it is not impossible for a correct interpretation to be rejected out of hand, only to be confirmed by later events! On such occasions it is best not to argue the point; communication is an imperfect art. Further, the material possibilities of the "text" that collaborators have produced delimit and transform the communication.

Asking the right question is also an excellent means of improving communication, but finding and formulating a question that is both intelligent and useful can present challenges. Questions that fit neatly into the semiotic structure of a conversation, and so are answered easily, *may be given preference over questions that are truly helpful*, especially when there are limited opportunities for posing questions. Troubling questions can make too many demands on the interaction, and they are also more likely to become "wrong questions" than are simple questions.

There are those occasions, however, when one must force one's partner to attend to one's interpretation, no matter how foolhardy it may seem. As John Dewey (1916, 127 and 186) stated, "Communication is a process of sharing experience till it becomes a common possession." Until a teacher "can let his mind come to close quarters with the pupil's mind and subject matter" the education process will be stunted, and cornering one's collaborator within an interrogation may be the only means of achieving such contact. Parties to intercultural conversations tend to be conservative, almost paranoid. As one method, I would begin an interrogation by first clarifying some matters that I thought I already knew (an incorrect presumption here will terminate an interrogation). In an attempt to reduce the number of uncertainties, I would then ask about possible but unlikely significations that I wished to entirely rule out of consideration. This carries the risk that I might appear to be dumber than I really was, but here I am speaking about my efforts to *really* communicate. Having prepared the ground, I would then proceed with the more subtle matters.

To illustrate, of five possible meanings to an utterance, two might be ruled out easily, one most probably could be ruled out, and two might vie for being the correct solution. I would commence with the possibilities that could be ruled out most easily, progress to the one probably ruled out, and finally push my principal inquiry. Even if all five possibilities were ruled out, at least I would learn that whatever the correct meaning was, it was not among those candidates. As part of the process, my collaborator would have excellent opportunities to view the structures of interpretation that I was employing and so make contact with them, increasing the tools available to him for communicating successfully with me. Such full-fledged interrogation is a skill in its own right, but it is one that must be handled carefully.

There are those occasions when the best means of communicating is not to say more but less. Too many questions and too much time spent on fine details can cause collaborators to lose sight of the larger context. At times, abandoning an inquiry can be a boon to comprehension. By clearing the slate, some *fresh* semiotic structures can be developed without remaining implicated in the impending chaos of the abandoned structures. Simply put, the recommendation here is to *trim the branches*. Conversations have a natural tendency to drift into tangents. If a problem arises with a tangent, do not try to repair it but return to the main topic. If there is a problem with an illustration, give it up promptly and try another, and never entertain third-order explanatory phenomena, that is, an exegesis of an exegesis or an illustration of an illustration. The intellectual energy available to collaborators in intercultural interaction is a limited commodity and needs to be preserved for the principal tasks, for it will surely be exhausted before too long. Indeed, the speed with which exhaustion sets in is one of the characteristics that distinguishes intercultural from ordinary communication.

## CONCLUSION

This chapter could well be subtitled, "The Confessions of a Confused Ethnographer." But these reported confusions are in no way unique to my competencies and practices. The communicative difficulties and strategies described here must be faced time and again by each person who must make sense of, and with, people from other cultures. In fact, these local interactional phenomena are relied on by all field researchers—philosophers, anthropologists, sociolinguists, Orientalists, and so forth—although it is rare that they report such difficulties, preferring to submerge them beneath the cogency of one or another professional narrative strategy. Even analysts of intercultural communication miss the radical importance of these interactional phenomena because their inquiries remain lodged in cultural comparisons and contrasts based upon generalizations; nevertheless, they rely on these or similar specific organizational strategies each and every moment of their fieldwork. This organizational work is "the missing interactional What" (Garfinkel and Wieder 1992, 203) of intercultural conversation.

Understanding meanings is not all there is to communication in conversations. Many issues on which pivot the success or failure of communication are narrowly fixated on the immediate local interactional concerns, and these obligations can overshadow the semantic issues. When the local concern with interactional organization predominates, the interest in comprehending a topic may be suspended temporarily. The competence involved in comprehending a topic and the technical skills necessary for formatting the interaction are different skills, and ethnomethodology can provide analysts with access to the latter skills. Although both skills are important to the success of a conversation and both are topics for investigation, the first rule of a conversation is survival. This is true not just for intercultural communication but for all interaction. The concentration here on intercultural communication is warranted by the serendipitous frequency of breakdowns in intercultural interaction, which can render these organizational items more observable and thus more readily available to analysts, but the organizational methods used here are not in any way unique to intercultural settings.

# SIX

# "THERE IS A GAP" IN THE TIBETOLOGICAL LITERATURE

Tibetological research usually commences with texts and not with people. Isolated manuscripts shipped back to European museums by colonial officials or textual studies performed by colonial administrators, some of them laid up with long-term illnesses and finding themselves with much time on their hands, formed the germ of Indology and Tibetology. Buddhist studies was conceived as a literary enterprise, as an offshoot of philology (Lopez 1998, 158), and it has been the hallmark of Tibetological practice since its beginnings to reduce the live philosophical praxis of Tibetan scholar-monks to their docile texts. Docile texts provided first access, and frequently the only access, since the linguistic skills of philologists were literary and not oral. When Tibetans were consulted, they were used mainly as adjuncts to their texts, and they became functionaries for the Tibetologists' own inquiries. They frequently lacked authority, and the lived indigenous practices that composed their expertise were either never recognized or ignored. Regrettably, the early Tibetologists did not emphasize oral skills, and so it would have been difficult for them to follow the rapid flow and repartee of Tibetan dialectical inquiry. Instead of holding a lens up to Tibetan philosophical culture, it was more as if they used binoculars.

Tibetological studies that are textually based miss, *by virtue of the disciplinary practices that identify their discipline*, the indigenous lived activities that should be a primary part of their investigations. The Tibetans' texts themselves are mostly reductions and idealizations of their debates along with pertinent sectarian discussions about those debates; what occurs in the actual debates themselves is much more dynamic, multiply determined, and messier than what is found in their texts. This messiness is disfavored by Tibetologists, who seek tidier stories that can be told without too many mundane kinds of complications. But the real world is always mundane, and even a topic as esoteric as Tibetan philosophy is embedded in its quotidian practices.

Prior to the current generation of scholars, Tibetologists operated from a secured vantage point that was only infrequently placed at risk by extensive interaction with indigenous Tibetan practitioners. In fact, young scholars were dissuaded from becoming extensively involved with any real practitioners of Asian philosophical reflection. Max Mueller (1823–1900), one of the founders of Indology and based at Oxford, forbade his students from even going to India to do their research (Nandy 1983, 17); instead of going where they could witness live practices, they were instructed to confine themselves to some of the texts that those practices produced. All specification of researchable problems and all matters of professional relevance were to be derived only from what Harold Garfinkel (2002, 122) has termed "the corpus status of its [disciplinary] bibliographies," which was given *precedence* over the interests of indigenous people. Even today, researchers who take their Tibetan studies too seriously may be accused of "going native" or of being unprofessional. It seems that professionalism includes a directive that no indigenous idea ever be taken seriously. While it is wrong to surrender one's independence of judgment (Liberman 2001), there are both ethical and scientific shortcomings to insisting upon a professional myopia that makes it unlikely one will ever discover what one needs to learn most: what one does not yet know.

During the classical period of Tibetology, Western scholars frequently spoke in the voice of the Master Narrator, a literary device inherited from the colonial era of social research, and any of their analyses relied upon what are basically taxidermal approaches, as if all of the live subjects had expired long ago and any that remain have no relevant competence. The Tibetologists' authority proceeds from impressive philological competence, won at the cost of extraordinary diligence, but it also proceeds from a careful cultivation of the standpoint of the universal observer whose transcendental status is ensured by means of literary devices. The observation of actual people engaged in live situations occurring naturally as part of their ordinary lives, made not from a "universal" vantage point but from the mundane vantage point of the actors themselves, is not a method used or even approved of by many Tibetological researchers. One of my early teachers of Tibetan, Professor Thubten Jigme Norbu of Indiana University, the elder brother of the present Dalai Lama, would deliberately mispronounce "Tibetology" as "Tibeto-ology," in order to satirize the self-importance of these Western academicians.

Once Buddhism was tamed by such epistemic strategies, Orientalist research was safe from contestation. Robbed of any agency, Tibetans themselves were asked to contribute only a little to this imperialist project, except for some translations of texts whose Sanskrit versions were lost. Only scholars thought to be "biased" or "romantic" accepted Tibetan philosophical practices as worthy of study in their own right. Blinded by their own Eurocentrism, Tibetologists were not fully capable of investigating one of the world's most remarkable philosophical cultures. But there was an irony here: the Tibetologists were for the most part dependent upon Tibetans to explain the most difficult portions of their philosophical and religious texts.

It is not that some Tibetan notions do not lead Tibetologists to vital insights, it is only that the insights they have had made only minimal contact with the naturally endogenous experience of Tibetans and is nothing like a Tibetan engagement with those same notions. Unless those notions can be captured ethnomethodologically in *just the way* that the Tibetan scholar-monks come to them, little of real interest can be learned. It is not that Tibetologists have not come upon anything profound; it is that *the profundities they have come upon are neither Tibetan nor Buddhist*: there is a "gap" between the Tibetological canon and the experience of Tibetans.

In one ethnographic inquiry after another there seem to be two alternative projects at hand. First, there exists an established version of a given social world, usually presented in a formal literature. According to Garfinkel (1979–80), "It is not that the established literature is wrong. It is that it is absurd." Because nothing outside of the concerns already addressed by the literature is permitted to enter the scope of what is being investigated, a myopia is assured. Its absurdity arises from its irrelevance to what the people, on behalf of whom the literature speaks, are actually doing. As Garfinkel and Livingston (2003, 25) have observed about professional researchers whose work is literature-based, "Peer-reviewed Literatures can always ignore lived work." An incommensurable alternative project is the ethnomethodological investigation that respecifies these academic topics in terms of the actual looks of the world from the perspective of these actors, capturing their horizon of meaning and their practical activities along with as many of their *particular details* as possible. Garfinkel (1979–80) advises caution here, "Fascination for what the people are really doing will get you into a lot of trouble because the authors of the established literature will become antagonistic." In our present case, there exists a large corpus of established Tibetological research that has topicalized Tibetan philosophical practices but has *missed* the in-the-course practices that compose the philosophical life of what Tibetan scholars are actually doing. And much as Garfinkel has described, they do not miss the in-the-course practices in just any way; they miss them explicitly because of the particular disciplinary practices that they impose upon the affairs they study. Consequently, "There is a gap in the literature" (Garfinkel 2002, 131).

Much of the education in Tibetan philosophical culture takes place on the public debate grounds of the monastic university, where Tibetans engage each other in a dialectical pursuit of philosophical understanding; hence, any methodology that is so exclusively concentrated upon textual analysis that it misses the associated social practice will *necessarily* fail to capture what most identifies this philosophical culture, which has its roots in ancient South Asian society. The Tibetologists' textual empiricism can simultaneously be considered a textual imperialism, since it is an exercise in ethnocentrism. Although it is true that the situation is changing significantly among the current generation of Tibetologists,[1] even the contemporary Tibetologists who today do travel extensively and live in Tibetan monasteries, villages, and settlements spend most of their time there in their rooms translating texts instead of participating in the actual philosophical practices of Tibetan scholars. It is rare for Tibetologists to study a text in the way that Tibetans do, although this is beginning to happen. Today we face *the disciplinary problem* of how we do more than simply replicate the achievement of Ippolito Desideri, the Italian cleric who lived in a Tibetan monastic university for some years during the early part of the eighteenth century and was the first European to apprentice himself to practitioners of Tibetan philosophical culture.[2] How do we teach ourselves to learn to see what the Tibetans are seeing?

Tibetology is changing, even rapidly, and much of the significant change has come not at the hands of Tibetologists themselves but at the hands of Tibetans, who have become increasingly involved in the mundane disciplinary activities of Tibetology itself. When I was a graduate student, there were usually one or two Tibetans who attended the international conferences devoted to Asian studies, Tibetology, comparative philosophy and comparative religion, etc.; however, they mostly sat in the back and observed quietly, except when they had been scripted into the proceedings. For most of the time I was a professor, an increasing number of Tibetans have been attending these conferences; and there were often enough of them that Tibetologists were forced to subject themselves to the critical scrutiny of Tibetans who might complain that a monograph was short-sighted or challenge them about one error or another. This was quite salutary for Tibetological inquiry. Today, many Tibetans have received academic degrees from European or North American universities, which facilitates their being full and equal participants at these gatherings. At the international seminar of the International Association of Tibetan Studies held in 2010, the conference organizer himself was a Tibetan and there were panels where the Tibetans were more than equal participants and where the discourse itself, the Narrative perspective of the field, had become more indigenous. The European-, Japanese-, and North American-born Tibetologists were occasionally required to engage Tibetans within the terms of a discourse that the former no longer dominated. On occasion, the debates of the sessions would shift into the Tibetan language, and the non-Tibetan participants had to struggle to keep up their equal participation.

For anyone studying Tibetan philosophy, the important question to ask is a *simple* one: *what is it that Tibetans do?* What is it that Tibetans do that preserves for them the productive life of their thought? Such a question can only be pursued by capturing "the role of rationality within the interstices of its dynamics" (Schrag 1992, 8–9), that is, by an "extended preoccupation with rationality as a *praxis*." There is in the Tibetological study of the philosophical practices of Tibetans what Garfinkel calls "a missed orderliness," an orderliness that the debating Tibetan scholars rely upon to produce, maintain, and exploit for investigating the nature of reality, for placing their ideas into formal statements, and for living their life.

The organizational matters and the philosophical matters that preoccupy Tibetan scholar-monks do not exist apart, independently of each other. Their separation is only an analyst's convention. In the real world, they come packaged together. To separate the logic out from the social is to be left with only an idealized, reductionist reason, which represents no one's philosophical practice. Instead, as Bar-Hillel (1964, 125) commended, we need to turn toward the wild "jungle of daily discourse" of philosophical discussion and face directly the forms of language and reason in use there:

> The deeper we go into the jungle, the more difficult it is to advance. More than once, the pathways we uncover re-grow with savage vegetation that threatens to return us to our former condition. Scholars are attracted in droves to the few areas where the sun has arisen, instead of continuing to open up the jungle.

Mundane situations can become very complex, and as the complications multiply, it becomes difficult not only to communicate the details we have identified, it is difficult to identify them. But to simply lift a formal philosophical assertion out of the context of its production and build our inquiry into reason around that is to engage in nothing more consequential than what Garfinkel called "an ethnography of sentences," and it is not a practice that will assist us to understand another's world. Heidegger writes (1991, 19), "This glib talk—superficially and off the cuff—of *axioms, principia*, and fundamental principles in a homologous sense is indeed precarious."

In fact, the desire for a homogeneous reason is another social demand more than it is a philosophical one; it owes its preeminence primarily to an obsessive interest in being perfectly certain, a characteristic of northern European philosophical culture, and Tibetans are more respectful of the necessary limits of formal analytic reasoning. Although Tibetan philosophical reflection is formally registered and carefully administered, the formal notions of truth with which Tibetan philosophical culture is working are less logocentric than those of European philosophical culture. Some European philosophers dismiss what is a vital *alternative* epistemological perspective highly critical of essentialist assumptions as being something that does not rise to the level of "philosophical." I was once arguing this very point with a phenomenological colleague at an annual meeting of the Society for Phenomenology and Existential Philosophy, and after several minutes of discussion, my colleague retreated to this argument: "The Tibetans cannot be doing philosophy because their ideas do not originate with the Greeks." Surely, this is myopia being elevated to a virtue.

In Garfinkel's (2001, 19) terms, a local orderliness works only with "the holy hellish *concreteness* of things." Once one has *located* the actual worksite of indigenous practitioners, one becomes swamped by the details. Further, when one begins to speak about those details, there will be no end to the telling that will be required. A serious risk is whether any audience will have the interest or patience to learn such a level of detail, a problem I encountered with the reception of the chapter about rhythms in formal analytic debating in my book on Tibetan dialectical practices (Liberman 2004). But there is no alternative to the effort to make one's way through "the jungle of daily discourse" that inevitably accompanies philosophical inquiry.

Tibetan scholar-monks are notoriously dismissive of Europeans who lack expertise in the ethnomethods of Tibetans, especially when they wish to "translate" texts by just sitting at their desks with dictionaries. They consider the endeavor to be a ludicrous and sterile exercise. University of Wisconsin Professor Emeritus Geshe Lhudrup Sopa, a scholar with the imprimatur of both the American and Tibetan academies, warns that the correct way to read a Tibetan text is within the context of the debates that the text fosters in the monastic courtyards. Properly witnessed, Tibetan dialectics is an end in itself, not just a means to knowledge. One of the orderlinesses "missed" by Tibetologists is that for Tibetan dialecticians *the practice is more crucial than the products*. When one fetishizes the results and turns them into cash in the economy of professional careers, the phenomenon itself is left far behind.

The topic of a Tibetan debate (for example, that entities are empty of inherent essences) is addressed by a practice of thinking; that thinking can *itself* be captured in (and as) the web of essentializations in which it is already entangled. In this way reificatory thinking can be exposed and held up to the light of their dialectical criticism. Moreover, the essentializations there are not merely opposed theoretically; the itinerary of the intellection that sustains them is followed so that the Tibetan scholar-monks can gain some ability to recognize *just how* a self-alienation of thinking takes place.

Tibetan epistemology can be thinking at the limits of reasoning itself, especially when the reflections of dialectically engaged philosophers are themselves escorted through their itineraries of reification. Their ideas are brought *within the dialectics* in order to confront some of the absurd ironies they have born along the way. The principal objective of Tibetan dialecticians is that their philosophical thinking should bring their inquiries to life. Since this is a collaborative project, some sociological methodologies are appropriate, despite the low status that sociology can sometimes have in the priorities of professional philosophers.

Capturing the *in vivo* work of Tibetan philosophers *as* these tasks is a matter that poses a number of methodological difficulties. In another context, Garfinkel (2001) has observed that the very concreteness of the local affairs can defeat any effort to come upon these ethnomethods. But Garfinkel strongly encourages us to resist the urge to take any of the easy shortcuts offered by restricting one's gaze by repeating one or another "principled version" of actual social interaction, and he advises us to remain addressed to the social interactions themselves. He suggests that it is alright to try to settle the matters of just-what, and just-how, a local cohort of social actors do what they are doing, so long as one recognizes that any time such a matter gets settled "it only gets settled for the time being. If you cannot take the two together [i.e., "the matter is settled" and the "for the time being"], then ethnomethodology is not for you" (Garfinkel 1979–80).

This is a severe discipline under which to undertake social phenomenological studies, but it is one that always keeps oneself open for what one does not yet know. This also gives to it an ethical merit that more imperialist social research methodologies lack. At the very least, the aim in micro-level studies of Tibetan philosophical practices should be to preserve and sustain *the site* of the Tibetans' own philosophical efforts. Above all, that site should not be lost, as it is for too much of Tibetological inquiry, for only within the intricacies of that site can any real philosophical life be understood and appreciated. In some circumstances, contemporary Tibetological scholarship has welcomed the detailed micro-interactional study of Tibetan philosophers, but on other occasions these methodologies have been resisted by "a paternalism that simply refuses, through the sheer force of will or the exercise of power, to acknowledge the existence of viable methodological perspectives and styles of scholarship" (Cabezón 1995, 242). At times their rejection has been enforced by the disciplinary control that philologists retain over the awarding of some research grants, scholarly appointments, approval of submissions for publication, etc.; however, the situation today has opened up considerably. It may be that ethnomethodology is capable of making a contribution to the current generation's effort to drag Tibetological praxis out of the nineteenth and into the twenty-first century.[3]

SEVEN

# CHOREOGRAPHING THE ORDERLINESS OF TIBETAN PHILOSOPHICAL DEBATES

Any formal thinking has local organizational requirements. Despite the fact that the orderliness of reasoning is a necessary preoccupation of philosophers, the practices for dealing with issues of orderliness are not readily apprehended, like the water that fish swim in, and this practical interest in local organization has been mostly overlooked by those who write about philosophy. Whatever else reason and logic may be, they are *tools* that philosophers can use to keep their reflections and inquiries organized. The organizational uses of the formal reasoning developed by philosophers is not

Figure 7.1

merely their accompanying interest, it is a central aspect of their professional work; in fact, it identifies what can be considered the "formal" in formal thinking.

This is especially true for collaborative thinking, which is most of the thinking that people do, including conversations, seminars, colloquia, public debating, face-to-face arguments, and whenever topics must be communicated, shared, and developed with one's colleagues. Before an idea can be understood, i.e., understood in common, it must be made over into a unity that can become a public possession, an object-in-common, which will serve as the focal point for their collaborative work and contribute to making that work orderly. Without orderliness, it cannot be formal analysis. In his prospectus for a proposed sequel to his *Ethnomethodology's Program*, Harold Garfinkel commenced his prospectus with this epigraph from Husserl: "How Something Comes to be Known. . . . Naturally the answer is: I could only understand it if the *relation* itself [that is, between the knowing and the known object] could be given as something that could be *seen*."[1] The important point and the reason for citing this passage is that the work of providing a local orderliness demands that what is to be made a common possession, made a social fact, must be available to and *witnessable* by all of the participants at an occasion. Even philosophers work in a public sphere, and so the matters they take up need to be organized in some public way. Accordingly, one of the first tasks that philosophers attempting to organize the orderliness of an occasion must do is to *make evident* what it is they are addressing. And this is true for every situation. For something to come to be known in common, it must be "*seen*." It is a practical matter: without clarifying an "*x*" that can be shared, there can be no commonality.

I have written a book on the topic of the orderliness of formal analytic reasoning (Liberman 2004) in which I take up the case of Tibetan philosopher-monks who are engaged in regular public debates on a variety of epistemological matters. The principal discovery of that monograph was that these philosophers use logic in order to make evident—to make seen—the thinking they are doing. So in this way the logic of their reflections *is also something social*, and formal reason itself can be respecified as a resource for social orderliness. Some formalization of thinking is necessary for thinking to keep track of itself, i.e., for thinking to know itself. More importantly, the use of logic and reason is necessary for facilitating the sharing and communicating of ideas. The immanent, local, and indispensable need for communicating clearly by developing notions in orderly and *publicly available* ways was an abiding preoccupation of every cohort of Tibetan philosophers that I studied. Their *first* task was to organize an orderliness for their ideas which they could use as a scaffold for their collaborative inquiries. The substantive matters that interested them came afterward.

For a number of years, at some point during my undergraduate courses on social phenomenology and ethnomethodology I gave the students a lecture on Tibetan philosophical debating that included many videos of actual debates, which I used for presenting to them how the Tibetans make their debating orderly and how they turn their serendipitous findings into objective, formal acquisitions, a process I call (after Husserl and Schutz) objectivation. This lecture usually came at a point when students were working on one or another of the course projects that form the topics of the chapters of this book, projects whose work-load made students unavailable for any reading assignment. And so the lecture was a kind of "filler" that permitted me to present ethnomethodological material without requiring any preparation on the students' part. It so happened that when I had a chance encounter with any of these students years later, they would always mention that lecture to me, ask about whether I was still studying those debates, and express to me how that presentation made an enduring impression upon them. A few students confessed that it was the only thing about my course that they remembered clearly, and in their minds, the students had associated closely that lecture with me.

Once or twice I had almost decided that since the lecture was peripheral to the course material, too much of a "filler," it should be dropped from my curriculum; however, the reliability with which students keep referring to that lecture always persuaded me to retain it. Consequently, I spent time reflecting upon what it was about the lecture that impressed the students, and I concluded that it was not the philosophy presented there, nor was it even the ethnomethodological analysis that accompanied it; rather, they were provoked and perhaps inspired by the way that the Tibetans' clapping and remonstrations, performed in such a highly rhythmic way, made their philosophical tasks compelling. That is, what attracted the students was the way the Tibetans choreographed their debating—the raw, *rhythmic properties* that are apparent in any and all Tibetan philosophical debating. Just as those rhythmic properties energize the Tibetan thinkers, they energize us. While their choreography is related closely to the substantive matters about which they are arguing and helps them to organize the orderliness of those arguments, it is not anything that in itself is conceptual. It is another one of those *nonconceptual* phenomena that are so very fundamental to how we organize our mundane lives together—a matter I addressed at the end of chapter 1—but that somehow do not draw very much attention from philosophers.

These nonconceptual matters of rhythm and choreography, whose presentation was important enough for me to devote a separate chapter in a previous book (cf. Liberman 2004, chapter 6), were almost universally ignored by readers and reviewers, Tibetologists and ethnomethodologists alike. Despite the fact that I had even prepared a CD-ROM that displayed the lived details of the very phenomena I wished to emphasize and included it in the hardback edition in an envelope inside the back cover, none of the reviewers made even a mention of how these nonconceptual matters contributed to the orderliness of Tibetan debating. I attributed this to a general bias among academicians in favor of *concepts* and *ideas* that they can latch on to, favorably or unfavorably. For the most part, nonconceptual phenomena live below their radar. In addition to that, the rhythmic work of Tibetan debaters is a culturally embedded and somewhat difficult-to-appreciate, "thick" phenomenon, the spirit of which is not easily captured by means of ethnographic reportage. It is always more difficult and more time-consuming to set aside the ideas and conceptual agenda that is one's professional interest (and meal-ticket) and instead commence learning an unfamiliar social world. Even Tibetologists' professional work for the most part consists of working with docile texts that do not talk back to them, and they can straightforwardly locate the conceptual matters that interest them most and provide a meaningful exegesis of the ideas they have located, without seriously entering the lived world of Tibetans.

Even if one were to try to take up some of the lived work of Tibetan philosophers *in its own milieu*, and not in the milieu of the reviews found in Western literatures, learning the in-the-course dialectical strategies and choreographic skills of Tibetan debaters is a complex task, a sort of advanced study of a specialized expertise, and so I did not fault the Tibetologists (whose special interest may not have include *gelukpa* debates) for not undertaking what would have required unusual effort. However, I did fault the ethnomethodologists because for them there was no excuse since their professional craft consists of penetrating, in each case, the specific local expertise at hand along with its local orderliness. Even the review of my book in the *American Journal of Sociology*, written by an accomplished ethnomethodologist, made no reference to the chapter on the rhythms of debating. How could the *most* ethnomethodological chapter of the book be overlooked by ethnomethodologists? My students' enthusiastic responses to the physical rhythms of Tibetan debating reassured me that my ethnomethodological analysis and ethnographic presentation were on the right track, and so I decided to revisit the topic and emphasize only the choreographic components of Tibetan debating for a paper for a meeting of the International Association of Tibetan Studies,[2] in the hope of drawing some attention to this overlooked topic. It is my hope that its inclusion in this volume may provide similar motivation for ethnomethodologists to consider the topic again, as well as offer an opportunity to take up one more occasion where nonconceptual events contribute to the organization of the orderliness of local affairs.

The rhythmic properties of their debating are central to the work that Tibetan philosopher-monks are doing, *including the work of organizing the orderliness of their philosophical dialectics*. These debaters are not very concerned about winning or losing a debate, their agenda is more collaborative than that: primarily, they seek to provide themselves with a stimulating and satisfying exploration of a philosophical topic. Here satisfaction usually means *becoming intoxicated with the cadence of their debating*, and it also involves coming to figure out how to confront each other in an immanent way with an important philosophical quandary so that some life can be breathed into an epistemological or ontological matter. A debate that has been choreographed well has vitality, and when ideas have vitality people will listen to the ideas more carefully; and good philosophy is produced when people listen to each other.

Any collaborative philosophical exploration will contain certain insights and also specific forms designed to carry those insights. The formalization of thinking becomes critical when two or more people think together. The capacity of propositions to integrate the analytic contributions of participants influences their selection of the forms. The analytic forms and the philosophical insights keep each other company, but there is no guarantee that the forms will convey the insights: the forms must be made to carry the insights. It is what people *do* with the forms that matters, not just the forms in themselves. The rhetorical features of philosophical dialectics are designed to insure that forms effectively bear the insights in ways that can be communicated clearly. Choreography is one of the rhetorical tools that Tibetan debaters use; without it, the philosophical discussion would not be recognizably Tibetan.

## COHERENCE IN DIALECTICS

Philosophers have not only truth concerns but also concern for the practical, organizational tasks that pertain to developing and sustaining a formal structure of thinking, for without that structure—ideas that are arranged so that they can be *seen*—they will have nothing at all. So they concert their efforts together and produce a local orderliness for their dialogue and for keeping their talk organized. From the very start philosophers address themselves to the local organizational tasks of establishing some facilities for communicating together and making their ideas coherent.

The sociolinguists William Labov and David Fanshel (1977, 70) suggest that the coherence of a conversation *is not found at the level of propositional statements*; rather, it is achieved among the actions of the interlocutors. Philosophizing can take place only after the parties have concerted their actions to provide an interactive basis for philosophical inquiry. The formal accounts of the philosophical matters are themselves employed for keeping the interaction organized. Although keeping the talk organized and keeping the philosophical reflection organized are separate tasks, it may be said that they work hand-in-glove. *The formal structure of reasoning* finds its way about via the orderliness that the work of keeping the talk organized has provided; the formal analysis rides the interactional order, as it were. But *that organizational work of producing a local orderliness* also exploits the formal accounts, utilizing those accounts' own organizational capacities. That is, to turn Labov and Fanshel's constructive insight on its head, conversational coherence can be established interactionally by means of those propositional statements that Labov and Fanshel denigrate somewhat dualistically; however, it is not only the truth-value of the statements that is vital here but the capacity of the propositions to integrate in an organized way the analytic contributions of the participants.

Husserl has addressed repeatedly, both in the context of the individual thinker and later in intersubjective thinking, how the proliferation of thoughts must be united "in one unity of consciousness" and that somehow "our glance is thereby directed towards the identical element, the $x$ of the meaning" (Husserl 1962, 384). It is part of the fundamental work of philosophers to produce that $x$ so that they have something to talk about. Only by objectivating their thinking and redrawing it into formal, public structures can they proceed with their philosophical work. This formalization offers them at least three benefits: (1) it allows them to *keep track* of their own thinking (much like the notations of mathematicians facilitate mathematicians keeping track of their thinking; cf. Livingston 1986); (2) it allows philosophers to *communicate* in a clear fashion about the ideas; and (3) it offers them a scaffold for building and collaboratively *accumulating* their ideas. Of course, to facilitate the public availability of their accomplishments some of their ideas require reduction. Not all of the fringe meanings will survive, what confuses—no matter how profound it may be—may be dropped, and whatever *can* be communicated clearly will be given priority, a priority it may not deserve. Husserl (1970a, 639–70) has spoken often about how the polythetic rays of attention get reduced to a monothetic ray, which may be the only thing that survives the occasion: "It is true of the 'conjunctive' (or better 'collective') synthesis, as it is true of the predicative synthesis, that it permits of nominalization, in which case the collective object constituted by the synthesis, becomes the simply presented object of a new 'single-rayed' act, and so is made 'objective' in the pregnant sense of the word." Simplification is part of the way that the philosophical work is made orderly, so that everyone participating can reorganize what is happening. In this way the forms, driven by local organizational demands, can transform what is thought.

Some of the readers who overlooked the chapter on rhythm in debating may have considered it simply to be a diversion into aesthetics, and for some serious scholars aesthetics, while interesting, is a topic that is not always taken to be vital for a philosophical or sociological interest, and so its consideration is optional. But in the case of Tibetan philosophers, the aesthetic properties of their debating are the heart of the matter and are vital for organizing their local orderliness. It is the way they manage to conjoin the two mental flows of the participants. The matters just referred to—the public availability, the communicability, etc.—are accomplished by means of the rhythmic patterning of the argumentation: *the logic must be made to dance*. Only when the rhythm of a debate carries the debaters along, rendering them not producers but witnesses to a spectacle, is a debate considered to be proceeding in proper form. This is in fact a fabulous achievement and is what most identifies Tibetan debate; and it is what my students have been responding to. It is fabulous because it requires that the debaters *really hear each other*. In order to dance, one must be tuned in to one's partner.

During one of my stays in a remote Tibetan monastery, located in the largest settlement of Tibetans outside of Tibet, I was asked by the principal of the Tibetans' high school to act as a judge for a forensic-styled public debate of teenage Tibetan debaters. This featured the standard Western format of a team of two debaters contesting a second team of two debaters under a regime of strict time limits, and the debates continued morning and afternoon on the stage of the high school auditorium. I was reminded of how a common feature of forensic debates is that each team debates without paying much attention to the arguments of the other team; at times it can be less an occasion for dialectics than it is for two simultaneous monologues. At the end of each debate it can seem as if two ships had just passed each other in the night. After the day's debates concluded and the winners were awarded their trophies, I was asked by the principal to make a few comments to the audience about what I had witnessed. As politely as I was able, I compared what they were doing with what was going on in the monastery just a few miles away. I observed that one feature of the monastic debates is that the debaters there always listen to each other carefully. In fact, they don't dare *not* pay attention. Since this feature was frequently missing in the Western-styled debates I suggested to them that they not sell their own culture too short; while the Tibetan form of dialectics is mostly medieval in origin, it has many qualities to commend it and should not be dismissed easily.

Communication is an important part of all philosophical discourse, and communication is well served when thoughts are respecified in objective forms that are made accessible to all. In a debate that has been rendered in a seamless rhythm, each party must know just how and just when to fit in their contribution with the others', and for that they must listen attentively.

In this fashion *the rhythm contributes to the objectivity of the discourse*. When a debate reaches the point where the ideas are so choreographed that they flow together seamlessly, it is as if the logic has been anthropomorphized into an autonomous force that transcends the contingencies of its local production. It is like a child's toy car whose rear wheels can be spring-loaded so that it is capable of running for a few feet by itself. The choreographic work is like the loading of the spring; and when the child places the car on a level surface and lets go of it, the witnessing of the run of the car across the floor is very much like the debaters' own witnessing of the philosophical apparatus whose rhythmic properties they have choreographed carefully. The result is an illusion that the philosophical matters presented therein are the inexorable result of a formal dialectical process that is objective, independent, and free of any individual subjective taint, i.e., it is the truth of a matter.

Husserl has recognized the importance of the physical materiality of monothetic, objectivated forms of thought and in his *Logical Investigations* has described the word sounds whose materiality is available to us all (Husserl 1970, 682). During the latter part of his career he gave more importance to the work of coordinating one's thinking with others, and in the *Crisis* Husserl (1970, 360) acknowledges the role of repetition and reversal in providing a unity of understanding: "In the unity of the community of communication among several persons the repeatedly produced structure becomes an object of consciousness as the one structure common to all." Establishing this "one structure common to all" is part of the *philosophical work*. Any formal analysis has a material tangibility to it—that is part of what is meant by "formal." When its public availability has been addressed, it is something that can be thought in common. And logic itself—made public (and repeated)—may be used by philosophers as a social organizational device, i.e., a means for organizing the local orderliness of their thinking.

Here we are not trying to reduce philosophy to social processes; indeed, our discipline as ethnomethodologists requires that we respect and preserve the integrity of the philosophical questions with which the philosophers are working. But the two matters of form and content exist alongside each other, *actively* with each other—actively *with* each other. The philosophical matters are even advanced by the organizational faculties that are brought into play by the cooperative collaboration of a cohort of philosophers; and people concert themselves in order to achieve some harmony, which is a prerequisite for understanding. It is common for philosophers to overlook this Durkheimian phenomenon, despite the fact that in their philosophical practice they rely upon its features.

It is pertinent here to remind ourselves that the formal analytic practices developed by the Greeks were developed as social practices: they developed as the discourse of juridical advocates in the Greek *polis*, most notably when such legal advocacy became the specialty of professionals. Those logicians who followed Aristotle increasingly turned away from analyzing arguments and investigating the semantics and structure of natural languages and instead turned to analyzing and interpreting Aristotle's formal analytic achievements (Bar-Hillel 1964, 122). And so, formal analytic philosophy was born.

The Tibetans also have formal analytic concerns whose locus is the public square, and they retain more of their affiliation to their public organizational tasks. The Tibetan term for "formal analysis" is *gtan tshigs*, which has been also translated both as "logical reason" and "syllogism." "*Tshigs*" alone has been translated as "enunciate," and "*gtan*" means "to put in order" or "arrange into a system," and it has the near-cognate *brtan*, which means "stabilized" or "firm." "*Tshigs*" can also mean "division; verse; something that is connected," and it is related to the word *tshig*, which means "word." Hence, it may be said that *gtan tshigs* is the setting of literal components into a stable order. This is the task of objectivating ideas about which Husserl has spoken. More specifically, it is the setting up of a course of reasoned thinking as a common accomplishment. At some level, all philosophy is collaboration since the task must be *to align the thinking*: philosophical dialectics is not only philosophy, it is a social practice. Logical formatting is a device which philosophers use to keep track of their thinking—that is, to retain in the objective memory of the occasion the developing accomplishments of their philosophizing.

## SOME CHOREOGRAPHIC TOOLS FOR OBJECTIVATING PHILOSOPHICAL IDEAS

How can people know when they are communicating adequately? When people are able to interlace their speech, each speaking the words of the other in a context that is shared, they most likely have achieved an adequacy of communication. When the other person has the opportunity to talk back and *learn to use the same words in similar ways*, meaning can come to be shared; but it doesn't happen on its own. It happens only when there are deliberate social practices undertaken to accomplish such a state of affairs. I am offering here an ethnomethodological respecification of *just-what* adequate communication can consist of. A competent interlacing of terms and utterances can furnish vital opportunities for establishing adequate communication, and the system of the give-and-take of utterances within the rhythmic flow of a typical Tibetan debate is one such system. A routine system like this requires of its practitioners more than merely intellectual understanding, it includes *practical experience* with the other's terms and the horizon of meaning that accompanies them. The interlacing of glosses and phrases does not guarantee adequacy of communication, it only provides opportunities, and the parties' success at organizing their affairs depends upon the specific interactive work they undertake with these shared terms. When a Tibetan debater reformats his opponent's articulations into a more objective form, he incorporates those words into the overall structure and the overall rhythm. This objectivation of the opponent's thinking assists the thinkers to correlate their thinking and to be on the same page.

The repetition used in debating helps to clarify a topic. A defender may repeat what a challenger has proposed and then confirm or reject it. The challenger is obligated to repeat any confirmation, etc. in order to make it publicly evident which position it is the defender has taken, much as an auctioneer repeats what a bidder has offered. This also provides the defender with the opportunity to consider or reconsider it. This repetition and re-repetition afford the debaters a format for erecting a certain rhythmic timing for their utterances, and once a timing is established all parties attempt to sustain it, so that the debate begins to dance. Along with this there are many punctutating flourishes used by the challenger—a single handclap after a proposition is publicly formalized, a backhanded slap when the defender has made a mistake, a churning or spinning of the challenger's rosary to intimidate the defender, and finally a loudly shouted "You are CONFUSED!" while circling the rosary over the head of a defeated defendant. Along with these flourishes and along with each uttered argument, the challenger dances back and forth—he may commence an intricate argument standing several yards away from a defender, and his arm will orchestrate both his assertion and the defender's reply. As the dialectics grows more intense, the challenger may finish a vital point hovering over the sitting defender's head, so that the obligatory handclap is completed just inches from the defender's nose. I have even witnessed debates where a challenger is so confident of having defeated the defender that he prances around the seated defender in a sort of victory lap. And most of this takes place while the utterances of the challenger and defender maintain conformity with the rhythm of the turns and pace of speaking that has been collaboratively established.

Let us examine a transcript from an actual Tibetan debate. This will permit us to examine our issue not as an abstract thesis, but as part of an *in situ* course of a developing reflection, thereby bringing these matters into sharper focus. The following conventions are employed in the transcript for this debate. "T" stands for "the person who clarifies the reasoning" (*rTags gsal gtang mkhan*) in a Tibetan debate, and "L" stands for the "respondent" (*Len pa po*). When there is more than one respondent, L' and L" distinguish their replies. A single slash (/) on two adjacent lines indicates the start of a conversational overlap, and a double slash (//) indicates the end of an overlap. Phrases that appear CAPITALIZED are phrases that are standardized performatives, tokens of the Tibetans' formal analytic argument. Finally, the hand-gestures of the clarifier of the reasoning are indicated by a ">~" for a regular hand-clap and a "=v=" for a backhanded hand-clap.

Illustration 1: Interlacing the Utterances

T   Now the apprehension of the habit of reifying entities and the apprehension of the object to be refuted—an entity's seemingly inherent essence—in order to identify that, one must identify the object to be refuted, an entity's inherent essence, right?

L'  Yes, yes. The mode of apprehending an entity's seemingly inherent true essence. One must understand well how such a true essence comes to be established.

L"  So, how one must establish in that way, this is one topic, right? Oh, we say that this must be identified.

10 T  NOW THIS FOLLOWS, right? Yes, so, we speak of the identification of 'just-how-it-is,' right? IT FOLLOWS THAT one must identify the object to be refuted, that entities are established as if they had inherent essences.

L'  We do say that one must have identified it. One must, one must.

T   One must identify it?

L'  One must.

It is apparent that all of the parties participate in the discussion. L' repeats T's formulation and by doing so gets a handle on the notions and the horizon of meaning they might be carrying. After some seven lines of informal discussion, in line 10 T reformats that discussion into a more formally analytic version, using the conventions of Tibetan debating ("IT FOLLOWS . . .") for reducing the general discussion to a more concise and more formal philosophical formulation. This makes *a public object* of their topic. Following T's formulation, L' confirms it, repeating T's words. It would seem that lines 15 and 16 are superfluous, since they offer nothing new; however, they play an important role in beginning to set their give-and-take to a predictable rhythm, something like setting a metronome when one plays the piano. By each party employing the terminology of the other, the parties hear each other clearly and are *not* two ships passing in the night.

The formal analytics of a smoothly functioning debate has particular nervous properties. The participants concert their utterances as rapidly as they can while still remaining in synchrony with each other, as if they were dancing the philosophy. They do this rhythmic synchronization while making publicly evident the positions that are being discussed, and this is accomplished by the challenger (T) objectivating the contributions of the defender (L) with extraordinary quickness. It is the responsibility of the challenger to convey whatever the defender says to a more formal version, but the process does not need to be tedious; their aim is to do it quickly, with some playfulness and beauty. Repetition is a major resource for them in their work of setting up the pacing for their debating. Repeating phrases not only adds further clarification, it revs up the engine. Tibetologists might never know this if they only casually observed some debating. This would explain why Tibetologists might criticize these debates as too routine and repetitive; but they have essentially missed the aesthetic agenda of the debaters, an agenda that contributes to making their thinking objective, improving communication, and energizing their debating.

Illustration 2: Repetition

T    The reasoning is not correct. >~

L    YOUR REASON IS NOT ESTABLISHED.

T    The reasoning is not correct.

L    YOUR REASON IS NOT ESTABLISHED.

5   T    IT FOLLOWS THAT the reasoning is correct.

L    I ACCEPT.

T    IT FOLLOWS THAT the reading is not correct.

Here T's first assertion is repeated in line 3, along with its formal rejection. Only after it has been introduced in its negative form (twice), does T reverse the formatting and assert it in a positive form, which L accepts. The repetition and reversal here facilitates the establishment of a crisp, clean rhythm for the dialogue. Such reversals can be quite elegant. While no new content is provided, the repetition of the assertion (line 3) and its subsequent reversal (line 5) can be used to synchronize their utterances. At line 7 T surprises L while confining himself to the established rhythm by proposing the negative thesis once again. Occasions like this can seem as if a dancer has performed a pirouette, and it adds rhetorical force to the dialectics. It is important to appreciate that when a debater *repeats parts of the argument in a manner that does not contribute to the rhythm of the debating*, the debater will be considered dull-witted.

CHOREOGRAPHING THE ORDERLINESS 199

The real metronome of Tibetan debating is the hand-clap. It sets the pacing of the dialogue, punctuates the phrases that are formal assertions, and can be used to accelerate the arpeggio of some formal argumentation. In this way it signals to one's opponents when to intensify their focus and begin to gear up for the principal argument. Not the least of its benefits is the way it can call to attention a debater who has been daydreaming. Although the reader has no access to the audio effects that comprise the metronome, here is a debate whose rhythm is being set up by the hand-claps:

Figure 7.2. The Hand-Clap

Illustration 3: Hand-Claps

T   Therefore, so it's written, "*By relying upon a correct understanding of the Four Truths and the Sixteen Attributes as it is explained in the two principal Abidharma texts,*"—

L'   Mm.

5   T   —IT FOLLOWS THAT one cannot thereby obtain liberation from cyclic existence. >~

L'   Yes, indeed.

| | T | One cannot thereby obtain it, right? |
|---|---|---|
| | L' | One cannot obtain it. |
| 10 | T | Because one would not be able to obtain it, IT FOLLOWS THAT to actually liberate oneself from cyclic existence, it is necessary to realize the meaning of emptiness. >~ |
| | L' | I ACCEPT! |
| | T | It is necessary to have this realization. |
| | L' | It is necessary to have this realization. |
| | T | That's why, according to the explanation of this system, it is positively necessary that a person who abides in the Middle Way fathom the meaning of emptiness. >~ |
| 20 | L | What are you saying? A person who abides in the Middle Way must do so. |
| | T | Because of this, TAKE AS THE SUBJECT Bhavaviveka. |
| | L | Yes. |
| | T | According to this system he is not a person who abides in the Middle Way view. >~ |
| | L | He is not. |
| | L" | He is not, it is said. |
| | L | No, no. |
| 20 | T | TAKE AS THE SUBJECT Bhavaviveka. IT FOLLOWS THAT according to this system, he is not a person who abides in the Middle Way view. >~ |
| | L' | /I ACCEPT. |
| | L" | /I ACCEPT. |

T commences with a noncontroversial assertion, which is customary in these debates so that the rhythm can get off to a decent start, and it is made formal by T's hand-clap at line 6. He is asserting that a mere liturgical appreciation of some elementary Buddhist practices is insufficient for gaining liberation. The repetition at lines 8 and 9 assists the rhythm of the debate and at the same time objectivates the thesis. After L has publicly accepted his assertion, T adds to it the contention that an understanding of emptiness is required for liberation, and this too is formalized by being given a hand-clap at line 12, which also contributes to the debate's developing rhythm. They repeat the proposal in an abbreviated form (lines 14 and 15), and then T offers a similar assertion, punctuating it with the hand-clap at line 18, which further contributes to setting the pace of the debate. By this time the rhythm is clearly established, and it is has been made an objective form with which the debaters must comply. Noncompliant replies that are delayed past the now established rhythm will be a cause for embarrassment, and possibly a scolding.

In line 23 T then proposes that a well-known Middle Way scholar does not subscribe to the Middle Way view (this is for the reason that he does not understand emptiness in the most appropriate way, a matter they had discussed earlier), and another hand-clap is offered that maintains the rhythm. This proposal is agreed to by both defendants, and in lines 28–30 T offers a fully formalized assertion and decorates it with a hand-clap in keeping with the established rhythm of the debate, and it is formally accepted. The debate is now quite tidy.

One of the iconic ways that a challenger can scold a defender is for the challenger to offer the defender *a backhanded clap* while crying out, "TS'A!" This is usually performed in a dramatic fashion when a defender has been inconsistent, has forgotten something, or has taken too much time in responding. This backhanded clap, offered by the standing challenger, is done extremely forcefully directly in front of the nose of the sitting defender, and it can be very intimidating. When it comes suddenly it can catch the defender off balance, especially when he has not yet realized that he is being inconsistent. It recalls Socrates's account of how negative dialectics can destabilize a thinker's reflections: "tripping them up and turning them upside down, just as someone pulls a stool away when someone else is going to sit down" (Plato 1961, 392). Here is an illustration:

Illustration 4: The "TS'A"

    T  If that is not necessary, the establishment of the pot's true existence—please listen. At the time one realizes that the pot's actual mode of being is not in accord with how it appears to exist by virtue of its own inherently true essence, IT DOES NOT FOL-
5       LOW THAT there is a realization of the pot's subtle falsity. >~

    L'  CHEE-CHEER [literally, BECAUSE OF WHAT?; i.e., 'No']

    T  TS'A! =v= IT FOLLOWS THAT a falsity is established in connection with the pot.

    L'  I ACCEPT. Your TS'A is groundless!

The "TS'A!" both energizes the debate and can have a logical function; however, in this case it only serves in the former capacity, and the defender is annoyed by the unjustifiable and possibly superficial use of the "TS'A!"—it is superficial because the defender was agreeing with the challenger. An unjustified TS'A is known as a *tsa tong*, or an "empty TS'A" and is one of the scandals of Tibetan debating. Since it bears an insult within it, and in fact is a means for publicly proclaiming a defender's logical inconsistency, its use in inappropriate circumstances will be criticized, as in line 9. What is most interesting is that *even in circumstances where the "TS'A" is not warranted, a defender will accept it without complaint when the "TS'A" plays a constructive role in preserving the rhythm of a debate*. This demonstrates the vital role of rhythm in these debates and how it can vie in importance with logical matters. Too many TS'As can make a debate ugly, at least when they offer no rhythmic contribution. In such instances a defender may show his annoyance by scrunching up his face, and his annoyance is with matters that are *both* logical and aesthetic.

When performed appropriately the choreographing of these TS'As— with the challenger's left foot raised as high as his waist with a conspicuous wind-up, or perhaps a double-TS'A while the rosary is flinging about—can be a matter of rhetorical beauty. They can also contribute to the playfulness of a debate. In such instances it can be said that they lend considerable energy to the debating and may even be the cause for the opponent to think more freshly.

There is a choreographic tool even more serious than the TS'A, and that is the "KOR-SOOM." This is usually uttered when a challenger believes that the defender has lost an argument, or the debate itself. This, too, has its genuine and gratuitous forms. The use of KOR-SOOM, which I have translated as "CONFOUNDED!" can be an effective rhetorical tool that may be used to keep a defender off balance (see line 13 of Illustration 5). But when a challenger puts forward too many of them without a substantive intellectual reason, it can destroy a debate. When its use is apt, it can be used effectively to set up the argumentation in a beautifully rhythmic way, especially when it is accompanied by hopping, spinning the rosary three times over the defendant's head, and other theatrics, such as when a logical pirouette is accompanied by an actual pirouette in the challenger's dance as he announces the "CONFOUNDED!"

When longer statements are repeated, along with the defenders' replies, they amount to rehearsals, and these may also be used to maintain the rhythm of a debate, especially when the rhythmic pattern has deteriorated and requires being reestablished. There is a particular kind of rehearsal that I call a "reversal," during which the negative form of an assertion is rejected and then immediately followed by its positive form, which is accepted. Although no new content is introduced, the integrity of *the rhythm of the debating* is reinforced.

Illustration 5: A Reversal

T   TAKE AS THE SUBJECT a sprout like that.

L'  Mm.

T   Yah, for them it does not exist in an unmanifested way at the time of its cause. >~

L'  / THE REASON IS NOT ESTABLISHED.

L"  / THE REASON IS certainly NOT ESTABLISHED.

T   TAKE AS THE SUBJECT a sprout that has already manifested.

L'  Mm.

T   Yah, IT FOLLOWS THAT the Samkhya accept that it exists in
10   an unmanifested state at the time of its cause. >~

L'  / I ACCEPT.

L"  / Indeed. I ACCEPT.

T   CONFOUNDED! An already manifested sprout according to how the Samkhya put it—

L'  Mm.

T has provides his formulation first in its incorrect, negative form. After he receives the defenders' concerted rejection, he then provides the correct, positive formulation of the same topic (lines 9–10). The defenders are able to chime in with their agreement together, thus emphatically sustaining the debate's temporalization. The rapid alternation between the negative and the positive formulations permits the debate to make visible its own rhythm as an autonomous object, that is, independent of the debaters who have produced it. In addition to its rhythmic contribution, many Tibetan debaters prefer to present first their proposition in its incorrect form, in the hope that a defender who is not thinking originally will go along with it and make an early error. The result is that defenders are kept very wary of every proposition. They must reply quickly, in compliance with the regime of rhythm that is in play, and yet they must also work out the longer term consequences of any rejection or acceptance. It produces scholars who are able to think quickly on their feet.

The predictability of the course of reversals can offer some time for reflection, and a few Tibetologists may consider it sophistic and beneath the level of a philosophical discipline; however, once again they are overlooking its rhythmic contributions. The same is true for the use of tautologies, whose purpose may only be to sustain the rhythm while all parties have a brief moment to consider the longer term consequences of their positions. The demands of a rhythmic regime can unduly constrain deeper reflection, and both reversals and tautologies are sort of work-arounds for the debaters. Citations may play a similar role, and offer excellent opportunities for the challenger and defender to sing together a familiar citation, which also energizes the debate while helping to maintain or establish the pacing.

While all of this is going on, the challenger is using his hands not only for the forward clapping and backhanded slapping but much as a conductor would control the level, pacing, and duration of the musical contributions of his orchestra. The physicality of the choreography keeps the debaters engaged and closely attuned to each other.

## TWO KINDS OF DEBATES

There are two styles of formal debating that Tibetan debaters employ—sometimes they "debate up" (*yar*) and at other times they "debate down" (*mar*). A debate whose protagonist debates "up" is a debate that builds progressively to an ever deepening and more complex reflection; the preceding, more simple arguments provide a basis upon which increasingly more elaborate arguments may be developed. As newer philosophical topics and insights are taken up there is some accretion in the overall structure of argumentation. A debate whose protagonist debates "down" is a debate that proceeds by progressively undermining the tenets a defender is attempting to uphold. It is a negative dialectics in which notions are deconstructed in a sort of Socratic way, and instead of the arguments expanding they seem to contract.[3] Each mode of debating has its function, and both rely upon choreographic elements.

Illustration 6a demonstrates a debate in which the initial part conforms to the "debating up" method, in which the thinking is furthered by adding more topics and the argumentation progresses from the simple to the more complex, and the latter part of the debate (Illustration 6b) proceeds via the "debating down" method. It is probably easier for debaters to set up the rhythmic pacing of a debate when the challenger debates up, and the debate in Illustration 6a utilizes the resources of this method for establishing a fully shared rhythmic structure that all participants are able to recognize and to participate in. In this earlier part of the debate, the challenger provides a sequential presentation of the following assertions:

Eye consciousness [posits] a pot

Wisdom of meditative equipoise [posits] the nature of things

Wisdom that realizes just-how-it-is [posits] the nature of things

Wisdom that realizes just-how-it-is [formulates] the nature of things

The groundwork for each subsequent assertion is prepared by the preceding assertion and its acceptance. The subject matter is kept clear, is understood in common, and a clean rhythm is established for their collaborative inquiry. Each subsequent assertion builds upon its predecessor in some way.

Illustration 6a: Debating "Up"

T   Yah, TAKE AS THE SUBJECT something like a pot. Yah, IT FOLLOWS THAT it is posited by an eye consciousness that apprehends a pot. >~

L'  I ACCEPT.

L"  That pervades isn't it?

T   Right?

L"  That pervades.

T   In that case, for example, TAKE AS THE SUBJECT something like the nature of things—

10  L'  [Rapidly] Emptiness, emptiness, emptiness.

L"  We can present the idea of something like emptiness.

T   IT FOLLOWS THAT it is posited by the wisdom of an Arya's meditative equipoise. >~

L"  THAT IS ACCEPTED.

T   Is it?

L"  Yes, yes.

L'  Yes, yes.

T   If that is said to be posited, TAKE AS THE SUBJECT the nature of things, IT FOLLOWS THAT the wisdom that realizes
20      just-how-it-is posits it. >~

L'   /I ACCEPT.

L"   /I ACCEPT.

T   Well then, TAKE AS THE SUBJECT something like the nature of things, IT FOLLOWS THAT it is formulated by the wisdom that realizes just-how-it-is. >~

L'   I ACCEPT.

L"   I ACCEPT.

T   Positively, TS'A! =v= You are contradictory! IT FOLLOWS THAT there is no such formulating.

Here the hand-claps punctuate the developing rhythm and signal each element of T's argument. Each clap requires either a formal acceptance or a formal rejection of the assertion it punctuates, which the defenders provide while adhering to the emerging rhythmic structure. Not only are the assertions formally presented and accepted, their presentation and acceptance is repeated at lines 6–7 and lines 15–17, and this contributes to the rhythm of the debate. These abbreviated repetitions, which lack a hand-clap, are a kind of syncopation that runs underneath the main rhythmic pulses sustained by the hand-claps, and they contribute to the attractiveness of the debate. More importantly, they serve to make evident to everyone just what is at stake. The initial assertion, that an eye-consciousness apprehends a pot, is not controversial, and it is common for challengers to commence a fit of debating with something innocuous since it makes it easy to get the rhythm going. The second assertion, that the wisdom of a person in meditative equipoise posits the nature of things (line 12), is also not very controversial; however, bringing "the nature of things" (*chos snyid*) under the rule of formal cognition raises some difficulties. The third assertion, that wisdom that realizes just-how-it-is (*ji ltar ba*) posits the nature of things (lines 18–20), is bit more problematic since it is the nature of realizing just-how-it-is to be non-dualistic and positing can involve a dualistic component; however, the pattern of accepting the challenger's propositions has created a momentum that the defenders find difficult to resist and they accept the thesis. At the end the challenger asserts something that is genuinely controversial—that the wisdom that realizes just-how-it-is would be (dualistically) formulating anything, or that emptiness itself is a matter to be objectified by formal cognition. When the defenders accept this (lines 26 and 27), T gives them a TS'A and a back-handed slap to bring their thinking up short. Why the TS'A here? It is given because emptiness is something that can be witnessed, appreciated, realized, understood, etc., but it cannot be contained within in the terms of formal thinking, and so it is not something that strictly speaking is formulated.[4] T's clarification in line 23, that an understanding of emptiness is not something that can be captured in a formulation, raises the irony of any philosophical examination of emptiness to the level of a public spectacle.

From this point forward it is not T's aim to proceed by means of accretion, nor even to resolve the irony; rather, it is his strategy to develop the quandary in the most stimulating and challenging way possible. In lines 30–32, T formulates the quandary in a way that on its face is illogical, and yet it captures very well just what philosophical practice is doing. Here T's epistemological reflection is running up against the limits of language:

> T Although there the nature of things may be formulated as arising through the force of appearing to the mind, it is not formulated
> 25    so.[5] It's this way is it not?

The defenders attempt to resolve the quandary by referring to the account of an authoritative text, but the challenger does not wish to minimize the fecundity of the problem here or solve the quandary in a facile manner; instead, he insists that the defenders remain attentive to *a face-forward confrontation with the irony*. When they attempt to explicate the matter, *departing from the established rhythm* of the debating, T scolds them and insists that their contributions remain in conformity with the proper form of Tibetan dialectics, and he provides them with the model they must follow by offering another formal assertion and its accompanying hand-clap, which conform to the ongoing rhythm of the debate.

> L' It is said that there is no such formulation that formulates emptiness as existing concretely in the face of the realization that cognizes the nature of things. Do you follow? According to the Great Digest -/
>
> T             / In the face of the realization . . .
>
> 30  L" No, no.
>
> L' Now we discuss it, do we?
>
> T Now we don't need too much talk!
>
> L" This is said—one does not formulate it as existing concretely; it's the same. It is formulated, but it is not formulated as existing concretely.
>
> 35  T IT FOLLOWS THAT the wisdom that realizes just-how-it-is, yah, does not formulate emptiness as existing concretely. >~

T has brought them back to face the irony, and they then accept his formulation (lines 46 and 47), but T challenges them to reflect *even more deeply* by offering another backward hand-clap, and a TS'A, and in this case the fact that the backward hand-clap *precedes* instead of follows the utterance of the "TS'A" adds to its rhetorical force:

L"  I ACCEPT.

L'  It does not formulate that.

T   =v= TS'A!

The TS'A is provided more to herald the aporia to which their thinking has come than to declare that there is an actual inconsistency. It is a kind of celebration of their having successfully brought the quandary to life.

From this point T changes his method of debating and begins to "debate down." The cherished position of negative dialectics in Tibetan debating is made evident by the fact that the most frequently uttered phrase in Tibetan debating, and the phrase with which the vast majority of debates commence, is "NOW IT DOES NOT FOLLOW." The phrase is a kind of icon of the deconstructive, negating aspect of Tibetan dialectics. During most debating down, the debaters' concern is not so much about the theses themselves but about the mental frameworks in which theses arise. This interest is very much in keeping with the philosophical agenda of the principal thinker of Mahayana Buddhism, Nagarjuna. There are many occasions where thinking may be furthered better by breaking down the arguments that an opponent has offered than by building up syllogisms that are capable of standing alone. Any incorrectness, illogical assertion, or inconsistent thought will be used as a vehicle for gaining access to the broader underlying framework in which the concepts are developed.

In the next part of our debate, L" (line 54) is unwilling to accept that any person with wisdom would consider emptiness to exist, since emptiness always refers to the *lack* of inherent existence of any notion; that is, emptiness is something negative, not positive.

Illustration 6b: Debating "Down"

50  T   IT FOLLOWS THAT emptiness is formulated as existing concretely—

    L'  What?

    T   —BECAUSE the wisdom that realizes just-how-it-is, yah, realizes emptiness as existing. >~

L"   What? It must be said that THERE IS NO PERVASION. Now what?

T    IT FOLLOWS THAT the wisdom that realizes just-how-it-is, formulates emptiness as existing.

L"   Mm.

60

T    BECAUSE the wisdom that realizes just-how-it-is cognizes emptiness. >~

L'   THE REASON IS NOT ESTABLISHED.

T    CONFOUNDED![6]

This way of debating permits T to pursue the core irony further, observing that any cognition necessarily has subtle flaws, rendering suspect the completeness of even wisdom's realization of emptiness as soon as it becomes a matter for formal cognition. T has come upon a fundamental irony regarding just how emptiness can be *thought*, and be known to be true:

T    When the wisdom that realizes just-how-it-is realizes emptiness as existing, IT MUST FOLLOW THAT the wisdom that realizes just-how-it-is is a subtle cognition that conceals as a customary practice. IT FOLLOWS THAT there is this flaw. >~

L'   It is not said to be this way. It's not said. This reason is not posited, is it?

70

T    EXPLAIN HOW is it that the wisdom that realizes just-how-it-is does not cognize emptiness as existing? [*ma rtogs ste–*] >~

Although it is true that all cognition involves a degree of concealment of the actual way something abides, the notion that there is something wrong about the wisdom that realizes just-how-it-is is a heterodox view, and L' is compelled to reject it, but then he is instantly faced with T's *ste* (line 70, pronounced "Tay!" and meaning "Explain it to me!"), another tool in the challengers' arsenal. The "Tay!" is very much like a quick parry in a sword fight, especially when it comes in the midst of some dialectics that is operating within the constraints of a predictable rhythm. It brings the flow of the debating up short. Here it is not simply the logical consequences that are paramount, but its particular location in the choreographed dialogue suddenly places a heavy burden upon the defendant. In this way, the quandary is provided its fullest possible philosophical life.

L"   . . . It does not exist.

The problem with this conclusion is that it brings the debaters perilously close to nihilism, a philosophical flaw that they are very concerned to avoid. In line 71, T accentuates this dilemma by posing a nihilist thesis, but L' is not ready to admit it.

> T   Oh, IT FOLLOWS THAT the wisdom that realizes just-how-it-is, in the face of the realization of just-how-it-is, emptiness does not exist. >~
>
> L'  According to who? "IT FOLLOWS THAT emptiness is nonexistent"—No!

By skillfully keeping the defenders hovering between their acceptances and rejections, T sustains the koan-like character of the inquiry and L' and L" are placed directly in the center of two mutually exclusive possibilities neither of which is correct, a condition to which the hermeneutics of emptiness is naturally predisposed. It is a vision of truth that is not something static and reduced to words but something active, in the way described by Walter Benjamin (1999, 418) when he wrote, "Every truth points manifestly to its opposite, and this state of affairs explains the existence of doubt. Truth becomes something living; it lives solely in the rhythm by which statement and counterstatement displace each other in order to think each other." The very instability of their reflections is the achievement in this debate, *and this instability is assisted by the choreographic tools that the debaters employ*, things like claps, TS'As, the use of "CONFOUNDED!," "Tay!" and the rest, including the rhythm of their remarks as it is sustained throughout their debating:

> T   =v= TS'A! IT FOLLOWS THAT for the wisdom that realizes just-how-it-is, in the face of the realization of just-how-it-is, there is no cognizing of emptiness as existing concretely. >~

When Tibetan debaters are debating down, their goal is not only to deconstruct the framework of the thinking but to do so *using the minimum amount of argumentation*, and this economy of argumentation enhances the impact of any irony. In our final illustration (Illustration 7), the challenger is able to create a stunning effect (in Socrates's simile, upsetting the stool) by simply changing *one word*. The change of one word is able to have a strong impact because the remainder of the debating remains in conformity with the rhythmic structure that they have collaborated in establishing. That the rhythm is left undisrupted disguises the fact that the logic has fallen apart, and the contrast is so dramatic that the defender practically chokes on his own thoughts.

The response of L in line 4 of Illustration 7 is a repetition of a citation that each of the debaters has already uttered several times, in a sort of celebration of their unanimity. It is a well-known textual passage and also bears the topic of the debate; and it has become a chorus in their choreography. T's rehearsal of the passage in line 6 is performed as if he was repeating a musical phrase, and this lulls L into a sense of comfort and safety.

Illustration 7: Negative Dialectics

T   There is what we speak of as the refutation of an object of attachment generated by an imputed conceptualization of an habitually reified "true" essence, isn't there?

L   "*Subsequent to being subjected to the three—the basis, its appearance to awareness, and the path of analyzing and meditating upon it.*"

T   In accord with "*Subsequent to being subjected to the three—the basis, its appearance to awareness, and the path of analyzing and meditating upon it,*" there is a type of refutation of an object of attachment produced by an imputed conceptualization of a reified "true" essence. It's the same.

L   Exactly, exactly, exactly.

T   And there must be a realization of emptiness. >~

L   I ACCEPT that there must be.

T   Oh, because "There must be?" IT FOLLOWS THAT there must not be! Right? BECAUSE "*Subsequent to being subjected to the three—the basis, its appearance to awareness, and the path of analyzing and meditating upon it,*" that is the way that the analyses of the lower tenets establish how entities are apprehended to exist by virtue of their own defining characteristics. In his system there are such fixations. >~

L'   Yes, sure.

At line 14 T stuns L with a direct contradiction of something about which they had just seemed to come to agreement. The rhythm of the debate could break down here, and L could retort angrily; however, by T returning to the harmonized phrase he affords L with no time to react, especially since L must also attend to his responsibility to maintain the flow of their argumentation. It is extremely skillful. By the time he has offered a reason and a hand-clap, L is ready to go along with him. But it is to no end, since after another rehearsal of the phrase (lines 22 and 26) and the assertion (lines 23–25), L's acceptance is met with T once again pulling the rug out from under their revised collaborated assertion (lines 31–33):

    T    When one refutes that sort of reified fixation, "*Subsequent to being subjected to the three—* /

    L    / That's right. //

    T    // *the basis, its appearance to awareness, and the path of analyzing and meditating upon it,*" IT DOES NOT FOLLOW THAT it is a refutation of the object of attachment produced by an imputed conceptualization of a reified "true" essence. >~

30  L    I ACCEPT.

    T    [Quickly spoken] IT DOES FOLLOW, BECAUSE it is a refutation of the object of attachment generated by the habitual, imputed conceptualization of a reified, "true" essence. >~

    L    THE REASON IS NOT ESTABLISHED. [I.e., No.]

As was the case with the previous illustration of "debating down," whichever way L turns it will be contested. The hope is that such negative dialectics will force a defender to extend his reflections beyond his customary thinking, which may be based upon received notions he has not fully explored. But this reflection will have to occur later, perhaps when L considers the debate while he is having his dinner, since here his immanent task is to offer a reply that conforms with the rhythm of the debating, something that L manages to do. Not knowing how to answer is a scandal that is worse than giving the wrong answer, and equally disreputable is not stating one's answer within the limits of the rhythmic contours of a well synchronized debate. In a successful debate, both the rhythm and the ideas flow smoothly. For that to happen, the debate must be choreographed well.

Tibetan debaters are usually not preoccupied with winning or losing, and Tibetan dialectics is not simply about the ideas; rather, the debaters are focused upon the ways that their ideas can be brought to life. These ways involve some ethnomethods that are conceptual and others that are nonconceptual, and each of them is an essential tool that Tibetan philosophers utilize in their debates. Their organization of the ideas, however, is not strictly a formal analytic matter; instead, the communicative competence depends upon the skill with which the debaters have choreographed their dialectical inquiry. Their success at highlighting logical dilemmas, emphasizing ironies, understanding clearly, indeed the objectivity of their discourse itself, all require the effective use of rhetorical practices that are part of the arsenal of Tibetan philosophers. As much as the intrinsic appeal of the philosophical matters themselves, the way that Tibetan debaters collaborate in choreographing their arguments suffuses their reflections with the energy needed for carrying out their inquiry while maintaining a sharp intellectual focus. In brief, it brings their thinking to life.

EIGHT

# THE PHENOMENOLOGY OF COFFEE TASTING: LESSONS IN PRACTICAL OBJECTIVITY

> There is no such thing as phenomenology, but there are indeed phenomenological problems.
>
> —Ludwig Wittgenstein (1978, 9)

If the perfect cup of coffee were something strictly subjective, then the purveyors of coffee worldwide would probably not invest as much energy and as many resources seeking to identify, locate, and produce its components as they do. There is no one who denies that drinking coffee is a subjective experience, yet there must be something about the perfect cup that is objectively there. When that something can be identified, coffee purveyors can learn how to reproduce it. The objectivity used by coffee purveyors is a practical objectivity and is essential for their work of identifying, locating, purchasing, processing, and marketing coffees. The meaning of an objective taste does not always remain constant throughout these activities, but it bears sufficient intelligibility to permit coffee purveyors to organize their affairs around it. Part of the work of these coffee purveyors is to tame and stabilize the intelligibility of the objective tastes that they market.

To undertake this work, coffee companies rely upon coffee tasters (*assaggiatori*, *catadores*) who identify for them the elements of coffee tastes and who search world-wide for flavors. The tasters rely heavily upon taste descriptors, and the nature of this reliance is the subject of this inquiry. Since the taste of coffee is never quite capable of evading subjective differences in palates, these taste descriptors are interesting social objects. Not only does a really existing taste differ from person to person, the taste for the same taster can differ from day to day. When you add to that the varietal differences within the several taste domains (acidity, sweetness, fruitiness, nuttiness, etc.), not to mention the always present possibility of *new* tastes, the stability of the taste palette becomes problematic. There are standard terminologies for these tastes to be sure, but each country (e.g., Italy or India or Brazil or Japan, etc.), each company (large and small), and each coffee purveyor has their own quiver of terms that serve their practical need to satisfy the expectations of their clients and consumers. Various national associations of coffee purveyors or tasters make serious efforts to stabilize these terms, to reduce the number of them to something manageable that addresses their marketing priorities, but such exercises never fully succeed, since the flavor of coffee is always changing, as tastes, blends, processes, soils, and species evolve. Even the advocates of strictly limited taste descriptors regularly violate those limits themselves, and coffee *tasters*—a remarkably independent lot—frequently ignore delimitations.

At the same time these descriptors cannot be so loose, their semantic lability so fluid, that the coffee tasters cannot conduct their business. A home factory, it might be in Trieste for example, must be able to send their buyers and tasters to Brazil with a quiver of stable descriptors that will enable them to find the tastes that the company markets, and what these descriptors mean in Brazil must be similar to what they mean in Trieste. Certain flavors that are capable of obtaining a premium price must arrive at the destination wharf with those same flavors, which are vouchsafed for by tasters at both ends. Some transcendent, objective knowledge must be brought into play. One of the many factors that militates against any caprice in tasting is the hundreds of thousands of dollars that will be invested in the objective accuracy of the tasting. "Smooth" is not just anything that arrives at the docks. How is this objectivity accomplished? The only way it can be accomplished is with the active involvement of subjective skills—here objectivity and subjectivity are in no way mutually exclusive. Accordingly, the study of the work of coffee tasters can be a laboratory for exploring the relations of subjectivity and objectivity.

Advertisements are not the best place to learn about tasting coffee, and yet that is where most consumers encounter taste descriptors, so consumers have developed some skepticism regarding the utility of descriptors. Take, for instance, this description found on a commercial bag of specialty Asia/Pacific coffee: "Traditions and growing conditions within the Asia/Pacific region are as varied as its coffees. Flavors range from spicy and full-bodied Indonesian beans to the balanced and lively coffees of the Pacific, to the sturdy, herbal beans of Papua New Guinea." This description is too broad to be helpful. While "sturdy," "herbal," and sometimes "balanced" are indeed descriptors used for these coffees, it conveys little specific information besides implicating the difficulty of reproducing such a variety of flavors.

What precisely do the terms, "spicy," "full-bodied," "sturdy," etc. mean anyway? Or should we ask what *can* they mean, since what they mean will be subject to the local work of the tasters in organizing the intelligibility of the descriptors? How does one recognize a "full" or "medium-bodied" coffee when one tastes it? And in this case, just how do "balanced" and "lively" go together with each other, and why are they not mutually exclusive? It raises at once an interesting phenomenon when it comes to coffee taste descriptors, and that is that once a quiver of descriptors is put into play the semiotic relations among the descriptors makes them self-elaborating to a degree. In this case "lively" tells us what the semantic contours of "balanced" might be, and vice versa. "Sturdy" suggests what kind of "herbal" we need to be searching for. The same label offers us further instruction: "Big syrupy body, flavors of fresh green herbs, and lingering spice notes in the finish." These are descriptors more particular to the coffee that is in the bag, but from these descriptors we can learn that syrupy is what the "full" in full-bodied entails, what herbal can be is given further qualification, and the advertisement mimics the standard "taste profile" to which a professional coffee taster addresses his or her aim, in that the concluding tastes are differentiated from the initial tastes.

So the consumer's education can commence. Unfortunately, the taste descriptors found on many labels are too erudite, and so oriented toward closing a sale, that they are the wrong place for us to begin to look for resources and offer a somewhat distorted version of the work of tasters. The level of descriptive detail required for the selection, purchasing, and roasting of coffee is more detailed than what can effectively be communicated to most consumers of coffee. One medium-sized roaster attempting to describe the taste of several cups of coffee to my students began to wax poetic and then brought his description to a sudden halt, and apologetically told us, "There is no way not to be an ass-hat if you are attempting to describe a flavor." Except that sounding erudite is the last thing most serious professional tasters are trying to accomplish. Of course, professional tasters have an interest in being accepted by other professional tasters, but this is achieved by accurately pinning down the taste of a coffee, not by the use of poetics. A professional taster is often able to recognize the quality of a bean (and sometimes even the origin of the bean) by the smell of the grounds before brewing. Their work is extremely precise, and clearly they are up to something different than the work of those who design the adverts for coffee merchandisers.

## A PALETTE FOR THE PALATE

Let us suppose that you have been told that a Caribbean coffee just brought to you by the waitress is well known for its chocolate-like tones. You will naturally use that information to interrogate the taste you find in your cup. Even if you don't find the chocolate, you will find yourself oriented to tastes that work in that region of flavor. It is as if the taste descriptor is riding on the tip of your tongue, diving into the cup, and orienting your taste to be particularly sensitive to a certain area of the taste spectrum. And with it you are able to discover those tastes. Those tastes are objectively there, but the subjective orientation—and even the language and conceptualization ("chocolate")—affects the experience. Suppose that after the first sip you hear one of your associates at the table declare, "There is some cinnamon." The very next dive of your tongue into the cup will carry "cinnamon" on its tip. By hearing a taste descriptor you are able to explore more extensively that region of taste, although it is good to keep in mind that as descriptors open up some region of taste they necessarily close off other regions. Taste descriptors are complicated mechanisms.

Let us look at the work of coffee tasters, relying on the corpus of videotapes that I (and my students) have collected during our investigations in Italy, Brazil, Central America, India, and the Pacific Northwest.

A  I had a very distinct retro-nasal cinnamon aroma.

B  I got more of a dry cocoa powder.

A  Yeah, it's kind of in that range.

Most tasters work collaboratively, even in situations where the tasting is performed silently. Here the tasters are talking about what they are tasting, and they appear to have located a flavor in common although they are still struggling to find a name for it. They need a name for it so that they can better coordinate their searching and locate the same region of taste. Although some may find it puzzling how it is that cinnamon and cocoa are so close in flavor, the "cocoa" opens up a scope of flavor to which "cinnamon" by itself might not orient a taster, and vice versa. Just as ambiguity in a poem can be more accurate than a more specific reference, a "range" of taste may describe more accurately a flavor that is still to be identified than either of the two descriptors that the tasters are using. *The tasters are learning from each other where to search,* and their most serious work lies ahead. Similarly, a range of inquiry is suggested in this colloquy:

A  It could be Kenyan.

B  It doesn't have that Kenyan berry to it.

A  It doesn't have the spice.

How is it that "berry" and "spice" operate in a similar part of the palate? And how is it that each of them informs and constrains the possible sense of the other? The tasters are directing themselves to something real—the "Kenyan" suggests a range of typical flavors, and the denial of part of that range further narrows their search. But the tasters have more work to accomplish. One can ask as well how it is that "grapefruit" and "strawberry" operate in some proximity in this colloquy:

A   A sort of tart grapefruit?

B   Yeah, like maybe strawberry a little bit.

It is the quotidian work of coffee tasters to keep refining their descriptors, as in "those small strawberries that have sweetness and some spicy acidity." Here is a slightly longer conversation among a group of tasters discussing a cup they have just sampled:

A   Leafy. Very bitter, very astringent.

B   I found it very dry and astringent right on the aftertaste. A grassy astringent that had a very strong taint.

C   The greenness of it, the grassiness really put it under 80 for me.

D   Chalky-chalky.

E   Smoky.

D   Yeah, like ashtray ash.

G   That ashyness—a very dry tobacco.

D   But I didn't find anything that said it was a defect; for me it was just not good.

There is much to observe in this colloquy. First, there is serious collaboration throughout, from the grassiness to the smokiness, and it is by their collaboration that the tasters increase the certainty of what they have discovered in the taste. One might be puzzled about whether "bitter" and "astringent" are here the same thing, or if not how they are different, and to what region they direct a taster. We realize in the final line that there is a difference between the bad natural flavor of a bean and a bad flavor due to some processing defect (such as mold during the drying process). But more puzzling is the use of the descriptor "ashtray ash" since presumably few people have ever actually tasted it. Many may have smelled it, however, and perhaps some smokers accidentally tasted it, but here we find a taste descriptor whose reference is more metaphorical than actual. And so one must entertain the observation that some, perhaps many, taste descriptors are metaphors. And it follows that some descriptors are more metaphorical than others. Yet here they are capable of accurately capturing the reality of a really foul cup of coffee. Another metaphor sometimes used is "rubbery." Can one find rubber actually in a cup of coffee? No, such metaphoric tastes do not exist by themselves—they exist only along with the particular tastes that they collect. And so we are led to this discovery: taste descriptors do not exist independently, in themselves; they exist along with the actual tastes that they are able to collect. While it is this latter that gives the descriptor its specificity, the taste may never have been noticed if it were not for the education the taster received at the hands of the descriptors, as they were developed during some collaboration with other tasters. It follows from this that nearly every descriptor can be considered to be a metaphor.

Of course, descriptors for an expert taster are very different than descriptors are for a novice. A novice might not find the "herbal" or grassy in our commercial advert, and may not even be sure about where to begin the interrogation. Even one barista we filmed seemed uncertain when he asked his partner, "Would that be astringency?" Coffee tasters often couch their descriptions in the interrogative mode due to some uncertainty, insecurity, and/or respect for the judgments of others. Many of the coffee tasters' descriptions are addressed to other tasters to whom they look for confirmation and some elaboration, *perhaps even for what they mean by their own descriptors*. How does one learn what "astringency" is, if one is unable to distinguish it from "bitter," or "acidic"? Definitive accounts for these terms do exist, but they are not always identical for every coffee microculture that develops. I have observed even professional tasters whose ears perk up when a competent account of something like the difference between astringency and acidic is formulated.[1] The same can be said for "honeysuckle" or any term with which a taster has not had any personal experience. Moreover, the use of one or two appropriate flavors does not generally provide a complete account of the taste of a cup of coffee. A more typical account includes a temporally changing description and runs more like this: "I think it's interesting, the flavor profile in this cup. One track is a very floral track. The other track a very freshly cut exotic woods. And the wood nose elevated itself to become more of what I call honeysuckle flavor that merged with those floral tones. I think that was really beautiful. It's a beautiful way that coffee works."

Having observed that the taste descriptors have their life in the tastes to which they direct the tasters' tongues and are more the work of tasting that they accomplish than what they can convey in the abstract, I concluded that I needed to join in some tasting myself whenever that was feasible. On one occasion, a sample had an instantly detectable flavor, but I was hard-pressed to give it a name. As I tasted it, I decided it was "fruity," and I shared my assessment with one of the amateur tasters nearby whose scorings would not be counted. This taster corrected me: "Floral." With this instruction I re-tasted the coffee and at once recognized the greater accuracy of his descriptor. While describing this discovery later in the afternoon, another professional taster offered me even further specificity: "It was a floral explosion." That captured it precisely, and with that I added a new coffee descriptor to my arsenal of taste descriptors whose sense I know and can use with some specificity. But the specificity was not located strictly in the descriptor; rather, the descriptor directed us to a flavor actually experienced, and it is only that real flavor that provides the specificity. *Taste descriptors not only describe the taste that they find, they find the tastes that they describe.* Further, they offer real assistance in expanding the range of tastes that one knows. The most central aspect of this study is identifying and describing just-how taste descriptors assist tasters to organize their knowledge of taste, and by so doing are used to enlarge and enhance the experience of the taste of coffee.

Such accomplishments require a good deal of work on the part of the professional taster. They must share the meaning of descriptors, use the differences to open up the scope of tastes they are addressing, settle and stabilize the sense of the categories of taste they are using, and as they are taming and stabilizing their professional apparatus—and stabilization is a necessary component of any order of knowledge—they also do battle with the regime of alienation that any reified system of tasting introduces. *The stabilization of meaning, the accompanying alienation of experience due to the formalization of knowledge, as well as the resistance to that alienation are all inevitable, and evident in the daily work of coffee tasters.* When the first taster to comment about a coffee says, "No one can deny there are a lot of adjectives for that coffee," or "It's a beautiful city," the aforementioned work has hardly begun. Within the colloquies of tasters one can observe this work, skillfully performed, in which subjective certainties morph into objective knowledge, and observe as well how those practical objectivities are put to work.

## REAL OBJECTIVITY

At its most basic, objectivity can be described by this observation, often repeated, made by a professional coffee taster: "The coffee has to speak for itself." This comment captures well the "object" in objectivity, and speaks to the notion of *Evidenz* so well elucidated by Edmund Husserl. For Husserl *Evidenz* is the source of truth, and it refers to an absolutely original experience, undeniable in its immanence (what is experienced most immediately and most proximately), that a person has. Without it, truth is merely something structural that lacks the experiential element that gives truth its name. *Evidenz* refers to the fact that "one can focus on immanent objects as objects of immanental experience" (Husserl 1969b, 286), addressing what is closest to one, pre-theoretically and as little mediated by conceptuality as possible. Husserl directed his students to focus their inquiries on *the thing itself*, and his student Martin Heidegger (1996, 30) said that phenomenology means "to let what shows itself be seen from itself, just as it shows itself from itself." But can such immanental experience really serve as the basis for objective truth when it is obviously something that of necessity must retain its subjective character? Even the most committed objectivist must acknowledge that coffee doesn't speak, people do. Can one imagine any taste of coffee that would not be subjective? On the other hand, is it possible for that experience itself to be unaffected by categorial objectivities, by the many notions and thought forms that are used for organizing knowledge and making knowledge formal, *formalities that guide our knowing*?

Many coffee purveyors seek formulaic methods for overcoming the difficulties introduced by this necessary subjectivity, and there exist coffee tasting methodologies that provide them with some success. The odd situation is that most coffee tasters retain their respect for the subjective experience of coffee—"It is so subjective, it's hard to disagree with someone about what they're tasting"—*at the same time that they seek more objectivity* in their evaluations of coffee. Simply put, professional coffee tasters want it both ways. If they want it both ways, it is because they need it both ways. This is for the reason that the objectivity and the subjectivity necessarily accompany each other.

There are at least two senses of objectivity. The first is the real objectivity that is the actually existing taste of some coffee; this is the objectivity that always has some subjectivity attached to it. There is another sense of objectivity that is a socially constituted objectivity, more abstract and less immanent, and which seeks to remove all traces of subjective experience. This objectivity doesn't just happen—it is socially constructed and therefore is an artifact. Both of these objective ways of knowing seek certainty, but from where does certainty come? As we saw in the earlier chapter on sketch maps, certainty occurs whenever some knowledge congeals and gains coherency, and some social confirmation, however tentative. As we also saw, some very certain certainties can prove to be wrong. Both of these two kinds of objectivities, and their certainties, can be observed in the world of coffee tasting.

The second objectivity establishes its sway by being authoritative, but this authority can eclipse some of the subjective experience that Husserl considers vital to truth. Theodor Adorno, who spent most of his career interrogating the relations between objectivity and subjectivity, and who could himself be described as an objectivist with subjective leanings, speaks of "the subjective in the object. What transmits the facts is not so much the subjective mechanism of their pre-formation and comprehension as it is the objectivity heteronomous to the subject, the objectivity behind that, which the subject can experience" (Adorno 1973, 170). The thing itself, which is heteronomous to subjective experience, which endures within the coffee bean, *but which is heteronomous also to objectivist methodologies* (i.e., the second of our two kinds of objectivity) is what transmits the facts. When describing Husserl's notion of objectivity, Adorno (2008, 71) speaks of "an objectivity that is not produced by the abstract mental operations of the subject," and for him the second kind of objectivity is included among the abstract mental operations of *the subject*. He writes (2008, 39), "The structure of [an objective] mode of thought is no longer imposed on it by the authority and sovereignty with which it creates and generates its objects from within itself, but by the shape of whatever confronts it." More simply put, the monologue of a formal system and the myopic thinking it fosters are continually disrupted by the object that is actually there and insists upon being experienced. While we may pine for a more positivist version of the object and necessarily employ a precise, orderly, elaborate, and active methodology for measuring it, Adorno (1973, 300–301) suggests, "That activity breaks men of the habit of experiencing the real objectivity to which they are subjected." This *real objectivity* is Adorno's name for the first kind of objectivity.

While one may wish to avoid the problematics that arise with the subjectivity of tastes, those problematics will necessarily be there anyway, and brushing them under the rug will only increase the difficulties that will arise. Adorno (1973, 189) says, "What we may call the thing itself is not positively and immediately at hand. He who wants to know it must think more, not less. . . . And yet the thing itself is by no means a thought product. The thing itself is non-identity through identity. Such non-identity is not an 'idea,' but is its adjunct." The thing itself, in our case taste, evades the system of descriptors that attempts to lasso it into a preexisting, comprehensive system of identity[2]: the taste is ultimately a non-identity in that it always and necessarily *exceeds* whatever one identifies. Coffee tasters are well aware of this. No successful coffee taster can afford to cease remaining open to the experience that is "still mute which we are concerned with leading to the pure expression of its own meaning."[3] The real objectivity of a taste is what offers us this mute experience that is nevertheless really there, and which it is the task of coffee tasters to bring to expression.

But the ideas of the system of descriptors are *always* at work, assisting us and constraining us at the same time. Our taste of flavor cannot avoid being affected by how we have organized our knowledge of taste, including the "universals" that professional tasters have established as part of their work. As Adorno reminds us (1973, 351), "The universal is not just a hood pulled over individuality, it is its inner substance." In other words, the objective *in our second sense* is always active inside the thing as perceived, so in this way as well, objectivity and subjectivity are conjoined. Once one learns how to give the thing its due, the authority of the system or method is challenged: "Thought which aspires to be authoritative without system lets itself be guided by the resistance it encounters" (Adorno 2008, 39). This resistance to our systematization is instigated by the real objectivity, which is the source of what can be known. This resistance is the taste that remains beyond our descriptions, and to be professional, tasters must give this resistance its due; however, as soon as they do so the coherency of the system (for example, the tasting schedule used to measure the flavors) is put in jeopardy. In the Panamanian tastings we studied, the extraordinary coffee responsible for the aforementioned "floral explosion" wrecked havoc with the stability of the descriptors' measures, and the Head Taster observed, "High scoring, well processed Geishas are making us rethink the scaling." The scaling (our second type of objectivity) is not objective by itself; its objectivity is a constructive social achievement.

## PHENOMENOLOGY

In order to gain some better tools for understanding what coffee tasters are doing, we need to review some basic concepts of phenomenology. Edmund Husserl (1982 (1913), 204) explored "the remarkable duality and unity of sensuous and intentive [acts]," which roughly speaking parallel our first and second kinds of objectivity. His point is that original sense experience finds itself entwined with the categorial objectivities that we use to organize our knowledge, even though the two remain different orders of phenomena. For our purposes we can consider the first order (the sensuous) to be "the objectivity of the subjective," as Fredric Jameson (1990, 124) phrases it in his paraphrase of Adorno. The second kind of act (the intentive) is the more formal categorial unity that gets projected upon the immediate sensuous phenomena and that provides it order and intelligibility, the universal that precedes the particular. That the sensuous and intentive acts are *both* unitary *and* dual speaks to the fact that the intentional sense can infect brute perception itself with its prearranged intelligibility, so that almost nowhere do we find simple, pure, uncommitted sense perception. It is a precarious way to proceed, but it is the way we live nonetheless.

In his *Logical Investigations*, Husserl (1970c (1900), 813–15) makes the distinction between "primary contents," which are those contents in which reflection is founded, namely sensuous perception that is straightforward, and "reflective contents," which are those categorical acts that involve identification of the object that is the focus of the senses' attention. This schema is revisited and amplified in *Ideas I*, where Husserl (1982, 202) refers to mental processes designated as primary contents and to mental processes that bear intentionality. The former are sense-data or "formless stuffs" and the latter are "stuffless forms" (1982, 204). Husserl (1982, 207–8) further elucidates the latter by explaining that they involve "the constitution of consciousness-objectivities," objective forms that are used by thinking for creating a unitary idea (let us say, "medium body" in a cup of coffee), which becomes a tool with which we reflect. In the world of brute sense experience "the unitarily encompassing consciousness of one and the same objective something" does not exist until we introduce it. It is certainly an odd objectivity that has its origin in reflection. Key to Husserl's analysis is the idea that the thing revealed is always revealed by means of these categorial objectivities *that are projected upon* the sense-data and thereby organize it. This phenomenon of projection, also known as intentionality (we actively "intend" the significance of a thing by interpreting it in the light of our way of understanding it), is perhaps phenomenology's most fundamental idea.

In the case of coffee, any taste descriptor along with its meaning can be projected onto the taste and used to organize the intelligibility of the taste. Taking the case of "bitter," once bitter is proposed as the sense of some tasted coffee, tastes that conform to that sensibility will be collected. Of course, it could be that there is no corroborating experience, but as soon as a taste is found and some category (even a different one) given to it, that category continues the work of organizing the intelligibility of what is being tasted. A category that is hardly more than a name can bear considerable indeterminacy, and it is for tasters then to reflexively provide the determinacy of the descriptor by virtue of the specific taste that it collects. Further, in the case of "bitter" for instance, what it can mean for a consumer of coffee can vary widely from taster to taster, and this complicates the situation. As one roaster explained, "Bitter is good, you know. Bitter is definitely a major descriptor of coffee. The bad part is that people walk in and they hear 'bitter' and they associate that with being bad. But there is a good bitter and a bad bitter." To gain an appreciation of the sense of projection as it is used in phenomenology, consider what a consumer who thinks of the bad bitter when hearing "bitter" might project into the tasting versus what a taster who is looking for the good bitter might project. The idea of projection is that each of the tasters uses what she or he is projecting to interrogate what is being tasted.

The notion of projection can be conveyed schematically by means of this diagram, which depicts a person actively projecting "→" his or her structure of understanding "(- - -)" upon an object "Δ". The structure of understanding is the lens through which she or he comes to know the object, and according to the phenomenological idea of projection this structure of understanding actively participates in organizing the object's intelligibility:

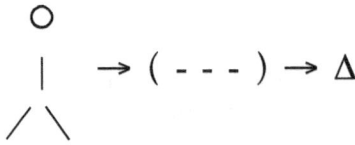

Figure 8.1

Since the tasting is inevitably infected by what is being projected, one might consider such tasting to be unfairly prejudiced, except that no tasting exists that does not involve this structure of thinking—i.e., the projection of some sense—and so this situation might as well be considered to be ultimate. What is extraordinarily interesting is that most persons quickly forget the responsibility they have had in producing what they know. It is as if their model was something more like this, which is a very different matter:

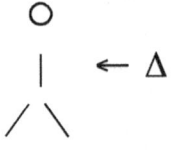

Figure 8.2

One taster remarked of a cup, "It doesn't bring enough flavor to the table. On my table it was improving toward the end," as if whatever was happening to the flavor was being done by the cup itself. It is more common, however, for tasters to qualify their observations with words like, "For me, . . . ," "To me, . . ." or "In my tasting, . . . ," which acknowledges the inevitable conjoining of the subjective and objective that occurs in tasting.

The work of categorial objectivities is the work of reflection itself, and involves any kind of naming that we might do. A botanist once told me that he would often wait until a student became familiar with a plant before he taught the student its name. According to his account, as soon as a student learned the name, his or her interrogation of the plant would cease. And yet another friend of mine, a philosopher, has praised what names can accomplish, saying that he would never be able to recall what he has learned about plants in his lifetime without the handle of their names. It is for certain that the objectivation provided by a name like "dune globemallow" or "glacial lily" serves us well by allowing us to organize, collect, and integrate what we have learned collaboratively about a botanical species. But once we have the name, there is a possibility that we will simply project what we already "know" by rote, and fail to learn what about the plant it is that we do not know, which amounts to a failure to *see* the plant that is there before us. Naming can be the termination of inquiry, *or* it can assist inquiry. Which of the two predominates has much to do with our own awareness of the process of knowing. As one taster declared during the tasting of a table of coffees, almost in a cry, "I'm trying not to think 'Pacamara' because it just makes my mind go crazy." This is a reference to all the meaning that the label of the cultivar "Pacamara" will impose upon the taste once it gets projected upon the coffee.

Another problem that generations of researchers who followed Husserl have been addressing is that once the categorial objectivities have congealed into a system, the elements of the system are free for their own semiotic relatings, an insight that has contributed to structuralist theories. Not only can the priorities of the synthetic unities of sense generated by any system of inquiry come to eclipse the real objectivity of an experience, they come to have a life of their own and lead the one who reflects to new and unanticipated abstract notions and syntheses of notions that may then get projected. Only after all of this are they "fulfilled" (Husserl 1970c, 509 and 533) by being given concrete content in some experience that they help to organize. Of course, sometimes we stumble upon new discoveries in just this fashion. Husserl's work was largely a response to how the human interest in rationalizing the lifeworld can lead to a nearly total separation from original experience. Husserl's cure for this was to temporarily put out-of-action the system of categorial objectivities one is using by exercising the phenomenological reduction, that is, by temporarily neutralizing the categories and the ways they have structured one's understanding of an experience. In this way one attempts to experience the occasion from a fresh perspective.

Coffee tasters accomplish something like this when they re-taste blindly a cup of coffee they have already evaluated. "We'll get to see it again," a Head Taster kept saying, which carries the implication that any questionable judgment will have another chance to be confirmed or contradicted. This new occasion presents the tasters with an opportunity to forget the details of how they organized the intelligibility of that cup of coffee. Alongside different coffees, in a blind tasting on a fresh table and on a different day, they may have a unique opportunity to taste the coffee unencumbered by the previous semiotics of the taste descriptors, or at least in the context of a newly devised system for organizing the intelligibility of the flavors they are tasting. Such opportunities are limited by the fact that most decent tasters will recognize at once the same coffee, and may reapply the old categories without necessarily knowing they are doing so. On rare occasions they may project those categories after having *incorrectly* inferred the coffee cultivar they are tasting, which is a recipe for disaster. The trick lies in learning how to keep tasting freshly, using the descriptors to scrutinize the tastes but without letting them get too much in the way of the tasting.

Doing just this is what Husserl (1969b, 287) calls *Evidenz*, which is the attention we pay to "the giving of something itself." This indicates that despite Husserl's extensive investigations into subjective acts of consciousness like projection, his ultimate interest rests in establishing what is objective knowledge. He acknowledges that "the essential form of the experience's flowing constituting is such that *evidences*, succeeding one another continuously and undergoing continuous modifications, *function together*," and he appreciates that "evidence. . . . has many diversities," gradations of clarity, and modifications by the other evidences that function with it. Accordingly, the acidity of a cup of coffee can have a significant effect upon its sweetness. Just as Husserl insists that "the evidence of the absolutely original *present* of a sounding tone. . . . functions, of essential necessity, in connection with an evidence of the *'just gone'* [tone] and an evidence of the originally *'coming'* [tone]," i.e., past and future, there is a temporality to tasting (both in the sequence of cups tasted one after the other and within the duration of a single cup) that affects taste and may not be captured adequately by the measurement tools. In a methodology of our second type of objectivity, one might want to separate out such categorial descriptors and give each of them—sweetness and acidity, for example—an independent rating. But in the actual world as it is lived, they do not function independently. So where does the real objectivity lie? Coffee tasters know that accompanying tastes affect each other, and they take this knowledge into account in their measuring, although they still record the objective scores independently by categories of taste on their forms, in conformity with the requirements of formal procedure.

By giving priority to the formal measurements and by routinizing the experience of the real objectivity of tastes, elevating the former to the status of what is objective and considering the latter to be something subjective, tasting methodologies reverse the status of the actual affairs, so that what is subjective (the devised system of categorization and its artificial unities of meaning) is accepted as objective and what is objective (the actual taste) is relegated to subjective status. Adorno (1974 (1951), 69–70) presents this sarcastic account of the situation:

> The notions of subjective and objective have been completely reversed. Objective means the non-controversial aspect of things, their unquestioned impression, the façade made up of classified data, that is, the subjective; and they call subjective anything which breaches that façade, engages in the specific experience of a matter, casts off all ready-made judgments and substitutes for relatedness to the object the majority consensus of those who do not even look at it, let alone think about it—in other words, the 'objective' itself. Just how vacuous the formal objection to subjective relativity is, can be seen.

For Husserl evidence entails the direct relating to an object, although Husserl (1969b, 286) acknowledges that evidence appears to be an achievement of human experience and that coming into contact with an actual thing involves a *performance*: "There are *no objects beforehand* and no evidences that merely take in what already exists beforehand. The evidences as functionings that constitute what exists, bring about the performance whose result in the sphere of immanence is called an *existing object*." This is to say that all objectivity involves some subjectivity, or that there is no objective objectivity, only subjective objectivity.

Maurice Merleau-Ponty spent the better part of his career as a phenomenologist exploring the relations of the subjective and the objective. In his remarkable chapter about this titled, "The Intertwining—The Chiasm," Merleau-Ponty (1968, 143) examines the ways that the subjective and objective are linked inextricably: "There is a circle of the touched and the touching, the touched takes hold of the touching." He recognizes that there are active components to both subjectivity and objectivity, and that no sooner does touching (or tasting) get involved that *what it gets involved with grabs it* and carries it further into it. Merleau-Ponty (1968, 139) speaks of "this strange adhesion of the seer and the visible" and admits that despite the *object*-ivity of the object the seer can never relinquish his/her involvement: "Since the seer is caught up in what he sees, it is still himself he sees: there is a fundamental narcissism of all vision." And yet if we want to taste the coffee better, we need to attempt to escape such narcissism. The taste in a cup of coffee does have agency; there occurs "the coiling over of the visible upon the seeing body," but according to Merleau-Ponty (1968, 146) what is objectively there is able to coil only because of my bodily, subjective engagement with it that the thing calls forth as it "makes me follow with my eyes the movements and contours of the things themselves." My engagement with the thing necessarily includes the full engagement of the categorical unities I have fashioned in my training as a scientist, scholar, or professional coffee taster—"the system of objective relations, the acquired ideas, are themselves caught up in something" (Merleau-Ponty 1968, 153).

The problem for Husserl's conveniently clean distinction between formless stuffs and stuffless forms is that in the actual world neither of them is ever to be found separately from the other.[4] The way in which subjective certainty (the Germans give it the name *Gewissheit*) comes to generate objective truth (*Wahrheit*) is a major focus of ethnomethodological research, and it is important to ground that research in the naturally occurring affairs of the real world since the standard Enlightenment model of epistemology, in idealizing the way objective knowledge is produced, has failed to accurately portray what typically occurs. We do not simply apply some proximate certainty to investigations that employ objective methodologies that gradually build up a body of objectively validated truth. The objectivities, which are social achievements—categorial unities achieved by means of what ethnomethodologists have discovered to be congregationally produced accounts that get ratified and objectivated (see chapter 3)—provide us with an appropriate technology, a social praxis, of indexical descriptors that expert practitioners use in organizing the local orderliness of their affairs. The objective schema *assist* that organization, just as the subjective attention to experience and to perpetual self-criticism of that praxis contributes to the truth that results. *There can be no question of doing away with either subjectivity or objectivity*: the question is only how they are to be employed. This means also that there can be no question of doing away with objective methods—they are the means by which serious scientific inquiry proceeds.

## OBJECTIVE METHODOLOGY

Why is it necessary to objectivate our knowledge? It is only by turning the results of our reflection into objects that we are capable of remembering them. It is only by objectivating them that we are able to communicate them to other people and use them to direct others to just-what we mean by them. And it is the only way we have to build upon what we have collectively learned, so that our knowledge is able to grow. Objectivity always entails a social component, and our research here is addressed to the public nature of objectivation.

One of the basic components of objective methodologies used in the coffee industry is the tasting schedule, a sheet or card that coffee tasters use for recording their evaluations of several components of the taste of coffee. These schedules differ from factory to factory, competition to competition, and coffee association to coffee association. Companies will naturally emphasize those taste descriptors of the flavors most important to their clientele, and countries will emphasize those descriptors that cover the characteristic flavors of their coffees, but they usually take the shape of a 1-to-10 (0–9, 0–10, 6–10) scale with some sort of bubble or hash-mark available for the taster to conveniently mark *in situ* while she or he is tasting. Tastes are usually divided and scored separately, despite some problems (mentioned above) with making them independent this way; however, the schedule may include more global categories that can handle the more synergetic effects of taste factors. Coffee purveyors are extremely concerned about flaws and defects, so there are usually some categories that cover these. There is some problem with rating the *quality* of taste along with the *intensity* of the taste, and with judging how a fine quality with little intensity should be converted to a 1–10 rating vis-à-vis a lesser quality with a greater presence or whose "taste gets more places."

The actual meaning of a taste descriptor is necessarily indeterminate, but within any given cupping its sense will be stabilized within the practice, by the practice, and *as* the practice, of any serious taster, who will be concerned to limit the variance in the descriptors being applied. Adorno (1973, 162) has discussed "the concept's immanent claim to its order creating invariance," and it is for the purpose of introducing invariance that the schedule of taste descriptors is employed, although it is an invariance that can vary from cupping to cupping. Nevertheless, it is quite common for tasters to independently rank a coffee similarly on a given descriptor, such as astringency, or to independently offer a flavor the identical narrowly specialized descriptor like "banana" or "butterscotch." Of course, to any taste (astringent, banana, etc.) there is always something further that can be discovered or said about it, and *it is this something further that is the work of coffee tasters to identify and describe.* Adorno (1973, 161) writes, "What is, is more than it is. This 'more' is not imposed upon it but remains immanent to it." This "more" is part of the banana flavor's real objectivity.

Let us look at this colloquy:

A  It had that deep, deep overripe fruit—slush—oniony, depending on how you read it. I actually thought that the slightly darker roast did this coffee a favor, rounded that out, mellowed that.

B  Compliant, viscous, marshmallows. It didn't have enough fruit.

C  I had to just keep scoring it up. I just returned to this coffee all day long.

S  Yeah.

T   Yeah.

C   I thought it was a Honey. I thought there were a couple of Honeys on the table, I'm not sure. It just had an expansive body, so fat.

S   Yeah.

C   So sweet. On our table I found a total consistency in the fruits in the cups. Heavily fruited, a lot of plum and raisin dark fruits, roast-related fruits, but, you know, really well developed. Yah a little bit of Pacamara character, too, but I don't quite know what it was. I didn't really get oniony.

D   Maybe too many flavors.

E   I'd bet a large sum of money that's a Pacamara.

C   To me, this is exactly what I want. Either way I love this coffee.

In this collaborative evaluation the tasters are seeking to nail down the "more" of what they all seem to have located, and this work is especially apparent at lines 17 and 18. It's not "oniony" but not far from it, and has associations with the flavors of another well-known coffee type. The tasters' work is still not completed, although it may be said that completing a description of taste to the point that there is no longer a "more" to contend with is an unachievable task.

The important thing about this work, as we have already noted, is that "The coffee has to speak for itself. You have to let the melody speak for itself." There is a recognizable objectivity to the coffee, but the very use of the word "melody" implies that it is an objectivity that is elusive. One taster amplified this metaphor of melody in his attempt to describe how the same taste can vary:

A   I think it's like, if you make an analogy, your favorite melody can be played either by a violin that has very high sparkling notes, or you can play it on a cello.

B   Yeah.

A   Because it has beautiful deeper tones. So this 2934 can be the cello; otherwise, it is a violin.

The Italian coffee taster Luigi Odello, who has written several bilingual books that elucidate the work of coffee tasting, expands this metaphor (Odello 2002, 122): "The difference between an espresso made with one type of coffee, compared with a good quality Italian Espresso made from a blend of at least 7–13 different types of coffee, has been likened to the difference between a concerto played on a piano and one played by a symphony orchestra." One might think that coffee tasters who use metaphors like this would not be seeking objective methods, but all of them are, for the reason that their investigations of coffee taste cannot proceed effectively without them.

With a tasting protocol in hand, it takes tremendous discipline to keep the mind focused on maintaining a uniformity of standards as one moves from cup to cup. One's own preoccupation to preserve conformity with *one's own* praxis of administrating the protocol can distract from the tasting and even restrain the effective employment of the descriptors. As a teacher, I observed that this aspect of the work of coffee tasters is not unlike the way I grade my students' papers: as I move through the papers my standards keep developing, so that the measures at work at the end of my grading can differ slightly from the ones that I applied in the beginning, making it necessary for me to go back and re-grade some of the papers. As coffee tasters proceed through a table of coffees, the standards that are pertinent become more apparent, and they must keep returning to re-taste and re-assess the coffees. Earlier descriptors can become less critical, and at times the tasters can be seen using their erasers nearly as often as they use the pencil tips. The ethnomethodologist Larry Wieder's (1970, 134) account of how people employ criteria can inform us here:

> Rather than having a stable meaning across a set of cases that are classified by their use, criteria are matched against cases by elaborating the sense of the criteria or the case to encompass the particular occurrences the name user faces. Explicating what members mean by their terms by stating criteria for using those terms would then be an inappropriate method, since criteria vary in their meaning over the occasions in which they are used.

Hans-Georg Gadamer's account (1975, 25) of good sense offers an approximate version of this: "It is a kind of genius for practical life, but less a gift than the constant task of adjustment to new situations."

Because of the indexical quality to the sense of coffee descriptors, it may take some time for a group of tasters to bring their practice of applying a tasting schedule into harmony on any local occasion, but they generally can get their use of descriptors remarkably well coordinated in less than a day. Many coffee companies have tasters on their staffs who are so accustomed to each other that they may know just what their colleagues are thinking with a minimum of words spoken, almost as if they are thinking with one mind. Coffee competitions schedule a calibration session before they perform any taste evaluations that officially count, and the tasters use such a session for bringing their practices of evaluation into better synchrony. To work effectively together, tasters must communicate effectively, and this entails coordinating their understandings of the meaning of descriptors on each local occasion. Once *they accomplish some stabilization of the meaning of the descriptors*, each taster can use the descriptors consistently, knowing what is meant by them *on this specific occasion*, and better ensure that what one taster means comes to approximate what the next taster means. By sharing the descriptors, using them to taste some cups, then report collectively about what they found, and then taste more cups, they are collaboratively producing a local social praxis.

Coffee tasters are good at remembering that their aim is not simply to produce a consistent methodology; they are there to taste coffee. Accordingly, there is a natural resistance to capitulating too easily to any regime of taste descriptors. Adorno has observed that it would be a distortion of objective methodology never to entertain any experience that is not covered by the methodology or is heterogeneous to the conforming model. So, there is always a tension at work in the taster's implementation of a protocol. Adorno (1973, 161) argues that to refuse to operate outside the boundaries of a methodology would be "to surrender, even pay homage, to the current cognitive ideal. Throughout, the ideal combines an appetite for incorporation with an aversion to what cannot be incorporated, to the very thing that would need to be known." An objective methodology that never entertains what may exceed its boundaries would be a caricature of objectivity, and there is no objectivity that fails to pay some price; but since it is necessary that we use a well coordinated, objective methodology, we are willing to pay the price. If we can recognize a moment of obsequious conformity as it happens, it can be repaired; but since it is a social praxis it soon acquires the somewhat intransigent force of habit, which contributes to our consistency and to the very possibility of moving through the evaluations with the objective methodology remaining in effective application. Not having an objective methodology is not an option. That being the case, not attempting to make that methodology as objective as we can manage is not an option either.[5]

The situation is further complicated by the fact that there are different palates, ever changing cuppers, different forms, different countries, etc. Professional cuppers recognize all of this, but most emphasize that in a competition it is not essential that every taster employ the same methodology in the same way—it is only important that they consistently apply their own methodology to all of the coffees they taste.[6] Despite all of this, it happens with some frequency that with a completely different cohort of cuppers, seven of eight coffees to be judged best will be the very same ones; an "8.4–8.5" measure for a coffee in India will mean something that is recognizable in Costa Rica. But given all of the potential for variance, a typical methodological solution might be to enlarge one's sample. A company wanting to know the precise taste preferences of their clients might commission a broad survey of its consumers, for instance, large enough to minimize any differences in palate, etc. But the problem may be that these consumers have little idea about what taste descriptors mean. For instance, what acidity or body is might be only notions pulled out of a hat when consumers are obligated to complete a tasting form by filling in the bubbles before the coffee is taken away. The resulting numbers, tabulated and processed with the best objective tools, might only disguise an underlying foolishness. People do not always know what they are tasting. The taste descriptors may be used to assist their tongues in locating one taste or another, but using a tasting schedule productively is a learned practice, and the meanings of the descriptive categories are prone to some slippage.

What is vital in using the tasting card is that the descriptors must be employed to guide the tasters to the same region of taste so that they can evaluate it collaboratively, describe its characteristics, and assess its quality. It is possible that the descriptors are less important for making the numerical measurements than they are for directing qualified tasters to a thorough exploration of the flavors that are uniquely identifying of a given coffee. This is what tasters do.

The objective methodologies can provide a focus and rigor to their work that is essential.[7] While there are different opinions about the priority of the ratings—ranging from "Always let the scores speak" to "There is a necessity for the scale, but personally I place more trust in the qualitative description that tasters write in the 'Notes' section"—no tasters can do their work without them. That many cards have a place for qualitative assessments, or that some schedules feature a dual scoring that offers some simpler numerical registration of the more intuitive judgments of tasters, suggests that the craft of developing these objective methodologies is very much alive. Most coffee purveyors recognize that they are operating with practical objectivities—objectivities that work for the practical circumstances at hand rather than aiming at timeless truths—and that their methods will require continual revision.

Another factor that complicates the standardization of the measuring is that it is inevitable that the taste of one cup will be affected by the taste of the other cups that are adjacent to it. Not only is the tongue affected, the mind is oriented by the inevitable comparisons regarding taste descriptors that will be made. But this is unavoidable so long as cuppers will taste more than one coffee at a cupping. Here are some pertinent comments:

"We were cupping at a table that had a lot better coffee."

"Following a Geisha,[8] it was too tart for me."

"I put the other one a seven for sweetness, but now there's this one, a *nine*."

"Five fruity coffees can wipe me out for the sixth new fruity coffee."

"It has a nice, juicy citric acidity, which I really like. And a very clear coffee. It had some floral notes on the aromas for me. It was very good, and I appreciated it very much, jumping from a Geisha to this coffee. It still fought its battle very well, I think."

When attempting to remain objective, it is wrong to allow oneself to be influenced by other tasters. The difficulty is that this is precisely how we learn most things, and if our task is to discover the taste of a coffee, at some point there must be some provision for collaborative work. Even if there is total silence during the hour of the tasting, in the talk among the tasters prior to the tasting and following the tasting the air is filled with pertinent taste descriptors, and once a descriptor begins to be used at a cupping it gains some authority that makes its further use likely. We have already remarked that there is plenty of nonverbal behavior at a cupping—smiles, brightened eyes, the smacking of lips, and the taster who is seen to return again and again to the same cup—which amounts to conversation of a sort. It is never a secret which tasters are the most knowledgeable, and those are tracked by most tasters in the room, not because tasters lack originality but because they wish to learn something. It is natural to learn from others.

During the post-cupping discussions, the collaboration can be vigorous. The corroboration that may be offered there is essential to the cupper's gaining certainty for their assessments:

A   Show me the acidity.

B   I hear that.

The collaboration is frequently productive:

A   Fruity.

B   Citrus. Orange.

C   Lemon in it.

And it can extend the horizon of the inquiry into the taste that is in play:

A  This is a lovely, lovely, lovely coffee.

B  Yep.

C  Yep. I love this coffee.

A  It's that jasmine, floral thing we had yesterday that I was a little skeptical of, but it had a wonderful flower that stays constant throughout. The sweetness was there the whole time.

D  It had elegant balance. It had everything going with nothing overstated. Everything understated, but there.

A  It could have used a little more zip.

E  It was a little one-dimensional, I thought.

A  Wow. Very, very pleasant, a nice coffee.

F  Elegant.

A  Elegant.

One can easily come to the conclusion that one would not want to sacrifice the collaboration for the sake of maintaining an independence of judging that is impossible anyway for the reasons that we have just reviewed. Objective methods are vital for the rigor of the analysis, but in the end they will not completely substitute for the congress of reason of expert coffee tasters teaching each other what is the taste at hand.

## THE WORK OF TASTE DESCRIPTORS

Let us summarize briefly what we have learned so far. The function of taste descriptors is not merely to describe but also to assist the tasting by directing and expanding the gustative inquiry. A descriptor is not merely the causal result of what is tasted—

$$\text{coffee} \rightarrow \text{taste descriptor}$$

Nor is it an imperialism of the objective methodology—

$$\text{taste descriptor} \rightarrow \text{coffee}$$

Rather, it is a reciprocal event:

$$\text{taste descriptor} \leftrightarrow \text{coffee}$$

The descriptors operate reflexively by finding in the coffee what they mean, and each is used to make the other more explicit.

Research into the use of descriptors that proceeds by merely *asking* tasters some questions about descriptors cannot give us access to the phenomenon at hand. It mostly gives us lectures. Instead, we need to witness coffee tasters *using* descriptors. Once we do that, we quickly learn that the descriptors are used not only for describing the taste but also for *finding* the taste. Our research task must include learning what is happening on the tongue, so this study is not only about learning what are the taste descriptors and how their sense gets stabilized; it is also about how the taste descriptors *expand the ability to recognize* the tasting itself.[9] This expansion of taste awareness is something that is accomplished *with* the descriptors. The descriptors do not stand independent of this work, with their isolated meaning already explicit and congealed; rather, they function always *along with* the taste(s) that they collect (syrupy, full-bodied, etc.), and the point is not merely to describe the taste of coffee but to *explore* the taste of coffee using the descriptors as tools. Our thesis, then, is that *the local work of coffee tasters is to manipulate the taste descriptors in a way that brings their tongues to confront directly the real objectivity of the cup of coffee.* I say "tongues," but I also mean "minds;" and my colleague Giolo Fele of the University of Trento has pointed out to me that the Latin word for taste and for mind is the same: *sapere*.

One cannot simply interrogate the meaning of some taste descriptors—spicy, caramel, "parchmenty"—in the abstract; instead, one needs to experience the descriptors along with the tastes that they collect. In recent years, the illegal smuggling (to avoid taxes) of choice naturally processed beans out of Ethiopia has caused a government crackdown there, resulting in a diminished supply of this highly prized bean in the world market. Panamanian growers are considering increasing their production of naturally processed beans in order to fill the gap, but they face a problem of reproducing the tastes of these Ethiopian naturals; however, to successfully fill the gap, they need to learn very specifically what those tastes are. Accordingly, a group of Panamanian growers posed the question to a collection of professional tasters: "What attributes are you looking for when you're buying naturals?" They received three replies. One was "This conversation can really be a long one. There are so many factors. You would not believe the different factors, from climate to variety to the fact that most of them are blends of coffees from different seasons—you can have four or five or eight different crop years." Another answer was "bright strawberry."

The third reply was the most interesting. The expert taster/buyer for a major U.S. coffee purveyor recommended that instead of their asking for an abstract, albeit professional, description, it would be much more productive for the growers to get together and order a variety of Ethiopian naturals and taste them for themselves. He added the counsel that they should taste especially for the cup that has really fantastic flavors. After that, he advised, they could discuss whether attempting to duplicate those flavors makes any sense. This is solid professional advice that recognizes that tastes are more important than the descriptors' objective meanings; nevertheless, those same objective descriptors will assist the growers to taste the flavor of the sample coffees in a comprehensive way.

The taste experience is elaborated by the chosen descriptors, which guide the taster's searching for the taste. While the descriptors' precise meanings may at first be indeterminate, the descriptors get elaborated reflexively by the tastes to which they direct the taster, and what they discover tells the taster what the descriptor meant all along. Descriptors collect the circumstances that it makes it reasonable for their being applied to any given cup. It is precise work.

## THE DOCUMENTARY METHOD OF INTERPRETATION

In order to better understand how taste descriptors are used, and especially how their related categorial instruments—regions of origin and cultivar types—are employed to categorize flavor, we need to review some basic principles about how people think. The sociologist of knowledge Karl Mannheim developed the notion of what he calls a "documentary meaning," which is the meaning of a document that bears "evidence that points beyond itself to something different" than what is simply there (Mannheim 1952, 47). In order to understand the meaning of a document or thing we have in hand, we look beyond it for a solution. Once that something beyond is located, *that* is used to make intelligible the thing that is in hand. Mannheim (1952, 81) writes, "What it does is to take some meaningful object. . . . and place it within a different frame of reference. . . . By being considered as 'document' of the latter, the object will be illuminated from a new side." According to Göran Dahl (1994, 105), one uses "pieces or fragments of an act or object in order to document an *ethos*," and that ethos is then used to make intelligible the piece or pieces. The ethos is something that is *not there*; it is a social invention that is extrapolated from the thing in hand, which is read not merely as a unique individual but as an instance or "case" of a larger principle. Even though it may be *the only* such case or "document" of a category, its significance may be derived more from the hypostatized principle that it fosters than from what it bears in itself.

For instance, if we are told that the coffee we are tasting is Indonesian, instead of simply reading the tastes on our tongue, we may draw from a principled model of Indonesian coffee and use that ideal to give coherence, consequence, and even nobility to the coffee in hand. We may retrieve information from what we already know about the ideal type "Indonesian coffee," to fill in the context or "secure the background against which the specific" thing in hand is interpreted (Mannheim 1952, 55). It will incline us to use other taste descriptors that are commonly employed with those "kinds" of coffees. The "ideal type," the "kind," the "beyond" is not really present, but it assists us in making what is present intelligible: "One single item of documentary evidence [can] give a complete characterization of the subject; if we are looking further, it is in order to have corroborating instances conveying the same documentary meaning" (Mannheim 1952, 57). Put in more simple terms, once we have a bug in our ear, no matter how it got there, what we usually find is more of what we already know how to recognize: our understanding proceeds in a way that is self-confirming.

That "something further" is essential for organizing our understanding, but it is not a strictly deductive process: "The whole goes before, and is not built up mosaic-like from self-subsisting parts" (Mannheim 1952, 70). "We understand the whole from the part, and the part from the whole" (74). As illustrations, Mannheim offers how we understand a text, a cultural era, and another person. Once we have grasped a person as having a specific character, for instance, his or her behavior will be understood in light of that preexisting nature: "Now I can apply the same technique of interpretation to every other manifestation of his personality as well—his facial expressions, his gestures, his gait, his speech rhythm; and as long as I maintain this interpretative approach, all his impulses and all his actions will exhibit [this] stratum of meaning" (47). The process seems circular, but according to Heidegger (1996) this hermeneutic circle is ultimate. The actual meaning of each chapter of a book is derived from the sense of the entire book—no one doubts this—but those very same chapters are responsible for the existence of the entire book in the first place. Any understanding necessarily finds itself embedded in this circularity. In tasting coffee, the various tastes lead to an understanding of the coffee, but when our understanding congeals into a characterization of the coffee, that characterization can become a self-fulfilling prophesy since further taste will be interpreted in the context of the characterization.

Harold Garfinkel has devoted considerable effort to elucidating this phenomenon, commencing with his 1967 book, *Studies in Ethnomethodology*, where he first presented his seminal explanation of the documentary method of interpretation and described the use of this lay method in a number of his studies (Garfinkel 1967, 78):

> The method consists of treating an actual appearance as "the document of," as "pointing to," as "standing on behalf of" a presupposed

underlying pattern. Not only is the underlying pattern derived from its individual documentary evidences, but the individual documentary evidences, in their turn, are interpreted on the basis of "what is known" about the underlying pattern. Each is used to elaborate the other.

Garfinkel offers many instances of its use, including the way U.S. Census officers assign occupational categories to people and the ways that survey researchers code and categorize replies to questionnaires. Garfinkel (1967, 95) finds "many occasions of survey research when the researcher, in reviewing his or her interview notes or in editing the answers to a questionnaire, has to decide 'what the respondent had in mind'" and Garfinkel concludes that they end up writing biography, even though the biographical labor is disguised by numerical encoding. This searching for and determining a pattern is "the work of documenting" one's understanding and the means by which understanding is "managed" (94). The stability of meaning that this procedure establishes comes at a price.

## REGIONS OF ORIGIN

Let us use what we have learned for investigating just how professional coffee tasters use the region of origin or cultivar type of a coffee in much the way they use a flavor descriptor. Regions of origin are widely used by tasters as palette stereotypes that offer them shortcuts for indicating a basket of flavors that a given kind of bean typically offers. Most tasters either work for coffee roasters or are roasters themselves, but in our research we have been able to observe a distinction in the use of regional categories between people who primarily roast coffee and people who are primarily tasters. The former generally know a great deal about taste descriptors, but when they cup coffees they are quicker to try guessing the region of origin of the coffee than tasters are. They may commence with some taste descriptors, but as soon as they collect enough descriptors to justify their naming a region from which the coffee likely comes they will do so; and once they have done so, they will use those regional labels to infer further information about the flavor of the cup they are blindly tasting. Moreover, since roasters generally have close relations with the retailers who market the coffees (or they do the marketing themselves) these regions of origin are included in most of the descriptions of coffees one will see in advertisements. In fact, since regions do have uniquely identifying flavors, one would be foolish not to inquire about the region of origin of a coffee that one is thinking to purchase.

Here are a few illustrations of this way of categorizing coffee flavor:

"It's probably a Sumatra. It could be a Celebes, but it's definitely an Asian kind."

"It emulated some good Kenyans with that citrus."

"It started to have some Pacamara character, because I got some tobacco juice."

"Could this be a Honey?"

This last one reveals the strenuous effort of a taster attempting to pin down the taste of a coffee with the aid of a possible cultivar type. Tasters can also be seen making a note of their best guess of the coffee type or origin in the margins of their tasting cards. In one case of a Geisha a taster, after smelling the grounds prior to brewing, made the mark "G" on the scoring sheet.

It may be that the more amateur the tasters are, the more heavily they lean upon region of origin stereotypes, but the practice seems to be ubiquitous. In one Pacific Northwest tasting, after two of the tasters (both roasters) spent three minutes discussing the possible origins of some coffee, a third taster, a noted expert, remained completely silent during their conversation and busied himself only with tasting, never indicating that he could even hear their discussion. When many of the student groups I sent out to study the use of taste descriptors filmed local roaster-tasters blindly cupping some coffees we located, what they returned with were tapes of "Guess-the-Origin," a game that sometimes featured a friendly competitive energy. These tapes were not very useful for the aims of this inquiry.

The phenomenon was so prevalent that we decided to make it a topic of study. We collected several coffees that were marketed under the regional origin "Kona" and attempted to see if tasters could describe what was identifying about the flavor of beans with that label. Some tasters concluded that Kona coffee featured a combination of lighter bodied coffees along with a degree of "brightness" in the flavors, but at times it seemed that "Kona" was little more than a gloss for "good." The flavors of this region of origin label remained indeterminate, although perhaps we did not pursue the research far enough. One taster offered this original assessment of one of the Kona cups: "It's got a robust, smoky taste—or tones, at least—with good body. *Very* unusual for a Kona coffee, which gives me reason to believe that that coffee's origin could be different. It's got dark, chocolate tones with a long aftertaste and some burnt nuances at the end." The originality of this assessment rests in the fact that his tasting of the real objectivity of the coffee forced him to question the heritage of the coffee, even though we had already authenticated its origin (it had been sent to us by the grower on the island of Hawaii, so it was not one of those Kona forgeries). He responded by suggesting that the original beans could have had Indonesian origin before they were planted in Hawaii. We checked back with the owner, who confirmed that it was true for some of the coffee planted in his plantation.

On another occasion a group of roasters and professional buyers identified a coffee that was spicy and citrusy as an Ethiopian Yurgachiev. After some conversation, they were satisfied with their finding. When we revealed the coffees to them after the tasting, and the Ethiopian Yurgachiev turned out to be a Columbian Cup of Excellence winner, they were quite surprised that any roaster could get that much citrus flavor out of a Columbian bean. The buyer at once recognized the potential of his discovery, since he knew just where he could purchase more of that coffee; and he offered my students and me a hearty "Congratulations people!" While analyzing this tape, I wondered whether if he had been employing a Columbian region of origin all along for his ideal type he would have come to appreciate the same taste in the same way. I also considered the matter of how he would be able to convey the sense of that taste to the roasters and the purveyors when he markets the coffee. This presents a pertinent corollary inquiry: which descriptors can most adequately convey the objective meaning of the taste while also pique the interest of some buyers.

Not only regions of origin but particular regimes of plantations—shade grown, high-grown—feature as stereotypes that assist tasters in organizing their knowledge of what they find: "That coffee has a lot of Altura." Altura, meaning high-grown, assembles certain taste characteristics, but once it has done so it can be used to collect further taste features; however, the tasters need to supervise carefully the reflexivity that is at work.

In the Panamanian tastings we studied, the celebrity coffee of the region is the Geisha, and this ideal type played an important role in how the tasters engaged with the coffees ("This is like a Geisha"). Or,

> This is our friend, the Geisha. Again, talk about an adjective rich coffee. It was a classic Geisha. It was like the Geisha that was like the first kind of Geisha that I have encountered. It had that strawberry and "Fruit Loops" kind of notes in it.

The name of the bean is used to normalize the discussion about its taste, and those tastes experience a further degree of objectivation by the use of the term "classic," which implies some stability in the meaning of the ideal type. One taster calls such a practice into question:

A  But does it make any difference to people's judgments?

B  No! The scores are the scores.

A  Yeah. O.K.

However, the desire and intention to work exclusively in an objective way does not ensure that this in fact happens. There are other colloquies with different practices. In the next one, A and B influence each other, so that both of them together come to know more than they might have known separately:

A  This is a Geisha clearly. It's sweet. It's clear and crisp.

B  This is a coffee that showed better yesterday.

In the next, the cultivar label has been made into an adjective:

A  Geisha uno. This is that classic Geisha, fruit basket vibrant. Intense /

B           / Geisha-like.

A  Yes, Geisha-like Geisha. Alright.

B  Like a Geisha all dressed up for Saturday night.

A  Yah, ready to go out.

[Laughter]

A  Puts a smile on my face every time.

The problem with recognizing a coffee is that tasters may draw from their prior experience with the type and extrapolate from the documentary type to the coffee being sampled. As soon as one recognizes the type, one can recall how one had previously organized its intelligibility and simply reproduce that without investigating the taste in a fresh way. What others have said about it or what is generally know about that type or region of origin is then applied routinely, and this can create problems and limit discovery. The Head Taster gave the issue this formulation in public discussion:

> And this Geisha thing. I don't know how many people here use Geisha as a flavor descriptor now, but I've heard it come up a few times, and certainly that's where I started with all three of these coffees. I went, "O.K. Geisha aroma," and then we go from there. So Geisha has sort of that set of flavors, that aromatic context of Geisha that can be off in the jasmine, floral, bergamot kind of

notes, or a basket of tropical fruits blended with strawberries or it's over in the stone fruit, syrupy overripe papaya notes. All those things have enough commonality that we identify them as Geisha. It's pretty easy to say, "That's a Geisha." But if this is Geisha that is low-grown, we have to ask ourselves what that really means.

The final "that" is rich with content. It can be the phenomenon that "Geisha" really is, but it also suggests the entire tasting praxis within which it has become routine to apply the category Geisha. Since most Geishas are high-grown, its application to a low-grown version for the first time seriously complicates the meaning of the descriptor. Of course, growers should be free to experiment with growing cultivars in varying habitats, but it may be that the tasters will need to discard the ideal type when categorizing the flavor and return to more standard taste descriptors. The Head Taster continued:

How do you score it in the context of that one kind of highly flavored notes that you get when you go, "Wow! That's great." I associate that with great flavors. Or when this coffee burped up all kinds of low-grown notes as it cooled off—it got ashy and rough and lacked finesse, the structure was broken down, and you got all the kind of stuff you would expect to get from low-grown coffees. So how do you score a low-grown Geisha? That's one question. The other question is if you're a Geisha producer from Panama, what do you want the result to be? Do you want this thing to show up on an auction platform somewhere, next to a cultivar that says "Geisha"?

And later, he summarized the predicament that a routinized use of cultivar types presented to them:

Well, here is the danger of these kinds of competitions, when you see these coffees again and again. One of the things you want to do for selfish reasons, for our own egos, is a greater tendency to recognize coffees that I've already encountered before, so I remember that coffee and that coffee and that coffee and that coffee. So, all of us by the end of the first day had "There are three Geishas," and we had that implanted in our minds, right? And we had a Pacamara, so we knew there was a Pacamara, and we've got that in our minds. So we started to think about these things, and you start to want to respect those experiences from day to day, despite re-roasting these coffees and having a whole new set of variables, and the human variables—everything changes, but you want to build a set of consistencies to pull it through. And your judgments are influenced by that desire.

This way of understanding taste is in fact not done out of desire or "for selfish reasons." It is the unavoidable structure of how people typically think, the hermeneutics of understanding anything; however, his account reveals a good deal about the praxis of tasting coffee. It may be that these hermeneutic difficulties are inevitable, but there is no doubt that the situation can be improved by an increased degree of self-understanding, and that might lead to more formal, objective protocols that better utilize these ways of understanding while minimizing their interference with the tasters' access to the real objectivity of the coffee. The phenomenon is most problematic when in a blind tasting a taster invokes a type that is incorrect, which does happen. While all tasters, as thinkers everywhere, wish for some certainty, being certain and being correct are not always identical. Our task, both as professionals and lay persons, is not to establish perfection but to organize ourselves so that our practical work can get done with competence while preserving a degree of creativity.

## THE TASK THAT TASTERS FACE

It is convenient when there is a descriptor ready at hand that we can use to keep our inquiry coherent, but tasters sometimes perform their work before any descriptors have done their categorizing, and so tasters face the sometimes daunting task of turning what can be an amorphous body of sensations into some intelligible order. They usually hesitate as they begin to face this task. When a taster finally comes to establish a descriptor, it will help for remembering the flavor, help for communicating it to other tasters, and provide a scaffold upon which further discoveries can be laid. But it frequently happens that no descriptor comes immediately to mind; and when one finally does, it may be best to linger with the indeterminacy instead of proceeding directly to projecting one descriptive category after another from a scoring sheet. When one cannot identify the flavor, it does not mean that no flavor is being experienced: "It's a scent I'm lost with right now, so I don't know what it smells like." "It's airy enough that you can't really grasp it. You can't get a handle on it." There may be an element that one recognizes as "refreshing" but is difficult to grasp: "It has more, yeah it has more . . . ," but the "what" of that "more" cannot yet be named; but that does not mean there is no "what" there. The most important work of tasters takes place *just before* the taste gets categorized, and part of the skill of their craft rests in keeping their experiencing of the taste open while they are categorizing it: "There is a sharper taste that I thought was vanilla, but it could be berries, I don't know. Give me another taste of it."

There will always be a degree of uncertainty regarding whether one's "decision" regarding taste is correct or not. This uncertainty or indecision can be a productive part of their work, even though at times it can fall prey to the other taste descriptors that one is hearing, which is one reason that cup of excellence competitions are performed silently; however, this silence is frequently filled with echoes of the descriptors that entered the tasters' conversations during the hours prior to the silent tasting or during cocktails the evening before. When people do not quite know what they are tasting, it is natural for them to try descriptors as candidate accounts with which they go and find with their tongues what can be meant. It is not only the novices that look to experienced tasters for direction—I have observed accomplished tasters look eagerly at novices to see if the novices are able to locate the specific taste in which the objectivity of the accomplished taster's subjective description rests. The uncertainty, the openness of possible sense, is substantial enough that the accomplished tasters seem to be hoping for some independent confirmation of what they have found, in order to lend credulity to its really being objective. Their aim is not to satisfy their poetic energies but to locate what is really objective in the taste, and they sustain a concern for the practical objectivity of the tastes.

This requires that they make contact with something that transcends the individual taster. Garfinkel (2007, 35) asks, "The Issue is: *Making contact with a transcendent: Just How is contact actually made?*" The achievement is necessarily one that involves the tasters' concerting their experiences so that a real *thing* can be identified, confirmed, and described. The "Just-How" of Garfinkel's question refers to the local methods that people use in concerting their efforts to access that contact. They do it, no one can doubt that; but just what is it that they do? When a taster marvels at the "adjective-producing" character of a coffee, she or he is inciting the other tasters to make contact with the transcendent taste for which they must still develop the appropriate adjectives. What is the work performed whose aim is to convert the ephemeral experience of taste into intersubjective meaning structures?

Taste affects the mind, but the mind also affects the taste; and each *assists* as well as *constrains* the other. If at times it leads the tasters to a sort of vertigo, it affords plenty of opportunity to develop their skills. At the point of one aporia, when the taste of a coffee could not be determined in a sufficiently objective way, a taster whispered to me, "This is where I learn the most about coffee taste." One taster writing for one of the trade journals of the U.S. coffee industry (Giuliano 2007, 11) summarized what is accomplished at a cupping: "The cupping table could be a place for coffee appreciation and inspiration, where knowledge is exchanged." Another taster described their task: "Our job as tasters is to be as objective as possible in defining the attributes that characterize the coffee we're tasting." This begs the question, *what is objectivity*; and when I asked it, the taster explained that the description needed to be objective enough so that an ordinary person walking in off the street would be able to find the same taste attributes that the tasters have found. This is a practical objectivity.

Professional tasters are practical about their work. As stewards of industry they have to be. Accordingly, in much tasting the very first tastes they seek are any defects that could corrupt a batch of roasted coffee. Some of the first comments that some tasters make have to do with the presence or absence of defects: "I don't detect anything that would make it seem under-roasted. It doesn't taste sour to me." Only following this task do the tasters turn to tastes that are more pleasing; however, their task it not to simply determine whether the coffee is pleasing but to identify just-what about it is pleasing. As a taster remarked in the middle of this task, "There is a fantastic coffee here, and it is our objective to describe its characteristics for the world." It is at this point that the tasters use the descriptors not so much for objectifying the flavor as for sharing the flavor so that they can collaboratively assess its quality in a comprehensive way. In one instance, the meaning of one descriptor, "Fruity," came to be settled by first negating it—"Not Fruity"—which opened up the search. Another taster suggested, "More Berry," only to be met with its negation: "Not Berry." Yet another taster offered "Apple," which was quickly picked up by a collaborator who proposed "Granny Smith," as the collection of tasters began to smile. Their colloquy was concluded by a taster who confidently stated, "Granny Smith skin," and received several nods.

If during their efforts they find something in the taste that resists being said, that perhaps even resists being organized into their discourse, *this* is where they focus their attention. Only later will they attempt to settle the meaning of the tastes that best characterize a coffee, but this is work that can never really be completed.

In this next colloquy, the tasters are *collaborating* seriously about locating just what it is about a coffee they like that is so pleasing:

A   Peer pressure. I had to lower it one point, so I ended up giving it a 98.

B   I just couldn't find anything wrong with that coffee. I tried and tried to find something wrong. I didn't want to give it a hundred, so I gave it a 97. But I could not find *anything* wrong with that coffee.

C    The strength of this coffee is really the high notes that supported it so well, not by just a one-dimensional jasmine. Viscous, with a really high quality. Lavender. You know, beautiful complexity of high notes.

D    Harmonious.

E    Yes, it had a structure to it. It had a base underneath it supporting it. Sometimes the really floral Geishas don't have enough strength to really stay on their own.

Their accounts of the taste begin as local rationalities. As they share them, some intersubjective accord emerges, and for these the tasters seek more universal expression. By the end, the particularities of the taste will come to have the kind of universality that one can read in a coffee advertisement. There is always a tension between the formal rationality and the local, particular expressions. According to Adorno (1973, 318) any universal rationality may be at odds with particular experiences and to some degree negates those experiences, or renders them invisible. As a formal descriptor defines an ideality with some clarity, the "something more" about the taste can get lost in it. Nevertheless, such universal components of experience are not simply added to it like butter to bread but penetrate to the very core of the tastes that are being tasted, if only because a taster cannot discover what is eluding the formal description until that formal description is in place. Once it is in place, a taster becomes more able to discover what does not confirm with that description, i.e., what more there is to its flavor that is unique. And the region of tastes to which the taster is attentive in the first place may have been grasped with the assistance of a universal descriptor. As noted above, Adorno (1973, 351) claims that the universal "is already part of a thing's inner substance by the time we engage it." That is, "The innermost core of the object proves to be. . . . the reflex of an identifying, stabilizing procedure" (Adorno 1973, 161), so *the objective component is not an alien at the scene* but, for better or worse, is part of the initial praxis that encounters the taste at its most progenerative moments.

## CONTENDING WITH "THE ROPE"

How do we keep the categorizing from obscuring the real objectivity of the coffee? This is a question that has its parallels in all human activity, in any systematization, in the law, and with the application of moral codes. Wittgenstein (1978, 17) has written, "Where do we draw the line between logic and experience?" This is to ask, what do we know from our formal analysis and its routinized understandings, and what do we know from our direct experience? Some stabilization of meaning is necessary for society to proceed in an orderly fashion, but will also introduce a regime of alienation; coffee tasters can be witnessed battling these regimes while they rely upon them. Their task is to learn how to use taste descriptors without getting used by them in the same way a mule is led around by *a rope through his nose*. This is an abiding goal whose impossibility does not prevent its being attempted. Coffee tasters are independent folks, as evidenced in the slogan of a popular Pacific Northwest coffee purveyor who inscribes on each of his pound bags, "A fiercely independent coffee purveyor—roasted in small batches." And there is a resistance of coffee tasters to objective codes that may increase the likelihood of their using those protocols in effective ways. Most tasters are alert for the risks posed by even the competent use of descriptors whose grip upon the taste may become too strong, like "the tightening structure of a grip which the concept conceives, limits, and delimits itself. The strangulating bottleneck is named in the concept" (Derrida 1986, 20). And so they must learn, and teach each other, how to keep the categorizing from obscuring the tastes and how to distinguish petty consistency from that consistency necessary for clarifying their work. The universality of the categories is not simply antagonistic, the objective order assists them in clarifying the tastes they are examining.

A taster must come to independent conclusions while learning from the other tasters. She or he must think about the taste without letting the products of the thinking close down the sensing. How are thinking and sensing related? Part of the tasters' discipline is *to remain open* to what they may not yet have experienced and which may reveal itself newly, even as the coffee cools. In work like this Adorno (1953, 153) recommends "dialectical thinking," thinking that attends both to what is universal and individual, to the objective and the subjective, and to what is both at once: "It is up to dialectical cognition to pursue the inadequacy of thought and thing." Since all solutions are suspect, part of the practice of dialectical thinking is to *keep the thinking in movement*. But at this stage, "dialectical thinking" is hardly more than a slogan; if there ever was a labile term in the English lexicon, dialectical thinking is it, and it remains for us to specify its circumstantial practices. It is thinking that bears an openness that is effective across a broad range of human endeavors. What can we learn about accomplishing this from the openness practiced by professional coffee tasters, who keep reminding each other, "We have to not over-think it, though"?

Perhaps feeling some need to justify his practices, one taster took it upon himself to explain to me, "In the end I'm still doing the math, but I don't let the math take over." In many cuppings, tasters can be seen going from the overall score they believe is the most accurate *back to* the individual descriptive categories, raising or lowering them as needed, rather than proceeding additively or deductively from the individual categories to the final score. While to a degree objective procedures depend upon their consistency and rigidity, reason sometimes requires judgment that can exceed the provisions of a given protocol. As Adorno (2008, 87 and 91) observed, "Without play there is no Truth." Every coffee taster I have met respects this; however, their strategies for handling the "rope" of rigorous method vary.

## EXHIBITING THE ORDERLINESS

There is an orderliness to every occasion, but it is not an orderliness that drops out of the sky—it is an orderliness that is organized by the people who participate in the occasion. Not only are the basic "structures" that keep the interaction orderly developed locally, on each and every occasion, the ways of properly thinking about the tasks that the people who staff the event are facing are displayed, witnessed and reproduced by those present. The effective order must not only be learned, it must be taught, and by teaching I mean here the exhibition of possible devices people can use for making their knowing orderly. Not only do people have to know something; they need to concert themselves so that *how* something is known (and not merely what is known) can be seen in its local "discipline specific coherent appearances as the organizational thing it is" (Garfinkel 2007, 35). What is known and how it is known must be made publicly available so that the parties there can learn to use them and come to share the developing methods for organizing the local orderliness of the event.

At most cuppings the tasters employ a tasting schedule, which typically offers a range of scoring on a 10-point scale. But the 10-point scale that actually gets used by them is a peculiar beast, molded and kneaded by the local organizational praxis at hand to fit the tasks that the tasters face. The 6 to 9 point range of the card is used much more than the other parts of the 1-to-10 scale. One professional association uses a card that only offers the 6–10 range, and in some of their cuppings only a portion of even that (7.8–9.6) seemed to be in play. This is a local organizational practice that must be learned, or rather, that the tasters must teach each other. Upon encountering such a local practice for the first time, one taster said, "I need to boost up my scores, since I'm consistently giving the lower scores." I have also been told, "Those people who do not want to draw any attention to themselves, they give a medium score," and cuppers are warned, "Watch out for 'safe' scoring." The fear of being caught out on a limb can undermine the originality of some tasters, and limit the usefulness of their evaluations.

The precise meaning of scores, as well as how they are used, is a local accomplishment. The 1-point difference between 7.9 and 8.0 is not identical to the 1-point difference between 8.4 and 8.5, so the scores can come to have very specific significance and idiosyncratic uses within the local praxis. As a cohort cups together over several days and those meanings and practices get displayed more comprehensively, more of the tasters begin to employ them in a similar way.

We have learned that taste descriptors are accompanied by the flavors they collect, and how the flavors come to be known by their names alone is also a local accomplishment that depends upon exhibiting the names in the correct context of practice, routinizing the way it is done, and allowing all of the participants to attune themselves to the public practice. Once a structure of descriptors is put into play, a natural semiosis occurs that quickly outstrips the participants' capacity to control it, and so they face the continual work of reducing the proliferation of meanings, redefining them, restandardizing them, making their use economical, etc. Just how the meanings they rely upon get stabilized and how this public semiosis is tamed is one of the topics for inquiry. Garfinkel (2002, 189) has demonstrated that these worksite practices are locally occasioned, hidden in and as their familiar efficacy, and are available only to practitioners (which means they are not available to disengaged or abstract reflection), and they are *developingly objective*.

Tasters cooperatively build up certain unities of meaning in a social process that is as passive as it is active. Once developed, the natural requirement for order can lead to more decisive regulation. Moreover, there always exists the possibility of gaining power by controlling these mechanisms of knowing, and this can lead to further regulation, depending upon the comfort level of the particular cohort of tasters. Since the tasters are constantly learning from each other, they generally are respectful of each other even when they disagree. On one occasion a taster kept nodding his encouragement to another taster who in fact was offering a contesting account of the taste of a coffee. He was nodding because he welcomed (and wished to encourage) more frank expression of others' experience since it broadened his own outlook upon the coffee.[10] The scope of what tasters are learning is quite broad, as it concerns not only the meaning of descriptors or the characterization of the coffees but the very system of reasoning and of the practical objectivity that is effective on that occasion. They learn all of these things by demonstrating in their talk and actions how such a system is to be employed; that is, what gets exhibited are not only the categories and their meanings but the praxis for applying them to the coffees.

## TASTING FOR PROCESSES OF PRODUCTION

Up to this point we have concentrated almost exclusively upon favorable tastes, although we did mention the concern that professional tasters have to search for defects in any of the coffees they sample. Defects are normally the result of mistakes in the processing. Since coffee is grown in humid climates, it is not always possible to prevent the beans from molding, especially in those drying processes where the beans are simply combed out on the ground in the open sunshine. Further, while most molds are offensive, there are a few that can enhance the flavor of the coffee (e.g., Indian Monsoon). Experienced tasters are able to detect tastes that could come from beans that are vulnerable to such problems, even when they do not have any defects. Tasters will comment that a coffee tastes "sweet but dangerous" or offer an assessment like, "Real floral coffee, dangerously fruity. This is a coffee I would never buy again because it just scares me." What scares them is that they might invest a considerable sum of money in a fine tasting coffee that arrives in a new shipment with beans that have fermented in an agreeable way. Since the same fermentation might not occur in a subsequent season, the financial risks are too great, despite there being decent flavor in the coffee.

This means that professional tasters are not merely searching for the taste, they are searching for tastes that are *reliable*, and they are tasting for the reliability: they are probing *beyond flavor* to whether the flavor they perceive is one that would be relatively easy for the producer to keep presenting in later harvests. Much of this depends upon the processing they can detect in the taste, matters that involve husking, cleaning, drying, and the like. As one taster commented, "I'm more interested in the question, is it a repeatable process of flavor or not?" With new and sometimes unproven processes of drying being developed every few years, their effects upon the reliability, good and bad, must be assessed and the likely reproducibility of any desirable identified tastes must be considered. The shipment of first-grade coffee that has "gone off" is one of the things a buyer dreads the most. A good taste for a professional taster is a taste that can be made a stable object in the world market, a taste that will reappear in an essentially similar form, year after year. A flavor that cannot be made available in a reliable way—and that is practical objectivity of the most concrete kind—will not be considered "a good coffee" and its scores will be lowered, even though a lay taster would not have the slightest notion that anything was wrong with the splendid taste in the cup. Here is a colloquy in which these matters became pertinent:

A   Those coffees scare me to death. I kept thinking that it's going to *really* break down any second here, and it didn't completely break down. It scared me. They have great applications in some places, but I would be terrified of it. If you have that application it's a great coffee—definitely aromatic, very engaging. For me it's not ferment, it's having some leftover /

B                                         / some pulp around it maybe.

A  . . . I'm scared to death of these applications. I gave it 8.45 at the end of the day.

C  I'm more interested in the question, is it a repeatable process of flavor or not?

D  For me it was a process.

E  Yeah.

D  But for F it was not a process. He thinks it's a washed and a particular variety.

C  Yeah. But I'm more interested in whether it is a *repeatable* process of flavor or not. Is it just the lucky break for the producer or is it something he or she can do year in and year out?

A  If that's a washed coffee, I'll promise you it will fail eventually, 'cause you can't get to those flavors, those permanent flavors, without getting one that's off the chart.

How is it that these tasters are able to recognize from the taste which flavors will be easy to reproduce and which ones are fortunate accidents? It is impertinent to suggest that it is impossible for them to know for certain, because they will be risking a great deal of their firm's money if they fail to spot the problem. They do not have the luxury of waiting for more definitive evidence, and this causes them to act with caution. Taster A above graded the coffee an 8.45, but it is possible that by itself its flavor may have merited a score more like 8.7; however, the very real fears about reliability and reproducibility lowered the score. How precisely can the value of such factors be calibrated along with the other things being measured? What consequence does this have for the objectivity of the resulting score? Rating one's prognostication of processing problems alongside the flavors is more unwieldy than the legendary difficulties associated with judging apples with oranges. The detection of even a suggestion of processing problems can throw a bucket of cold water upon a robust evaluation. Here the assessing for processing is collaborative:

A  I really like this coffee. Very fruity, had a lot of depth, clean. I liked the end of this coffee. It kept its sweetness all the way through to the end. To me it was a very nice, well-balanced, very fruity cup, very creamy.

B  Ripe fruit and berry soaked in sherry. You had that alcohol taste with mellow wine notes. What kept me from scoring it higher were those acidic notes at the end, and those terrify me.

C   It was so acidic that for me it did go to ferment.

B   Yeah, it turned, but it was [nods agreeably].

D   It really seemed like an African.

Coffees that are naturally processed, i.e., processed without water, are especially vulnerable to fermentation and result in beans whose flavors vary more greatly than washed coffees, although there can be some extraordinary tastes in these variations. One taster explained, "I want to address one thought. . . . I'd classify this as a natural. He left all the skin on it; he left all the fruit on it. It's very rustic. How they age, and how well they're able to dry naturals here, you get the raisin dry, you get the hard dry of a Harrar. They are dangerous coffees in how they age for a buyer. How a coffee ages over time. They may buy it one year, and they may fall for it. It was fruity, and I liked it, but I get that pulpiness and pulpy texture." Is it adequate to persistently judge these natural coffees lower than washed coffees because of the reliability issue? This question poses a problem for tasters, and competitions may require different solutions than tastings by buyers who are looking only to make a purchase (although most competitions are accompanied by an auction). Another taster summarized the situation like this: "It probably deserves a high value, but the fact that I could get one cup out of six where I could have a problem makes me worry about consistency all the time. But it's very interesting coffee. I'm not sure it's always appropriate in a competition to go straight, so I want to like the coffees more. But I think they're dangerous. They can be very good, so you see some very high scores, but the consistency is a very dangerous issue."

In the face of the variety of things that need to be measured, in light of the difficulties of comparing one region of origin or cultivar against another, coffee tasters are sometimes asked whether there any universal criteria for judging coffee. This question can sometimes lead to fascinating discussion, and a reply may be like this one: "There are some universal criteria for evaluating quality, which is like a clean cup, consistency, and balance." "Clean" is an important part of a taster's descriptive lexicon. It refers to the existence of any taints in a coffee, but its semantic field is broader than most descriptors and so it requires more local specification before its semantic range can be adequately restricted. The second component, "consistency," may be a bit less universal than this taster is proposing, since naturally processed coffees, which "are more variable in flavor than wet-processed beans" (Knox and Huffaker 1997, 12), may not even be rated for consistency since their very nature is not to be consistent. As a Head Judge explained, "Do we score naturals exactly like we would score a washed coffee, or are we going to make some accommodation for them? We won't rank them in with the other coffees, but if they end up with high-end scores, there will be the possibility of putting them in the auction. It will be edifying for those who haven't had a lot of these naturals. People are making these coffees, selling these coffees, and buying these coffees." As for the final universal criterion mentioned, "balanced," I have placed the situated study of the production of the sense and reference of this descriptor on the list of topics for future research.

Long-range foresight may also be employed by tasters in evaluating a new cultivar whose potential may still lie ahead:

A   I didn't want to punish this coffee because it's at the borderline, and I don't know how it's going to be in the future. I want to give it a score now, and I like it now.

B   89. I liked it. At the very end, when I went back I would worry about it.

C   Yes I'm sure it has a place. There's going to be a market for it, but I don't think it's going to have universal appeal. But that's O.K.

Taster A here is viewing the coffee as an evolving species, which indeed it is. But just how does such an intangible factor enter into the numerical evaluation? The formal ideal at cuppings is a hard-nosed and empirical one, in which only the taste at hand is judged; however, we have just seen that there are exceptions to this principle. Taster A pays lip-service to the requirement for empirical judging—"I want to give it a score now"—but it seems not much more than a token, and it may be that his empirical assessment gets elevated to handle the problem. The limitations of the objective methodology are constantly managed by the larger rationality of the taster, in ways that are always practical and sometimes ad hoc.

## THE TASTING SCHEDULE

The tasting schedule offers a classic account of coffee taste and its signed indications are a good place to begin the process of evaluating some coffee; however, what a tasting card promises lies ahead of whatever is on the card and does not depend upon any dictionary-styled definitions it bears already in hand but in how the taste categories on the card are used to interrogate some coffee. A category appearing on the card is only a first part that must be matched up with a referent that emerges in a course of actual practice using the category with the real objectivity of the coffee. This is in accord with the description Garfinkel (2002, 188) offers: "The first segment ignores the reflexive accountability of the work. It ignores the reflexively, naturally accountable details" of the practices, i.e., the actual work of understanding taste. To be complete, the first part—the formal descriptor—must collect as a second part some actual taste, and without the second part the first part is meaningless. Emmanuel Levinas (1981, 151–52) presents a similar discussion when he explains how anything that is "said" is always accompanied by a "saying": "Thematization is then inevitable, so that signification can show itself. . . . in the betrayal which philosophy is called upon to reduce. This reduction always has to be attempted, because of the trace of the sincerity which the words themselves bear and which they owe to saying as a witness, even when the said dissimulates the saying in the correlation set up between the saying and the said. Saying always seeks to unsay that dissimulation." Here Levinas is describing how the saying "as a witness" is necessarily reduced to a thematization. While thematizations are required in order for the saying or thinking to know itself, this capacity for self-recollection is not accomplished without *a betrayal* of the depth of what is known in "the saying" as it is occurring in real time. *Both* the depth of what is perceived and understood *and* the need for organizing, communicating, and developing that with the aid of practical objectivities are needed.

Tasting schedules are designed in a variety of ways. A form that is pertinent for a commercial grade of coffee will be difficult to use for higher, more specialty grades, and each purveyor and company will require a form that uniquely services the tastes and expectations of its clientele. Odello (2002, 46) writes: "Many cards have been devised for coffee, and they are mainly used in roasting companies to evaluate coffee lots to be purchased or to test the quality of their blends."[11] What is critical for any tasting schedule is that it be manageable, and we have seen how tasters have learned that there are limits to how complicated these forms can become before they introduce confusion and grow unwieldy. What is needed for adequately assessing an Italian espresso is different than what is needed for assessing an American drip coffee.[12] But in all cases the categories on the tasting card have a real battle to undertake in individuating the aspects of flavor and giving adequate value to each of the components, all of which is decided *before* the unique tastes of the tested coffee are encountered. Here is a colloquy in which a variety of flavors are competing for attention:

A   The most interesting attribute is this coffee was a really, really clean process. It really got the whole *universe* of flavors, and bergamot for me was the most important of all.

B   That's what I got.

C   Yes.

D   Highly elegant, highly elegant.

E   It must be the acidity. Was it the citric acidity?

A   I think it was, from my perspective more malic than citric. More malic. But bergamot was around for me.

F   Actually ginger, "gingerish." With all of that sweetness.

A   Really clean.

How are the categories on the tasting card to be divided to handle in an even-handed way the merits of the cleanness, sweetness, and acidity, not to mention the variety of the more specific flavors that the tasters are suggesting as they try to pin down the taste? It is important to keep in mind that as the tasters are rating the coffee, they are usually holding the tasting schedule with one of their hands as they lift the cupping spoon with the other hand (or they are squeezing the schedule between an elbow and one side of their rib cage while they hold the pencil in the hand on that side, even as they take a sip of fresh water to clean their palate). Trying to record their scores while not dropping the spoon is another learned skill. Frequently, they are reading *from* the card, which serves as a handy table of their recollections, *to* the cup. This work is not accomplished easily, and their attention is constantly moving back and forth between the table where the cups of coffee sit and the tasting schedule they are holding. Even managing the tasting in a way that the schedule does not keep slipping to the floor is a learned practice. One must add to these physical acrobatics the work of stabilizing the meaning of the descriptors on the card since new tastes may be continually disrupting the ways that the taster has organized the intelligibility of the descriptors. A tasting cannot be performed effectively until a taster has made routine some personal practice for using the card.

In one colloquy this problem was discussed:

A   Compared to yesterday, the environment today was more challenging to really get to the heart of these five coffees from yesterday.

B   Mm-hm. Mm-hm. [Nods agreement.]

A   And another thing, when it's so hard to concentrate it is hard to get to the finesse of the coffees. For me this plays a role. I have to work harder to get really to the bottom of these fine aromas with that type of environment.

B   Yah.

The difficulty he is having in concentrating is related to the mental acrobatics he is attempting, to which must be added the larger struggle each taster is battling to retain his or her originality in the face of the evolving regimen of a given protocol. To simply submit to the formal organization risks undermining the originality of the subjective capability of the taster, upon which a successful evaluation depends. Adorno (1973, 170–71) writes, "To give the object its due instead of being content with the false copy, the subject would have to resist the average value of such objectivity and to free itself as a subject." Free itself from what? From any mechanically implemented compliance with the reduced or abstract objectivities suggested by the schedule. This implies that it is by *enhancing* the role of subjectivity that objectivity can be witnessed. That is, *the real objectivity of the coffee requires an active subjectivity that engages it*, and objective taste cannot be established by excluding subjectivity. *Both* the subjectivity and the objectivity must be vigorous, and they are not necessarily mutually exclusive. One needs to permit the significance of the measuring tools to evolve, while remaining fair and consistent so that one is actually retaining a standard.

This naturally creates conflicts that require intensive mental effort to resolve, and this effort *can distract a taster from the coffee*. When an inequity in the evaluation is recognized, it may be necessary for a taster to arbitrarily raise or lower scores. As a taster once confessed to me, "Everyone always ends up gaming the chart." After using a tasting schedule myself for a morning and most of an afternoon's tastings, I found the mental labor of keeping the meaning of the schedule tamed and consistent to be so intense that in order to taste the coffee I had to just forget about the schedule and return to the table and simply decide which cups I wanted to drink. Afterward, I overheard one taster remark to another, "That was the toughest table for me in a long time." During the debriefings another taste referred to it as "that crazy table." There was something unruly in the flavors that kept changing the sense of the descriptors, and we had our hands full with learning how to keep applying them consistently. The craziness was related to the endless reflexivity of the intelligibility of the schedule in the face of some coffees for which the schedule may not have been well suited.

Every schedule will facilitate some evaluations and render others problematic, but they are very necessary to the science of tasting. In the words of one taster, "I strongly believe in having a very set form that actually works for you. But the ideal doesn't exist." What is critical in his comment is that it *actually works* for the taster. The schedule's efficacy rests not in itself but in what the taster does with it. "You come up with your own little shtick in order not to lose control," and losing control is an ever-present threat. Retaining control without the taster inflicting damage upon her subjective originality is the challenge that tasters face, each and every time.

## TASTE PROFILES

Up to now we have been treating the flavor of coffee as primarily an intrinsic, unchanging quality to be found in a given cup; however, this is a simplification of how the taste in a cup of coffee works. The taste of coffee is continuously transforming from when the coffee is steaming-hot all the way until it has become cold, and these changes in taste can be considerable. A competent account of the taste of some coffee by a professional coffee taster includes a detailed description of the flavors at each temperature of the cup, so that what is offered is simply not a naming of flavors, but a profile that tracks which flavors were dominant at each temperature along the way from hot to cold.

We have observed descriptions like, "It was consistent from start to finish" or "Very consistent flavor from beginning to end"; they indicate that the tastes of the cup examined did not vary over the range of temperatures. This would be a plus as far as the reliability of the coffee is concerned, though some of the most interesting coffees offer intriguing taste profiles and surprises that can enhance their value. Therefore, it is important for the professional coffee taster to closely track changes in taste during the cooling, such as a fruity taste that turned tart at the end, and during the post-cupping discussions it can be fascinating to listen to the detailed profiles that tasters offer each other, especially when they independently offer nearly identical taste profiles. What tasters especially want to notice is whether any desirable flavors that appear at the start disappear altogether by the time the cup has cooled, since this would lower the value of the coffee, besides also dashing the hopes of the consumer. One taster summarizes, "When the temperature went down, there was a struggle for the exotic jasmine flavor to rise above the cocoa flavors." In a contrasting case, a taster half-expected that the flavor would deteriorate, so he kept close track of it and was pleased to discover that most of the flavor held up: "It's got a nice little basket of fruit in the nose. It's sweet. For me it's that kind of edgy coffee that I kept going back to taste. I kept thinking that it was going to really break down any second, but it didn't completely break down."

Sometimes the best flavor or flavors of a coffee may not reveal themselves at first, and so some patience is required, along with *a capacity for suspending judgment* until the coffee has had a chance to display itself:

> A   While the cupping was transpiring it was developing, developing, developing, which makes it very difficult for a coffee that is slightly under-roasted. I didn't think that the roasting killed this coffee—you just need to apply more patience to it.

B  There were no greenish underdeveloped notes— /

C                                                    / No.

B  —when you haven't roasted the center part to the point of caramelization.

One taster offered this general advice: "You should judge a coffee by what it brings to the table at the end." His advice can be observed in many of the colloquies: "It was a lot better when it cooled. I was all set to harm this cup, but I was really shocked by how clean and clear it was when it started doing its thing." And, "It had a creamy body. At one temperature I loved it. Then I kind of ignored it for awhile and came back and went, 'Oh, that's a really solid coffee.'" In this next colloquy the coffee won praise for its taste when it was cold:

A  I went back and had it dead cold, just stone cold, and it was like strawberry soda. It was so pleasant.

B  I was going to say it was very consistent throughout the temperature range. There never was a point where it died off or wasn't very sweet and fruit filled.

C  I was going to say the opposite because actually in the middle temperature I had it, the cups seemed to show some inconsistency behind that veil of acidity, and I was wondering. And then as it got cool I couldn't find that at all.

D  I think that at one point it had a slight herbness to it, like a veil or something, but as it cooled it was holding off well. I just thought that for awhile it was sort of losing it.

A  I suppose that every coffee has got a low point in its cycle from hot to cold somewhere.

For each assessment like, "I thought it got a little more clarity, and got more sweetness upon cooling," there can be one like, "It fell apart upon cooling for me. It got rough and tar-ry and harsh," and one of the hardest parts of the tasters' collaborative work is to sew any such dissonant accounts together. What is for certain, however, is that the tasters are always concerned to read a dynamic, unfolding event, and are not just searching for a few static flavors that a coffee might offer, in the way one has coins in one's pocket. Accordingly, from the start the tasters are aiming at the full taste profile of the coffee. Coffees whose better flavors are short-lived are not rated so well: "To me there was a period when it was really flourishing, and then it disintegrated." "It betrayed me. It didn't hold up." And the behavior of the flavors can be very complex and subtle: "It is remarkable when we first had the aromas come. And then for a while they were gone, but they were painted behind this field of pulpy, fruity flavor." With these kinds of complexities, it can be difficult to decide how to measure the flavors. Do you rate highest the flavors that come at the first, middle, or end when the coffee has cooled? How is the best flavor to be measured against the strongest, or the one that endures the longest? Or do you pick that moment, whenever it occurred, when the taste knocked your head off? A great deal of the complexity of a taste can get lost inside of the number to which it is reduced. How much does one deduct from a cup whose best flavor disappeared by the end but whose flavor was truly extraordinary, as opposed to the numerical value of a slightly less desirable flavor that endured longer? Moreover, the same taster may not apply his preferred way to prioritize these with perfect consistency. One taster who mostly preferred flavors that could endure to the finish declared, "I thought I was going to kill it, but I scored it at its best moment basically, because at that moment it had some very nice qualities," and another summarized, "I got some tobacco juice, and then I got a very, very sweet berry syrup. Those two were co-present and battling each other. I had an onion initially, just a bunch of extremely weird flavors, but I tried to score it at its best moment."

One more complicating factor is that not only does the degree of roast of the bean (most simply formulated as light, medium, or dark) simply affect the flavor, the roast affects the entire taste profile and how the flavors behave over the full range of temperatures of the coffee while it is in the cup. And it should be mentioned at least that roasting not only involves length of time and the degree of temperature, roasting has its own profiles; that is, skilled roasters will slightly raise and then lower the temperature, and then raise it again—for instance, extending the time of a roast by letting certain beans sit in a lower heat for a longer period—in the hope of tweaking the flavor in just the way that renders the best parts of the taste dominant. But it is not that such a produced taste will simply be dominant as a sort of stasis or enduring quality, the dominance of a taste will reveal itself differently during different parts of the taste profile of the cup from hot to cold. A question coffee purveyors face is "Can we reproduce the roast easily?" or was it "just a one-time lucky break"? Of course, the goal is usually to give a coffee its best opportunity to excel, and tasters are always trying to assess whether the roast of what they are sampling has enhanced or burned off the desirable flavors. When the tasters were contemplating whether the promising flavor of a sampled coffee might be improved by a different roast, one of them proposed, "I don't think you can blame anything in the roast in the coffee either. That coffee is about as good as you can get it in the cup."

## THE ROAST, AND OTHER THINGS THAT ARE NOT-THERE

The optimum way to roast a particular coffee bean can be a matter of some contestation. Generally speaking, dark roasts can remove flaws in a coffee and tone down some of the naturally occurring unpleasant aspects of the flavors. Lighter roasts have the benefit of allowing finer quality flavors to survive the roasting; for instance, too much roasting can undermine the characteristics of coffees whose flavors dwell on the fruity side. Nevertheless, you need a good caramelization for a coffee to have some sweetness. I have heard many tasters complain that roasters who wish to save money roast inexpensive beans that have taints very darkly, so that the defects are burned away and the coffee can be sold at a decent profit. This, some claim, is a practice so widespread that dark roasts have become very popular, almost the default expectation of consumers, who are able to handle the bitterness of the partially burned flavors only by adding copious amounts of cream and sugar. One thing that characterizes Italian espresso blends is that mostly they are consumed straight, and the coffee has to fend for itself. The principal shortcoming of over-roasting beans, in the view of some tasters, is that the very best and unique flavors of the bean have gone up with the smoke. Surely, it is a pity to over-roast a quality bean. A Pacific Northwest roaster commented, "They fried everything to the point that nothing was bad, but it was dark, and that is what happened in this cup. It doesn't matter what it was—it could have been Jamaican bluebug walnut fruit state, but they fried it."

It is also possible for there to be interesting flavors that on their own might be too overbearing but when moderated by stronger roasting may become desirable. The roaster just cited commented, "I actually thought that the slightly darker roast did this coffee a favor, rounded that [flavor] out, mellowed that." The question of roast surely cannot be resolved here, but neither can the appropriate roast always be resolved at a national or international cupping. While it is the aim of the roasters there to present each coffee at its best, it is not always practicable to fine-tune the roast for each and every bean, and the general level of roasting tends to be similar, which may favor some beans and disadvantage others. Therefore, occasionally *tasters will compensate* for what they think would become a better flavor if it had had a more appropriate presentation. That is, they need to read *something that is not-there* into the evaluation, and this can be problematic.

It is really for the tasters and roasters back at the coffee companies' factories to finely hone the roasting for the taste profile most sought by the companies' clientele, but the organizers of competitions are necessarily faced with making their own decisions about roasting. Some may think that it is most fair to roast every bean the same, but others contend that a bean should be judged by the flavor it can present when it receives its most suitable roasting. One taster summarizes, "The tendency for a competition is to put coffees in a roaster and roast them all exactly the same. Fine, but I tend to agree with A that if you're trying to optimize these coffees and show them at their best, then someone needs to work on that roast to try to do the best that that coffee can do." But it does happen that the roasting can damage the taste of all of the beans in a cupping: "The coffees were not at their best today." And such opinions can be voiced very strongly. For the purposes of a phenomenological analysis of tasting, it should be observed that the tasters are not always tasting the flavor that is in the cup and which their tongues encounter—although that is their usual claim—they are tasting in the context of considering what effect the roast has had upon the flavor and what artifacts that roasting has created that require some compensatory consideration. The "not-there" is very much there in the minds of tasters:

A  I don't feel I'm qualified to score this coffee because I feel that the roast did not do justice to the work of the producer.

B  Same opinion.

Some sort of "not-there" is a component of most thinking. As we reviewed during our discussion of the documentary method of interpretation, when seeking to tame the intelligibility of any local *thing*, one must take into account a wide variety of factors, some of which are read into the situation and are not immediately evident; nevertheless, the factors that are not evident can be decisive for the sense of the thing. While they may be appropriate for some occasions, their partly imaginary character leaves the thinker more prone to errors in judgment. In one competition it was the concerted opinion of the tasters that a roast was *too dark* for them to be able to fully evaluate the more unique flavors of the beans of some premium coffees, and the demand went back to the head roaster to use a lighter roast on the next day's samples. Possibly the roaster felt chastened, but in his caution he roasted the next day's beans *too light*. First "They were overroasted," and the tasters kept wanting to imagine better flavors than were in the cups; and later they did not permit the brewing of genuine coffee: "I don't think we actually made any cups of coffee on our table. We made something. We made some brown water." They sent the beans back to the roaster to find some "mama bear" level of roasting that would permit the flavors to be assessed. But it seems that whatever the roast, there is always some component due to roasting that is not-there, like a ghost at the party; nevertheless, that component makes its way somehow into the evaluation: "Chewy. And I got very consistent cups. I think there is a better roast place for me. To me this is more oniony than I wanted it to be. But fruit, nice notes of dark fruit flavor, dark cherry and dark plum. So stable! It was good, good, good."[13] This taster's "good" may have been made better by his offering some scope for what a better roast might have accomplished. Another taster observed, "I kept imagining this coffee taken out of the roaster 25 seconds earlier." On another occasion there was a flavor highly unique but not very intense, which stimulated the imagination of many of the tasters. If one dwells too long in considering how a better roasting might have amplified a unique flavor, it could affect one's scoring.

It should be stated that a more suitable roasting is not the only possible factor that is not-there. Tasters consider as well what the bean might have become if it had aged a bit longer, or had a different preparation. Also, they might project possible constructive uses for a taste they have detected, uses that are also not-there. Any contemplation of a valued use—perhaps to add to a favorite blend of coffees or for use in a specialty cup—might elevate a score. In one case, the taster was provoked to imagine a bean's taste in an espresso extraction: "I like the fragrance. It was a bittersweet cup with a little tangerine and orange. I thought it would make a real interesting single-origin espresso." In order to fully appreciate the skills tasters employ in their craft, it is important to consider not only the tangible practices one can witness them doing but also the horizon of meaning to which they are oriented while they are making their assessments of the coffees. While the perfect cup of coffee may not be attainable, it is more easily imaginable. And so tasters find themselves scoring things that are not in the cup, such as accounting for too little ground coffee in the brew, compensating for water that may not have been hot enough, etc.

## THE LEARNING

The final observation in this ethnomethodological account of coffee tasters' practices is that most professional tasters are concerned not only with describing the taste of the coffees. *They are interested in learning more about the taste of the coffees than they have already identified.* And this means also learning more about taste in general. A cupping is a lot like a school, and the tasters are continually teaching each other about what they are tasting. It is for certain that collectively the tasters are able to taste a good deal more in the coffees than they would be able to achieve operating alone. For this reason, tasters eagerly engage each other in discussions about the coffees, and in most circumstances they are also diligent students. They listen respectfully, tolerate—are even eager to hear—dissonant assessments, and keep themselves attuned to what in the taste they may have missed (perhaps a flavor that appeared when it was lukewarm) or that is new to them. For these reasons tasters are attentive to other cuppers.

Another thing that tasters learn at a cupping are new descriptors, or descriptors that provide more specificity to a precise flavor than do the descriptors that are presently in a taster's quiver. Tasters solicit each other's participation to serve as sounding boards for the aptness of new ways of describing tastes they may have developed, and it is not only the coffee they are drinking that keeps the tasters attentive to what is being said. They recognize that there is always that "something more" in a flavor that they may have missed, and they are eager to learn what it is, how to recognize it and how to describe it.

The local producers, whether in Hawaii, Costa Rica, India, or Brazil, etc. also want to learn from tasters, since they may not recognize the unique aspects of the coffees they have become accustomed to for much of their lives. As one coffee producer told the tasters, "We want to learn more about what we're doing. It is very important to have you here because you can tell us whether we're going in the right direction." Another producer said, "Just for educational purposes we need a real assessment of those coffees. And whatever you can say about those coffees will be very important."

There are few commercial enterprises that feature better a comparable degree of collaboration and willingness to learn what is not yet known than is found at cuppings, although a few of the larger companies have been reluctant to permit us to study their in-house cupping practices. It should be noted that cuppings themselves have an iconic, almost sacred, status in the coffee business, and it is possible that this is largely due to *the intensity* of the collaborative learning and exploration of tastes that goes on at cuppings. In respecting the cuppings, the tasters are respecting their own collective efforts to extend their experience beyond what has already been achieved. Fortunately, because they are constantly engaging in this learning and teaching, and because it is done as a very public matter, persons like ourselves who are interested in learning about taste have an excellent place to go, since as they teach each other they teach us as well.

CONCLUSION

# RESPECIFYING HUSSERL'S PHENOMENOLOGY AS SITUATED WORLDLY INQUIRIES

At the conclusion of "The Origin of Geometry," Edmund Husserl took a moment to consider his phenomenological project in the broadest possible relief and posed a philosophical anthropological question: "Do we not stand here before the great and profound problem-horizon of reason, the same reason that functions in every human, the *animal rationale*, no matter how primitive he is?" This inquiry into how *Homo sapiens*, the hominid who knows, uses the tool of reason is Husserl's fundamental project. For him the abiding obligation of humanity is learning how to think, a path that we are only part of the way along, and philosophy's first task is to assist this investigation of the modes and methods of reason's employment. In his *Cartesian Meditations*, Husserl (1969, 4) assesses the important turn that reason took in the era of Descartes, a turn that involved the discovery of the contributions of subjective consciousness to science: "Changing its total style, philosophy takes a radical turn: from naïve Objectivism to transcendental subjectivism." Here Husserl's philosophical gaze has an historical dimension: "Should not this continuing tendency imply. . . . for us a task imposed by history itself, a great task in which we are all summoned to collaborate?"

In these few pages I offer a contemporary enhancement of this historical project of reason that includes a suggestion that many philosophers will find scandalous—that the employment of what are ethnomethodological methods can assist philosophy in discovering and investigating the uses of reason in the world. And I would assert that if philosophical inquiry ignores what social phenomenological and ethnomethodological researchers have discovered, they are more likely to remain trapped within the vertigo of their own eloquence.[1]

Husserl (1982, 5) commences *Ideas I* with the observation that "Natural cognition begins with experience and remains *within* experience," and he contrasts this natural theoretic attitude that is confined within what is most immanent with the transcendental attitude that makes the natural attitude itself a theme for examination. Eugen Fink (1995, 4) emphasizes that Husserl's scientific aim is to escape "the confinement of the natural attitude" by exploring "the constitutive becoming of the world in the sense-performances of transcendental life." That is, Husserl's aim is to learn how to think beyond naively accepted notions, especially our own or those of our own discipline. Husserl accomplishes this by making the "how" of thinking thematic. In *Formal and Transcendental Logic* Husserl (1969b, 153) provides this account of his program:

> Our chief purpose is to show that a logic directed straightforwardly to its proper thematic sphere, and active exclusively in cognizing that, remains stuck fast in a naiveté which shuts it off from the philosophical merit of radical self-understanding and fundamental self-justification, or, what amounts to the same thing, the merit of being most perfectly scientific, the attainment of which is the *raison d'être* of philosophy, above all as theory of science.

These two aspects, "self-justification"—which can include logical justifications and calculations along with the evidence of originary (*Originarität*) experience—and "radical self-understanding" are essential to Husserl's phenomenological project, which Husserl speaks of as finding a way to reason that does not eclipse original thinking as we retain the achievements of the ever finer calculating techniques that we develop. It is vital to recognize that the development of techniques of analysis must be accompanied by the more transcendental gaze of "radical self-understanding" that observes the role of subjectivity in constituting and stabilizing the intelligibility of our scientific inquiries. It takes more than "the logicians' 'straightforward' thinking" to make our reflection scientific! Science also requires a capacity for recognizing the ways that we ourselves continually construe the sense of the world we study.

In the course of his investigations, Husserl kept observing how thinking keeps becoming caught within the confines of its own webs, mistaking what is local and naive for something more universal, and he kept devising methods for discovering what there is in the world that might have been missed by the methods being employed. He observed that some European scientists "were misled into taking these formulae and their formulae-meaning for the true being of nature itself" (Husserl 1970a, 44) and considered it a crisis that these very same methods—not because of some flaws but due to their brilliance—exclude the most original evidence and lose sight of the most fundamental meaning of their inquiries: "Here the *original* thinking that genuinely gives meaning to this technical process and truth to the correct results (even the 'formal truth' peculiar to the formal *mathesis universalis*) is excluded" (Husserl 1970a, 46). Accordingly, Husserl's solution is to describe painstakingly and in its minutest details the "things themselves" *just as* they are given to thinking. The social phenomenological and ethnomethodological research programs I recommend here remain faithful to his project, although they have some important respecifications to contribute.

At bottom, Husserl's phenomenological method relies upon a scrupulous honesty in describing just what is witnessed, without excessive conceptual embellishment or distraction by extraneous theoretical interests: "Throughout phenomenology, one must have the courage to accept what is really to be seen in the phenomenon precisely as it presents itself rather than interpreting it away, and to *honestly* describe it" (Husserl 1982, 257). We remain committed to this pure description of what is immanent.

If aspects of Husserl's vision require respecification, these are respecifications that serve to revitalize the phenomenological project. Of the first generation of Husserl's commentators, Maurice Merleau-Ponty was among the most faithful; yet Merleau-Ponty identified a number of weaknesses in Husserl's penchant for systemic totalization, his emphasis on the monadic individual, and the priority given to the formally conceptual over what is more than conceptual. Inquiries undertaken while retaining as their primary focus Husserl's foundational questions cannot be taken to undermine Husserl's project even when they locate answers that require some reconsideration of Husserl's theorizing. Husserl himself never considered his discoveries to be settled method, since he kept revising his system, decade after decade. Merleau-Ponty (1968, 116) writes, "Husserl himself never obtained one sole *Wesenschau*[2] that he did not subsequently take up again and rework, not to disown it, but in order to make it say what at first hand it had not quite said." Since Husserl himself kept respecifying his project, it would be foolhardy for us to freeze phenomenology in a final form circa 1938 that would disallow our own faithful respecifications. During a conference in Memphis on "Husserl and Derrida," after Derrida offered his own respecification of some Husserlian matters, a notable phenomenologist rose to excoriate several aspects of Husserl's work. Derrida paused, and then strongly cautioned the scholar that nothing Derrida has accomplished would have been possible without what he had learned from Husserl, emphasizing that he remained an Husserlian. In the same way I too remain faithful to Husserl's questions, if not to all of his answers.

Husserl's phenomenology asks us to look behind our naïve absorption in the world to examine the nature and role played by the thinking that has organized, and keeps organized, the intelligibility of that world. He suggests (Husserl 1969b), "The geometer, for example, will not think of exploring, besides geometrical shapes, geometric thinking," and he insists upon making such thinking his theme by scrutinizing the operations of sense-constituting subjectivity there in its finest details. According to Husserl's vision of science, without this radical self-understanding there can be no science. And this necessarily requires a clear, "purified" (of immanent contaminants), encounter with "original evidence" (1969b, 154), or as he states in *The Paris Lectures* (Husserl 1970c, 6), "It is the spirit of science to count nothing as really scientific which cannot be fully justified by the evidence. In other words, science demands proof *by reference to the things and facts themselves, as these are given in actual experience and intuition.*" It should be noted that the emphasis upon objectivity here is as great as is the emphasis upon subjectivity; in fact, Husserl's primary interest is in the object. But the object is always a subjectively understood object, and any science that denies, *a priori*, the subjectivity that is really there is only a caricature of being objective. There exist no objective objectivities, only subjective objectivities, which Husserl described as early as *Logical Investigations* (1970c, 765) as "the complete self-manifestation of the object."[3] The *a priori* sphere of pure reason will not take us as far as truth, which requires the evidence (*Evidenz*) of the world. "All predicative and conceptual rational cognizing leads back to *evidence*. Properly understood only originary evidence is the source of legitimation" (Husserl 1982, 339).

The thematizing of the subjective, the "transcendental criticism of cognition," is a "criticism of the constitutive sources from which the positional sense and the legitimacy of cognition originate" (Husserl 1969b, 171). Here Husserl (1969b, 173–4) offers us one of his definitions of phenomenology: "The thematizing of the subjective—more distinctly: of the intentional-constitutive—a thematizing whose essential function is still to be clarified, shall henceforth be designated as *phenomenological.*" We are still occupied with research whose aim is to further this clarification, and that is what makes us phenomenologists. But on the way we have had to shed a few of Husserl's idealist proclivities.

Above all, Husserl was concerned to avoid the danger that reification poses for clear thinking, and he sought methods and disciplines that assist thinking in keeping itself open for what is most important to be thought: what is not yet known. Dogmatism of any sort is to be avoided, whether of philosophy or science. As Merleau-Ponty (1968, 39) phrased it, radical self-understanding cautions thinking not to reduce its openness upon the world nor "to reduce in advance our contact with Being to the discursive operations in which we defend ourselves against illusion," to not sacrifice insight for the sake of a narrow certainty. In making our knowledge consistent, clear and distinct, we must not forget to see; the alternative is a dogmatism of reflection with which "philosophy concludes the moment it begins" (Ibid.). And yet that could describe most of the philosophy and most of the science that we know, including much of our own.

Perhaps the greatest guidance we have received from Husserl is that the coherence of the objects that we investigate come from the unity of sense that we fashion for it. Husserl's investigations into how a unity of meaning is fit together and sustained have provided us with some of our best directives for research. He has described carefully how the multi-rayed intentions of any inquiry, over its temporal course, are made objective in a monothetic act (Husserl 1982, 286), so that they can (first) be retained in our own memory and reflection and (second) be communicated successfully with the cohort of scientific investigators with whom we collaborate. Once these many-rayed intentions are reduced to a single ray, the horizon of inquiry narrows and an habitual acceptance sets in that facilitates the work of conceptual synthesis but risks losing sight of the phenomenon.

> The developed method, the progressive fulfillment of the task, is, as method, an art which is handed down with it; but its true meaning is not necessarily handed down with it. And it is precisely for this reason that a theoretical task and achievement like that of a natural science (or any science of the world)—which can master the infinity of its subject matter only through infinities of method [i.e., the infinite pursuit of its method] and can master the latter infinities only by means of a technical thought and activity which are empty of meaning—can only be and remain meaningful in a true and original sense *if* the scientist has developed in himself the ability to *inquire back* into the *historical meaning* of all his meaning-structures and methods, i.e., into the *historical meaning of their primal establishment*, and especially into the meaning of the *inherited meanings* taken over unnoticed in this primal establishment, as well as those taken over later on. (Husserl 1970a, 56)

There is not the space here to rehearse Husserl's investigations of noetic and noematic phenomena and their relation to each other, but these vital phenomenological inquiries serve as the prototype for our understanding of how we organize the intelligibility of phenomena and how thought becomes aware of itself. Noema (what is meant) do not actively constitute objects but they facilitate the constitution of meaning by collecting the products of our acts of awareness in a way that reflexively keeps them on task and capable of making our understanding deeper. Adorno (1982, 175) describes the noema as something "impaled on the isolated intention, which encounters it" as "the shadowy fetch of that thing;" it is the object intruding upon thought as thought is engaged in encountering itself. The noema, and also the names and concepts to which it gives rise, are the tools with which sense-shaping (*Besinnung*) works in determining sense and in stabilizing those determinations, in the face of the continually shifting gestalts and semiotics of the real world. While Husserl recognized the importance of intersubjective relations in this knowing, his inquiries were kept too exclusively individualistic—a holdover from the epistemological practices of the European Enlightenment, including its Cartesian and Leibnizian incarnations. Husserl set into motion all of these insights in the context of his description of internal time consciousness, so that his epistemological observations were not frozen outside of time but kept *in situ* as they operate in the course of real activities.

Ethnomethodologists have learned that these activities of finding the meaning, stabilizing it, and objectivating it[4] are social from their inception. The account that has each individual separately working out an understanding and then sharing that understanding as part of an interconcatenation of subjective understandings is a tale from European folklore; affairs occur in this fashion only in rare circumstances. Instead, thinking is a public activity,[5] and the processes of sense-building (*Sinnbildung*) are less deliberate and less conceptual than most epistemologists would have it. The taking up of these inquiries into sense-shaping as this shaping is situated in the actual world are what ethnomethodologists refer to as "studies," and they are guided by what is there in the world to be discovered. Of course, the worldly work of the lifeworld discovered is itself guided by categorial intuitions that function much in the way Husserl has described, but these categories are developed *socially*. We cannot discover anything, think any *thing*, without using categories to organize that thinking and searching; and these categories are amenable to social production and social forces; but therein lie the difficulties, for *the employment of those very categories that provide order can simultaneously obscure the originality of our thinking*. So the phenomenological question, Husserl's phenomenological question, becomes *how* do we use and need categorial intuition? But it is less useful to answer that question abstractly than it is to discover categorial intuition at work in the real world, and it is here that ethnomethodological inquiries can commence. We need to investigate, by scrutinizing real worldly affairs, *just what* are the ways that categories of thought aid experience and also *just what* are the ways we can keep our categorizing from obscuring the object that we mean to know. For categories necessarily do both, and they do them together. So the research strategy being recommended here is to *find* chemists working in their laboratories, *locate* and observe people using rules in playing games, *witness* real testimony in the court, etc. That is, let us investigate sense-furnishing by looking at actual and not imagined occasions where sense is being furnished.

This is consistent with Husserl's longstanding insistence upon returning to original experience and to the things themselves; however, Husserl called for such return much more frequently than he himself visited actual sites of sense-furnishing. The Husserlian commentator James Dodd (2004, 3) confirms Husserl's intention, reminding us of "an emphasis not only on the theme of sense or meaning, but above all on the place and importance of the experience. . . . in which we grasp something as 'itself,' in its 'genuine sense.'" Accordingly, phenomenology exceeds semiotics to the extent that it not only takes up the mechanisms by which sense is assembled and preserved as its theme, but it is also addressed to *the practical work* of gaining insight by which the genuine sense of an object is witnessed and made one's own. The important consequence is that phenomenology's interest is as much in the object as it is in the subject and "belongs both to subjectivity and the world" (Dodd 2004, 214).

Theodor Adorno, who composed his first book on Husserl's phenomenology, emphasized that the phenomenological task was to give the object its due instead of being content with the copy we have by means of our representations. Adorno offers a program for integrating the subject and object not by uniting them conceptually but by discovering them in the world where both the subjective and objective aspects are found together. Adorno (1973, 316) uses the illustration of the exchange of goods: "Both [subjective and objective] acts converge in barter, in something subjectively thought and at the same time objectively valid, in which the objectivity of the universal and the concrete definition of the individual subjects oppose each other, unreconciled, precisely by coming to be commensurable." That is, *instead of resolving the antinomy of subject and object by formal theoretical fiat*, Adorno searches for a perspicuous case in the world where the problem is resolved as part of the natural course of affairs.[6] If the subjective is easily removed in formal scientific accounts of the objective world, it is somehow more evident in the actual settings of the real world. Adorno (1973, 300–01) complains that *this real objectivity* is missed by theoreticians: "Positivist scientific bustle breaks men of the habit of experiencing the real objectivity to which they are subjected." Only the object itself can guarantee objectivity. As Husserl (1970c, 765) has commented, "The object is not merely meant, but in the strictest sense *given*," but first we need to locate it! We need to trace out the *ratio* as it is engaged with the world, but we require a good deal more than the limited world afforded us by Husserl's favorite illustrations of the "tree" and the color red. We are going to need some sustained "studies" of real worldly phenomena in-the-course of their real, *in vivo* worldly activities. It is here that some ethnomethodological assistance may be helpful; if it renders our reflections too mundane, it is only because our worlds also are too mundane. Moreover, they are immensely more complicated than the tree or color "red" that Husserl took up; these examples may have served well as an inaugural heuristic, but it is time that phenomenology matures to take up the activities of sense-building in its natural complexities.

In his *Cartesian Meditations* Husserl suggests just this sort of turn. He claims (1969a, 9),"The genuine concept of science, naturally, is not to be fashioned by a process of abstraction" but by "'immersing ourselves' in the scientific striving and doing that pertain to them, in order to see clearly and distinctly what is really being aimed at." This seems close to what I am recommending here. Husserl (1969a, 10–11) notes that what best identifies science is that it is a "striving for grounded judgments" and that "the scientist intends, not merely to judge, but to ground his judgments." It is for certain that the crux of scientific praxis rests in this sustained attention that is paid to the potential for grounding each judgment every step along the way. Accordingly, "Science always intends to judge expressly and keep the judgment or the truth fixed, as an express judgment" (Husserl 1969a, 11). That is what makes "a proof" a proof. However, the proof does not bear this grounding in-itself, although it is frequently made out as if it does; rather, the grounding is an ongoing, live collaboration that emerges as scientists interact and communicate with each other. They provide grounds for each other and with each other. Their objectivity is a social accomplishment, and as such it can be studied in its details. Husserl (1969a, 10) refers to such studies, but they are only mentions of them and not themselves situated worldly studies: "If we go further in this manner (here, naturally, we are only indicating the procedure), then, in explicating more precisely the sense of a grounding or that of cognition, we come forthwith to the idea of evidence." But what is "natural" about "only indicating the procedure," (Husserl 1969a, 10) instead of following the procedure up to witness for oneself the site's contingent details?

In *The Crisis of the European Sciences*, Husserl takes up the matter of the geometry that was given by tradition to Galileo. He emphasizes that Galileo was always addressed to the real objects of the physical world and had yet to substitute for them the "pure idealities" with which contemporary geometers are engaged. Husserl (1970a, 24) writes, "We note that he, the philosopher of nature and 'trail-blazer' of physics, was not yet a physicist in the full present-day sense; that his thinking did not, like that of our mathematicians and mathematical physicists, move in the sphere of symbolism, far removed from intuition." Galileo at Pisa may have been engaged with the theoretical consequences of Aristotle's theory of motion, but that was not what was essential about his work; rather, the discovery of the praxis of experimental settings, the way that embodied inquiries can be pursued—and made the core of physics, as its science—was Galileo's achievement. Philosophers of science can today employ ethnomethodological methods of research for capturing[7] and describing the steps and practical procedures that cohorts of physicists (or of any field) use in taming their scientific experiments; researchers can undertake a fine-grained analysis of the lived work of sense-production and sense-organization as the very matter it is for those practicing scientists, step-by-step. As Wittgenstein (1977, 9) suggested, "There is no such thing as phenomenology, but there are indeed phenomenological problems." Phenomenological problems are best pursued as situated studies.

I cited above Husserl's *Formal and Transcendental Logic* where he implores us to study geometric thinking as well as geometric shapes, about which he (1969b, 119) insists that "our experiencing itself and its productions" must be made our theme. Ethnomethodologists wish to amend this proposal by suggesting that examining geometric thinking in the abstract, or in the context of imaginary reflections about what Galileo was really doing, is insufficient—we need to examine the actual experiences of real geometers fully engaged *at their worksite*, and then study the sense-constituting work as it really operates in the midst of their scientific practice.[8]

In the present volume I have offered many illustrations, but I wish to emphasize only two of them now. Ethnographic treatises are very fond of speaking about rules in the most abstract ways, as if rules were always clear, straightforward, and followed faithfully. Over the course of a decade of classroom instruction, I placed video cameras in the hands of my students and instead of relying upon what conventional orthodoxy may say about rules, I had the students view the videotapes repeatedly to discover *just what was* rule-governed activity in an actual game. The students discovered that the collaborative building of a unity of sense, the reflexivity of understanding, the real processes of objectivation and stabilization of meaning over a temporal course, etc. could be investigated not as theoretical abstractions but as *naturally occurring phenomena*.[9] Such phenomena were able to provide much more complexity and detail about matters of phenomenological interest than do idealizations about rules. Moreover, as scientists we had additional confidence about what we identified and described when it was derived from our actually *seeing* phenomenological *events* in the real world. Our findings were consistent with science researcher Michael Lynch's (1993, 274) description of the ethnomethodological injunction to "master the practices studied (rather than simply learning to talk 'about' them) and by its complete disavowal of all established methods for mapping, coding, translating, or otherwise representing members' practical reasoning in terms of established social science schemata." The strength of this research program is to let the sites themselves teach us what we need to know instead of relying principally upon our finely worded accounts.

One of the first things ethnomethodological researchers discover is that there are fewer formal concepts at work than philosophers and formal analytic social scientists presuppose, and those concepts that are central to an occasion are less determinate than might be imagined. They also learn that on occasion indeterminacy can be a resource for members' discoveries. By formal concepts we refer here to "predicative and conceptual rational cognizing" (Husserl 1982, 339), the *ratio* at work in formally developing the themes of an inquiry. The organization of sense and intelligibility operates at more than the strictly conceptual level, and this "more than"—"the 'more' which the concept is equally desirous and incapable of being" (Adorno 1973, 162)—has naturally asserted itself as a topic in ethnomethodological investigations. For example, Lynch (1985) and Livingston (2008, 153–56) take care to describe the embodied, hands-on practices of the local laboratory organization of chemists that are critical for the success of laboratory science, and are discovered only as unforeseen shop contingencies only *after* the actual worksite is accessed. The chemist's skills in handling a catheter, for example, may not be conceptual but they are consequential. What was most obvious to my students who undertook *in vivo* studies of games-with-rules was that the players' local work of organizing the rules was not exclusively a rational phenomenon.

The respecification we are seeking here is captured well by Merleau-Ponty (1968, 38): "We are catching sight of the necessity of another operation besides the conversion to reflection, more fundamental than it, of a sort of *sur-réflexion* that would also take itself and the changes it introduces into the spectacle into account. It accordingly would not lose sight of the brute thing and the brute perception and would not finally efface them." This is consistent with Husserl's advice from *Cartesian Meditations* (1969a, 38–9), which Merleau-Ponty cites later in his text (Merleau-Ponty 1968, 129): "It is the experience. . . . still mute which we are concerned with leading to the pure expression of its meaning."[10] The principal contention of this essay is that one is better able to do this by studying naturally occurring phenomena at their worldly sites, a move that many phenomenological philosophers make only sparingly.

Aron Gurwitsch was an exception, and his discussion of phenomenal fields (Gurwitsch 1964) provided direction for ethnomethodologists who research nonconceptual aspects of organizing the orderliness of local affairs. Gurwitsch used many analytic strategies of Gestalt psychology, which was earlier brought into philosophy by Max Scheler; however, while Husserl showed some interest in these Gestalt studies, he preferred to remain "the theoretician of reason and remonstrates against the irrationalistic implications of Gestalt theory" (Adorno 1982, 160). Husserl could do so only by keeping his distance from the real events of the lifeworld.

By contrast, let us consider the uses of flavor descriptions by professional coffee tasters. This *in vivo* study tells us more about phenomenological matters than can many treatises of epistemology! Professional coffee tasters use taste descriptors to organize their experience of tasting coffee. The interesting thing about these formal descriptors is that their true sense does not exist apart from how the tasters use them in their tasting. Since their sense is continually shifting in subtle ways and they are always subject to being used in new ways, there is an interesting lability to these descriptors they are very serious categories, and it is common for hundreds of thousands of dollars to be dependent upon their proper and accurate employment. So, there is an objectivity to them, but it is an objectivity that has its origin in the real taste of a cup of coffee, which is a splendid example of what Adorno calls (see chapter 8) *real objectivity*. Further, the formal taste descriptors assist the tasters in *finding the taste*. But the tasters really do find the tastes that they describe, and they find them again, even half a world away. Yet the descriptor never exhaustively describes the taste—the taste as a real objectivity is always capable of offering something more to a skilled taster. And so, I discovered that *tasters are continually engaged in teaching each other more about what there is to be tasted*. And these are not imaginary tastes; they are objective tastes.

Adorno (1973, 318) has written:

> The general rationality [is] at odds with the particular human beings whom it must negate to become general, and whom it pretends—and not only pretends—to serve. The universality of the *ratio* ratifies the needfulness of everything in particular, its dependency upon the whole; and what unfolds in that universality, due to the process of abstraction on which it rests, is its contradiction to the particular.

It is this *ratio*, along with its universality, that we wish to *capture as a local production*. Note that there is a role for universality here since the particular is dependent upon the whole and "unfolds in that universality," but our more serious question is how, specifically, is it dependent? To simply refer us to "the process of abstraction on which it rests" is too vague a suggestion to offer us real assistance, and we need to specify just what takes place beyond simply uttering the word "process." The beauty of the coffee study here is that with dozens of hours of digital video of coffee tasting, I can identify and describe those details that specify *just what* is the real objectivity, the something in the taste that resists being said, *and* how their categorical objectivities assist the tasters in finding it. There is indeed an objectivity that is not simply the product of abstract mental operations of the subject, and this is the real objectivity. As John Caputo (1997, 80) has said of Derrida,

"Derrida is not trying to bury the idea of 'objectivity' but, a little like Kant, to force us to formulate a more sensible version of it." My study of coffee tasters facilitates gaining sight of this more sensible version.

The study, immersed in the real worldly practical activities of professional coffee tasters, can identify and describe how tasters cooperate in building up certain unities of meaning, in a collaboration that is as passive as it is active. It can capture the details of how they stabilize the sense of their taste descriptors, at once preserving the concept's contribution to understanding while cultivating an openness that prevents the categories from closing the taster off to what more there is to discover in the objective taste. Also, I can study the effects of any narrowing of what can be thought that is caused by the employment of any concept. The work of coffee tasters in stabilizing slippage in the sense and reference of their descriptors is real, practical, commercial, and endlessly revealing about thinking and objectivation. While Husserl's reflections on objectivation are our guide, these events tell us more than Husserl could have been able to know.

Here the relations of subjectivity and objectivity are located as real worldly phenomena and not as hyperactive abstractions. While the relations of subject and object raise immense complexities, at least these complexities are real ones. Naturally, coffee tasters themselves have an interest in routinizing their professional work and in making their results as objective as they can, and their strategies of practical reasoning can be studied as well. Most large commercial roasters and professional associations of coffee tasters have developed, as an always and ever evolving method, schedules for recording their taste evaluations, and these results are frequently tabulated in quantitative forms in order to assist them in objectifying the tastes. Without such methods and schedules, the coffee industry would hardly be able to function. Objectivity serves not only truth interests but also the vital practical demands of institutions, among which is a concern for providing for the adequacy of intersubjective communication.

A final aspect of ethnomethodological studies of sense-building *in vivo* is that by taking up the practical work of professionals (coffee tasters, scientists, software and IT designers, etc.) we the researchers can actively solicit the professionals' collaboration in developing further aspects of study, a research process referred to by ethnomethodologists as "hybrid studies." By fusing our and the professionals' interests and intelligence, we researchers can be guided by the professionals' expert knowledge of what they are doing, and, at the same time, since these practitioners may not always be aware themselves *just what* and *just how* they are doing what they do, the ethnomethodological researcher can assist them to identify the most vital features of their work. Neither party can make as much progress, phenomenologically speaking, alone as they are able to achieve working together.

In this way phenomenology's interest in the real experiences of the lifeworld lends itself easily to sharing the real interests of worldly practitioners, making those practitioners lay phenomenologists in the process.

These kinds of "studies" necessarily reveal aspects of the world that require respecifications of Husserl's phenomenology, and I have already alluded to many of these respecifications. Principal among them is that we need to shift the priority we give to the thinking done by individuals to the thinking that we do in concert with others, for the very good reason that most thinking in the world is of the latter kind. Alfred Schutz (1970, 134) suggested,

> We are still dealing with the fiction that this problem can be studied for a supposedly isolated mind without any reference to sociality. We are of course aware that this procedure involves the unrealistic assumption that our knowledge of the world is our private affair and that, consequently, the world we are living in is our private world.

Humans are a species being, or like pack dogs and dolphins our activity is fundamentally collaborative. The notion that we must ground our knowledge and our certainty on the Cartesian/Leibnizian homunculus allows the individualist biases of European metaphysics to impose an extraneous order that will fail to capture the public dynamics of thinking and sense-furnishing in the way they occur in the real world. This may have been excusable when we lacked the methods for scrutinizing the details of the local production of sense and orderliness, but there are no longer any excuses for ignoring these aspects of sense-furnishing.

Husserl did not ignore these aspects; however, he accounted for them by adding "intersubjective" phenomena on top of a structure that was already formed on the basis of individual subjectivity, which for him and for many phenomenologists always retains priority. While Husserl recognized the need to amend his account of transcendental subjectivity, his remedy was insufficient; according to Husserl (1970c, 275) we are presented with "a phenomenology that finally understands itself as a functional activity in transcendental intersubjectivity." His account had tremendous plausibility, but only so long as it remained primarily theoretic. Its good sense as epistemology is achieved by the clear, logical account of rationality it is always able to provide and by how readily communicable that account is for those receiving it. But a concern about maintaining the clarity of that account can militate against a full acknowledgment of the many arational and irrational ways that people organize themselves in working out the orderliness and intelligibility of the world. Just because order is preferred over chaos does not make the world orderly. As soon as social phenomenologists began to investigate the world, a much more complicated story was revealed. The visibility of that story depends upon one's inquiries remaining situated in the world.

A problem corollary to this, which also requires respecification, is Husserl's doctrine of absolute origins. That such origins rest solely in the experience of an individual, that we should be able to locate the absolute origin of anything, that meaning originates in the mind and not in the looks of the world as events unfold are all idealist prejudices that must be abandoned. Everything in the world is derivative, rationality is only one aspect of meaning-production, and knowing is hardly as deliberative in building itself up as Husserl's model supposes. And especially, most meanings have their beginnings in the public life of persons and emerge from that life without the sort of personal authorship that constitutive phenomenology imagines.

Aron Gurwitsch (1966, 432) learned to give more priority to intersubjectivity than to subjectivity: "The object may be said to derive its existence and the meaning of its existence from intersubjectively concatenated and interlocking experiences; and we may speak of the 'intersubjective constitution' of the world: that is, of the world as originating in intersubjectively interlinked experience." And Gurwitsch (in Grathoff 1989, 230) later came to conclude, "It is more than ever my conviction that Husserl's phenomenology cannot solve the problem of intersubjectivity, especially that of transcendental intersubjectivity, and this is its undoing." While we can retain Husserl's vital notion of originary understanding, which seeks to preserve the site where our first insight into sense, meaning and truth occurs, we need to give up its metaphysical trappings and recognize that all signification has its precedents, and that many of those precedents occur in the natural social interaction of parties who live and act together in public space. Once we loosen the hold of some of these *a priori* theoretical beliefs and begin to examine the world itself in everyday life, we will find these originary moments of intelligible life almost everywhere we turn, and our project will be to describe them. Garfinkel (2007, 27) argues that we are mistaken when we reduce local details to formal analytic generalities and suggests that "with this policy [Husserl] obscured and lost the origins of the sciences in their lived details of the shop floor."

Finally, it should be acknowledged that Husserl's abiding concern for constructing a comprehensive and total system that could purport to account for everything may be some hubris derived from the culture of the European Enlightenment. No doubt we are still too close to this outlook and share too many of its interests and inclinations to be able see our way clearly here, but Husserl's own continually revised comprehensive programs offer proof of the autoimmunity of such totalistic philosophical ventures. The sovereignty one detects in the voice of most nineteenth- and twentieth-century philosophers, and also during the great era of paternalistic social anthropology that established social science, has close affinity with the theological-political basis of European life and with the conceit that it is possible to control everything from a center. In order for any of the genuine insights found in sovereign thinking to survive, they will have to cope with some disassemblement of their tightly fabricated self-certainty and accept that they cannot provide for *everything* by relying upon their own foundations, theoretically construed. Taking care to ground one's thinking in directly intuited evidence and performing that grounding in expressly public ways is an essential part of scientific praxis, and necessary if the collaborative work of a scientific community is to survive and develop properly. Social phenomenologists are guided by Husserl's many inquiries and, like him, remain opposed both to extreme relativism and to the realistic assumption that the world we conceive exists independently of our cognitions, in just the way we conceive it. And they remain motivated by Husserl's principal advice: go *to the things themselves* and keep engaged with the worldly activities found there. These worldly activities may be more complicated, and even more chaotic, than some would prefer, and there are no guarantees that we will be able to capture them adequately in our ethnomethodological descriptions. Throughout these investigations, I remain compliant with this summons of Merleau-Ponty (1968, 39) as well as with his modesty regarding what it might be possible to achieve:

> [Our reflection] must descend toward the world such as it is instead of working its way back up toward a prior possibility of thinking it—which would impose upon the world in advance the conditions of our control over it. It must question the world, it must enter into the forest of references that our interrogation arouses in it, it must make it say, finally, what in its silence *it means to say*. We know neither what exactly is this order and this concordance of the world to which we thus entrust ourselves, nor therefore what the enterprise will result in, nor even if it is really possible. But the choice is between it and a dogmatism of reflection.

# NOTES

## INTRODUCTION

1. For a comprehensive summary of Garfinkel's rigor, see chapter 5 of my book (Liberman 2007), *Husserl's Criticism of Reason*, "Garfinkel's Uncompromising Intellectual Rigor." (Italian readers may wish to read the Italian translation of this chapter, which may be found in *Quaderni di teoria sociale*, Perugia: Morlacchi editore, No. 11: pp. 103–152, 2011).

2. See Garfinkel 2002, 245–61 and Garfinkel and Livingston 2003.

3. At the very first seminar I attended (at UC Irvine in 1970), I complained that there was no way that anyone could read such tomes in only one quarter; he replied, "I realize that. But that does not change the fact that until you do read all of them, you won't have any way to understand what it is we're doing here."

4. This was a plenary address presented to the annual meeting of the Society for Phenomenology and the Human Sciences, in November, 2010.

5. Recall the citation from Garfinkel's 1977 class, "If anybody comes in with a theory, I'll burn it publicly."

6. The wording "the water you're swimming in" is an analogy that Harold used frequently. It was also the practice of Harvey Sacks to insist upon beginning to discuss ethnomethodology only when the transcripts were completed.

7. From my course notes.

## CHAPTER ONE

1. For a discussion of authochthonous, cf. Gurwitsch 1964, 30–36.

2. An early, pertinent study of failure to stop at stop signs was made by Eric Livingston (in 1987). In his examination of an intersection with four-way stop signs, he found that a smooth, orderly flow of traffic required that motorists routinely violate traffic regulations. In a study of a four-way stop sign intersection elsewhere in Eugene, my students and I discovered this to be a common occurrence.

3. In the same way the corporate orientation of Australian Aboriginal interaction, or the individualist self-orientation of ordinary European-American interaction, is not the result of any social psychological essence but of the practical methods for mundane interaction that are available to Aboriginals or European-Americans at the scene (see Liberman 1989).

## CHAPTER TWO

1. Garfinkel would say that maps are "self-elucidating."

2. Phenomenological researchers can learn to be capable of describing and analyzing a lifeworld in which inconsistencies are commonplace, and not confine their analyses to worlds that are artificially made to appear more contingent than they really are.

3. Thomas Mann (1965, 498) describes such a vaporization of clarity in *The Magic Mountain* in an iconic way when he speaks about Hans Castorp as he gazes into his dinner plate after nearly skiing himself into oblivion and death during a blizzard a short time before, an occasion during which Castorp had briefly attained some long-sought-for clarity about his life: "An hour later what he had thought even that self-same evening was no longer so clear as it had been at first." That certainties readily become uncertain or confused may not necessarily diminish the truth of a certainty that for a moment we had experienced.

4. Although it does so, we can never do away with analytic thinking since it is ubiquitous. It is essential to our lives; however, in these circumstances recovering the embodied looks of the journey is the method that drivers following sketched maps preferred.

5. Cf. David Lewis, *We, the Navigators, the Ancient Art of Landfinding in the Pacific*, Honolulu: University of Hawaii Press, 1994; Edwin Hutchins, *Cognition in the Wild*, MIT Press, 1996; and Geoffrey White, *Voyaging in the Contemporary Pacific*, Lanham, MD: Rowman & Littlefield, 2000.

6. See chapter 4. There is an additional dynamic at work in face-to-face conversations that is not strictly rational, and that is the practice of objectivating the meanings that parties are able to share in a way that makes them accessible to everyone present. Since what becomes part of dependable, established and publicly acknowledged understanding can be used as tools for preserving local orderliness, accuracy of understanding is sometimes sacrificed for greater smoothness in social relations. On occasion, parties can find their way to a sense that no one anticipated or intended. One might say that a social rationality is at work, but it is nothing like an analytic rationality.

7. For an account of the documentary method of interpretation, see Garfinkel 1967, 77–80.

8. Eric Livingston (2008, 24) reports the same about the understanding of people who try to solve jig-saw puzzles.

9. I am reminded of this observation by the fifteenth-century Tibetan epistemologist, Tsong Khapa (1999): "We concretize our apprehension of each object, and then mistake it for the truth."

## CHAPTER THREE

1. The phrasing is one that Harold Garfinkel used frequently in his lectures. Cf. Garfinkel 2002.

2. Durkheim 1915, 431–32.

3. Since the students know that their research study is about rules, they are probably more careful than usual about reading the rules, but even this is not a force effective enough to motivate them to read all of them.

4. All of the names used are pseudonyms.

5. The term "candidate formulation" is Garfinkel's.

6. The term "game-furnished conditions" is Garfinkel's.

7. Throughout the transcripts in this book, overlaps and talk that is very closely knit are indicated with slant marks (/ and //) placed at the precise places where talk ends and commences.

8. How would one code shrugging? Social analysts who use coding may ignore interactional phenomena that are ambiguous or difficult to code.

9. For a thorough discussion of gratuitous concurrence, see Liberman 1985, 197–202.

10. This insight and its wording belong to Harold Garfinkel.

11. Indexical meanings are meanings that have their efficacy only at a particular place and time.

12. Schutz (1978, 36) remarks, "Parsons replaces subjective events in the mind of the actor by a scheme of interpretation for such events, accessible only to the observer."

13. See Liberman 2009.

14. Why do social psychologists rarely address knowledge such as this? Is it an elephant in the room?

15. For more details on "melody-ing" cf. Sudnow 1978, 66 and 96–96, and Sudnow 2001.

16. Marcel Proust, *In Search of Lost Time*, Vol. IV, 2004, 88-91, 96–99, 100–101, 108–09, and 117–19.

17. Cf. Liberman, "Proust the Social Phenomenologist," forthcoming.

18. One can call this observation an ethnomethodological theory, and it is a theory that has arisen naturally from the description. Shall it be rejected because it is a theory, as some ethnomethodological researchers are inclined to recommend, somewhat dogmatically? For instance, see Livingston (2008, 246): "[These] are matters I leave to theorists. For myself, such discussions are distracting." Is this kind of theorizing distracting? Of course it is; but distraction like this is *inevitable*. So long as one continues to think, one's insights will take form and necessarily become sedimented into an immanent structure that will *necessarily* clash and even control our developing intuition. Not only is theory a necessary part of reflection and investigation, a level of theoretical organization is unavoidable. What is to be avoided is allowing the theorizing to become extravagantly divorced from the described details so that it takes on a *raison d'être* by and for itself. It poses the most serious dangers to investigation when the researcher has invested him/herself in a career that depends upon the theory's fate and allows him- or herself to become separated from the in-the-course real worldly practices that motivate the theoretical reflection. When that happens theorizing is a force for bias and becomes too "distracting." But researchers who deny that they ever theorize are engaging in self-delusion. The point is to keep a tight reign on theorizing by remaining vigilant about its effects; to think that one can avoid theorizing altogether is a naiveté that can be even more dangerous for original inquiry.

Recollect the several times during this descriptive account that I have stopped to characterize the essential forms of what I found, in order to be better able to retain them and sustain those insights for the duration of my inquiries. No sooner is even a partly abstract, naturally theoretical summary made that it insists upon its own interests and its own semiotic possibilities that guide all subsequent inspections, and so my theorizing begins to interfere with my sight. Once this happens, my study becomes one more self-fulfilling prophesy. The only way to mitigate this is to spend more time watching players play games, while cultivating as much embedded openness to their practices that one can. This is a methodological discipline (cf. "Garfinkel's Uncompromising Intellectual Rigor" chapter 5 of Liberman 2007).

## CHAPTER FOUR

1. An earlier version of this chapter appeared in the Journal *Text* (Vol. 19, No. 1, 57–72, 1999).
2. One example would be Garfinkel's "accepting the credit you never bid for": when a student accepts with pride a teacher's compliments about the merit of a question whose sophistication was exclusively a product of the teacher's own interpretation and ensuing class discussion, all of which is credited to the student.
3. This topic is taken up more concretely in the succeeding chapter.
4. The "just-thisness" of any local occasion. Cf. Garfinkel 2002, 99fn16.
5. There are context-building resources that are intrinsic to the language system, and these are exploited by speakers. These formal, grammatical, and other constraints within discourse are treated by parties to be resources as much as they are constraints upon social practice.

## CHAPTER FIVE

1. This chapter is based on a plenary paper that was presented at the meeting of the International Association for Ethnomethodology and Conversation Analysis held at Bentley College in Waltham, Massachusetts, in 1992. An earlier version of the chapter appeared in *Research on Language and Social Interaction* 28, No. 2, 117–46.
2. The use of the gloss "channel" here is metaphorical, and there is no substantively existing, independent thing like a channel.
3. All transcripts are translations from the original Tibetan.
4. *'Dug zer gi red*.
5. *rkang pa dang po gnyis*.
6. The brackets indicate that what they enclose bears a meaning that is still to be collected from the conversation. What is more, at the time I did not know what it ["*mngon par zhen pa*"] meant.
7. I found the story compelling enough to translate for publication in an American magazine.

## CHAPTER SIX

1. A reviewer of my 2004 book for the journal *Sophia*, Yaroslav Kamarovski (2010), rightly criticized me for castigating Tibetologists with too broad a brush and correctly pointed out that the current generation of Tibetologists is less Orientalist

and less insular disciplinarily than the generations of academics who established the field of Tibetology.

2. As coincidence would have it, Desideri resided in the same Tibetan monastic university in which I spent more than two years.

3. This chapter was originally presented at the 2004 meeting of the American Sociological Association's Section on Ethnomethodology and Conversation Analysis, in San Francisco.

## CHAPTER SEVEN

1. The ellipsis here is from Garfinkel's original text. He did not include a reference to which of Husserl's texts he was citing, and I have not been able to locate this precise citation, although there are many passages similar to it. It is possible that Garfinkel has written it from memory.

2. The paper, "Choreography in Tibetan Debating," on which this chapter is based, was presented in Vancouver, Canada, in August of 2010 at the 12th Meeting of the IATS, which holds its international meeting once every four years.

3. I am indebted to Jeremy Manheim for first bringing this distinction to my attention.

4. Think, for instance, of the first stanza of the *Tao Te Ching*: "The truth that can be told is not the eternal truth."

5. *'Jog kyang mi 'jog.*

6. "CONFOUNDED" (*kor gsum*) is a formal token that Tibetan debaters use for declaring publicly the defeat of an opponent. Here the two defendants cannot agree on how to argue because they are faced with an inescapable dilemma: to cognize something is necessarily to reduce it to something that has been conceptualized, but anything that is conceptualized cannot be ultimate in the way that Buddhists assert is the realization of the emptiness of anything having inherent essences.

## CHAPTER EIGHT

1. An acidic taste comes immediately and disappears more quickly than an astringent taste.

2. This is a system that is "able to be certain that the totality of all that exists and can be thought can be deduced from a single unified factor" (Adorno 2008, 39).

3. Edmund Husserl, *Cartesian Meditations*. I have used the translation provided by Alphonso Lingis in his translation of Maurice Merleau-Ponty's citation of this passage of Husserl in Merleau-Ponty, *The Visible and the Invisible* (1968, 129).

4. As with most of Husserl's penetrating insights, he usually recognizes the complexities and inconsistencies of his own theoretical efforts and even contributes to the elucidation of them. His drive for clarity and his proclivity to bolster the systemic properties of his theorizing prevents him from always taking his own insightful self-criticism as far as he should.

5. This topic has been explored extensively in Hans-Geog Gadamer, *Truth and Method* (1975). See especially p. 251.

6. Perhaps across the chain from producer to processor to buyer to roaster to purveyor, it may be more important to establish more congruency in descriptor application and tasting protocols.

7. Investigation of the rigor of some of these methodologies is in progress, in association with Professor Giolo Fele of the Università di Trento, Italy.

8. A Geisha is a cultivar developed in Boquete, Panama, that features a pleasant blend of sweet tasting fruity flavors.

9. In Italian "*il sapere dei sapore*" translates "the ability to know the taste."

10. It is my experience that tasting original coffees is inherently a humbling experience; accordingly, any professional taster who has been at work for many years tends not to be so egotistical as to think that she or he will always get the taste right or that there is not always "something more" to be learned. Coffee tasting is not a zero-sum game.

11. Researching the ethnomethods employed in the design and assessment of *blends* is another rich topic that requires further detailed empirical study.

12. While I was drinking a *latte* in a Neapolitan espresso bar, the barista asked me how his latte differed from a standard American latte. When I described how tall a typical "giant latte" in the United States can be, he was incredulous. When he expressed a doubt that anyone could handle that much caffeine, I tried to put him at ease by saying, "No, no, they use the very same amount of coffee—and the difference in the quantity of liquid is achieved by adding boiling water to the containers."

13. One thing that is very impressive about this taster's assessment is that despite its complexity, he never referred to his notes or taste schedule once during his account of the taste. This would indicate that it was a genuine, original experience, and not merely an artifact of an accounting driven procedure.

## CONCLUSION

1. I have borrowed this phrase from Claude Lefort, in his "Editor's Foreword," to Merleau-Ponty (1968, xxix).

2. "Essential insight."

3. In *Cartesian Meditations*, Husserl (1969a, 42) becomes very specific about this: "The 'object' of consciousness, the object as having identity 'with itself' during the flowing subjective process, does not come into the process from outside; on the contrary, it is included as a sense in the subjective process itself and thus as an '*intentional effect*' *produced by* the synthesis of consciousness." Accordingly, "'Nature itself' thus acquires the value of a concept that is being constituted synthetically" (Husserl 1969b, 117) and "is categorically formed in the judging" (118).

4. For Husserl on objectivation see 1969a, 53; 1982, 367; and 1969b, 247.

5. See Liberman 2004.

6. For a discussion of how ethnomethodology uses perspicuous settings, see Garfinkel 2002, 181–82.

7. Preferably in digital video form, which is not to advocate a facile technological fix but to praise the ethnomethodological descriptions of the local interaction details of sense-building that are made possible by scrutinizing dozens, and sometimes hundreds, of times each act and turn of speaking of parties who are collaborating to

make sense of an occasion. Husserl did not have these recording devices to assist him to study naturally occurring phenomena in real time, devices that did not develop in a meaningful way until the 1950s.

8. See Garfinkel 2002, chapter 9: "An Ethnomethodological Study of the Work of Galileo's Inclined Plane Demonstration of the Real Motion of Free Falling Bodies," 163–285.

9. In fact, the need for focusing one's examination on naturally occurring phenomena is more than just heuristics: I have learned that the critical phenomenological and ethnomethodological theme of reflexivity is impossible to teach by merely talking about it; one has to get caught up within real, site-specific occasions where reflexive understanding is actively at work, and witness it in the course of its work. This is not so difficult to do, since such sites are practically everywhere. Theoretical descriptions of reflexivity will almost always fail, which is why epistemology should be captured as a real-world process and not only as the abstract reflections of an isolated individual.

10. I am using here Alphonso Lingis's translation of the French translation of *Cartesian Meditations*, rather than the Dorion Cairns translation, found in Merleau-Ponty 1968, 129.

# BIBLIOGRAPHY

Adorno, Theodor. 1973 (1966). *Negative Dialectics*. New York: Seabury Press.
——. 1974 (1951). *Minima Moralia*. London: Verso.
——. 1982 (1956). *Against Epistemology: Studies in Husserl and the Phenomenological Antinomies*. Translated by Willis Domingo, Cambridge, MA: MIT Press.
——. 2008 (1965). *Lectures on Negative Dialectics*. Cambridge, UK: Polity Press.
Bar-Hillel, Yehoshua. 1964. "Bgidat Halogicanim" ["The Logician's Treason" (in Hebrew)], *Iyyun* 14, 120–25.
Benjamin, Walter. 1999. *The Arcades Project*. Cambridge, MA: Harvard University Press.
Benveniste, Emile. 1971. *Problems in General Linguistics*. Coral Gables, FL: University of Miami Press.
Bohm, David. 1980. *Wholeness and the Implicate Order*. London: Routledge.
Brown, B. A. T., and E. Laurier. 2005. "Maps and Journeys: an Ethnomethodological Investigation." *Cartographica* 4 (3), 17–33.
Cabezón, José. 1995. "Buddhist Studies as a Discipline and the Role of Theory." *Journal of the International Association of Buddhist Studies* 18 (2), 231–268.
Caputo, John. 1997. *Deconstruction in a Nutshell*. New York: Fordham University Press.
Carbone, Mauro. 2004. *The Thinking of the Sensible*. Evanston, IL: Northwestern University Press.
Coulter, Jeff. 2009. "Rule-Following, Rule-Governance, and Rule-Accord." *Journal of Classical Sociology* 9 (4), 309–403.
Dastur, Francoise. 2010. "Phenomenology and Anthropology." *Philosophy Today* 54, 5–14.
Derrida, Jacques. 1973. *Speech and Phenomena*. Evanston: Northwestern University Press.
——. 1976. *Of Grammatology*. Baltimore: Johns Hopkins University Press.
——. 1978. *Writing and Difference*. Chicago: University of Chicago Press.
——. 1986. *Glas*. Lincoln, NE: University of Nebraska Press.
de Saussure, Ferdinand. 1959. *Course in General Linguistics*. New York: Philosophical Library.
Dodd, James. 2004. *Crisis and Reflection*. Dordrecht: Kluwer.
Durkheim, Emile. 1915. *Elementary Forms of Religious Life*. New York: Free Press.
——. 1938. *The Rules of Sociological Method*. New York: Free Press.
——. 1983 [1914]. *Pragmatism and Sociology*. Cambridge: Cambridge University Press.
Elkin, A. P. 1933. "Studies in Australian Totemism." *Oceania* IV (1), 65–60 and (2), 1–131.
Fink, Eugen, and Edmund Husserl. 1995. *The Sixth Cartesian Meditation*. Bloomington: Indiana University Press.

Gadamer Hans-Georg. 1975. *Truth and Method*. New York: Seabury Press.
Garfinkel, Harold. 1952. *The Perception of the Other: A Study in Social Order*. PhD. dissertation, Cambridge, Mass.: Harvard University.
———. 1966. University Lectures (3/31/66 and 5/12/66). UCLA.
———. 1967. *Studies in Ethnomethodology*. Englewood Cliffs, NJ: Prentice-Hall.
———. 1974. "Lectures on Games-with-Rules." UCLA graduate seminar.
———. 1975. "The Boston Seminar." Transcript of the seminar given at Boston University. Los Angeles: Department of Sociology, UCLA.
———. 1977a. "Lectures for Soc 148." UCLA undergraduate class (2/16, 2/21, 2/28, 3/2, & 3/9).
———. 1977b. "Lectures for Soc 248." UCLA graduate seminars (4/18 & 5/11).
———. 1979–80. "Lectures on Ethnomethodology." UCLA graduate seminar (Soc. 218A, Fall 1979; and Soc. 218B, Winter 1980).
———. 1991. "Respecification: Evidence for Locally Produced Naturally Accountable Phenomena of Order*, Logic, Reason, Meaning, Method, etc. In and As of the Essential Haecceity of Immortal Ordinary Society." In G. Button (ed.), *Ethnomethodology and the Human Sciences*. Cambridge, UK: Cambridge University Press, 10–19.
———. 1992. "Two Incommensurate, Asymmetrically Alternate Technologies of Social Analysis." In G. Watson and R. M. Seiler (eds.), *Text in Context: Contributions to Ethnomethodology*. Beverly Hills: Sage, 175–206.
———. 2001. "Plenary Talk" to the Conference on Orders of Ordinary Action. Manchester, England, July 10, 2001.
———. 2002. *Ethnomethodology's Program*. Lanham, MD: Rowman & Littlefield.
———. 2007. "*Lebenswelt* Origins of the Sciences." *Human Studies* 30, 9–56.
———. 2007. "Four Relations Between Literatures of the Social Scientific Movement and their Specific Ethnomethodological Alternates." In Stephen Hester and David Francis (eds.), *Orders of Ordinary Action*. Hampshire, UK: Ashgate, 13–29.
Garfinkel, Harold and Kenneth Liberman. 2007. "Working Out Durkheim's Aphorism." *Human Studies* 30, No. 1, 3–7.
Garfinkel, Harold and Eric Livingston. 2003. "Phenomenal Field Properties of Order in Formatted Queues." *Visual Studies* 18 (1), 21–28.
Garfinkel, Harold and Harvey Sacks. 1970. "On Formal Structures of Practical Actions." In J. C. McKinney and E. A. Tiryakian (eds.), *Theoretical Sociology*. New York: Appleton Century Crofts, 337–66. Reprinted in H. Garfinkel (ed.), *Ethnomethodological Studies of Work*. 1986. London: Routledge, 160–93.
Gendlin, Eugene T. 1992. "Thinking Beyond Patterns." In B. den Ouden and M. Moen (eds.), *The Presence of Feeling in Thought*. New York: Peter Lang.
Giuliano, Peter. 2007. "Counter Culture Coffee and the Art of Come-One-Come-All Cupping." *The Specialty Coffee Chronicle* (March/April).
Göran, Dahl. 1994. "Documentary Meaning—Understanding or Critique? Karl Mannheim's Early Sociology of Knowledge." In *Philosophy and Social Criticism* 20, No. 1/2, 103–121.
Grathoff, Richard. 1978. *The Theory of Social Action: The Correspondence of Alfred Schutz and Talcott Parsons*. Bloomington, IN: Indiana University Press.

———. 1989. *Philosophers in Exile: The Correspondence of Alfred Schutz and Aron Gurwitsch, 1939–1959.* Bloomington, IN: Indiana University Press.
Greimas, Algirdas J. 1990. *The Social Sciences, A Semiotic View.* Minneapolis: University of Minnesota Press.
Gurwitsch, Aron. 1964. *The Field of Consciousness.* Pittsburgh: Duquesne University Press.
———. 1966. *Studies in Phenomenology and Psychology.* Evanston, IL: Northwestern University Press.
Halliday, Michael A. K. 1992. "How Do You Mean?" in Martin Davies and Louise Ravelliu (eds.), *Advances in Systematic Linguistics.* London and New York: Pintger Publishers. Pp. 20–35.
Hanks, William F. 1966. "Language Form and Communicative Practices," in John J. Gumperz and Stephen C. Levinson, *Rethinking Linguistic Relativity.* Cambridge: Cambridge University Press.
Heidegger, Martin. 1992. *Being and Time.* Trans. by John Macquarrie and Edward Robinson, New York: Harper & Row. 1996. *Being and Time.* Trans. by Joan Stambaugh. Albany, NY: SUNY Press.
Heritage, John. 1984. *Garfinkel and Ethnomethodology.* Cambridge: Polity Press.
Husserl, Edmund. 1962 (1913). *Ideas.* Translated by W. R. Boyce Gibson. London: Collier-Macmillan.
———. 1969a (1929). *Cartesian Meditations.* Translated by Dorion Cairns. The Hague: Martinis Nijhoff.
———. 1969b (1929). *Formal and Transcendental Logic.* Translated by Dorion Cairns. The Hague: Martinis Nijhoff.
———. 1970a (1900). *Logical Investigations.* Translated by J. N. Findlay. London: Routledge.
———. 1970b (1936). *The Crisis of the European Sciences and Transcendental Phenomenology.* Translated by David Carr. Evanston, IL: Northwestern University Press.
———. 1970c (1929). *The Paris Lectures.* Translated by Peter Koestenbaum. The Hague: Martinus Nijhoff.
———. 1982 (1913). *Ideas Pertaining to a Pure Phenomenology and to a Phenomenological Philosophy.* Translated by Fred Kersten. The Hague: Martinus Nijhoff.
James, William. 1890. *Principles of Psychology, Vol. I.* New York: Henry Holt.
Jameson, Fredric. 1990. *Late Marxism: Adorno or the Persistence of the Dialectic.* London & New York: Verso.
Kamarovski, Yaroslav. 2010. "Review of Kenneth Liberman, Dialectical Practice in Tibetan Philosophical Culture: An Ethnomethodological Inquiry into Formal Reasoning." Sophia.
Khubchandani, L. M. 1990. "Paradigm of Power Versus Understanding." New Quest 83, 287–94.
Knox, Kevin, and Julie Sheldon Huffaker. 1997. *Coffee Basics.* New York: John Wiley and Sons.
Labov, William, and David Fanshel. 1977. *Therapeutic Discourse.* New York: Academic Press.
Liberman, Kenneth. 1982. "The Economy of Central Australian Aboriginal Expression: an inspection from the vantage of Merleau-Ponty and Derrida." *Semiotics* 40, 81–160.

———. 1985. *Understanding Interaction in Central Australia: An Ethnomethodological Study of Australian Aboriginal People*. London: Routledge.

———. 1989. "Decentering the Self: Two Perspectives from Philosophical Anthropology." In Arlene Dallery and Charles Scott (eds.), *The Question of the Other* (1989 Issue of the series, "Selected Studies in Phenomenology"). Albany, NY: SUNY Press, 127–42.

———. 2001. "Ethnographic Practice and the Critical Spirit." In David Bromley and Lewis Carter (eds.), *Toward Reflexive Ethnography*. J. A. I. Press, pp. 93–116.

———. 2004. *Dialectical Practice in Tibetan Philosophical Culture: An Ethnomethodological Inquiry Into Formal Reasoning*. Lanham, MD: Rowman & Littlefield.

———. 2007. *Husserl's Criticism of Reason, With Ethnomethodological Specifications*. Lanham, MD: Lexington Books.

———. 2009. "The Itinerary of Intersubjectivity in Social Phenomenological Research." In *Schutzian Research: A Yearbook of Mundane Phenomenology and Qualitative Social Science* 1. Bucharest: Zeta Books, 149–164.

———. 2012. "Semantic Drift in Conversations." *Human Studies* 35, No. 2, (DOI) 10.1007/s10746-012-9225-1.

Livingston, Eric. 1986. *The Ethnomethodological Foundations of Mathematics*. London: Routledge.

———. 1987. *Making Sense of Ethnomethodology*. London: Routledge.

———. 2008. *Ethnographies of Reason*. Hampshire, UK: Ashgate.

Lopez, Jr., Donald S. 1998. *Prisoners of Shangrila: Tibetan Buddhism and the West*. Chicago: University of Chicago Press.

Lynch, Michael. 1985. *Art and Artifact in Laboratory Science*. London: Routledge.

———. 1993. *Scientific Practice and Ordinary Action*. Cambridge: Cambridge University Press.

———. 2004. "Misreading Schutz." *Theory and Society* 5 (1).

Mann, Thomas. 1965. *The Magic Mountain*. New York: Alfred Knopf.

Mannheim, Karl. 1952. *Essays on the Sociology of Knowledge*. London: Routledge, 33–83.

Merleau-Ponty, Maurice. 1962. *Phenomenology of Perception*. London: Routledge.

———. 1964. *Signs*. Evanston, IL: Northwestern University Press.

———. 1973a. *Consciousness and the Acquisition of Language*. Evanston, Ill.: Northwestern University Press.

———. 1973b. *The Prose of the World*. Evanston, IL: Northwestern University Press.

———. 1968. *The Visible and the Invisible*. Evanston, IL: Northwestern University Press.

Moerman, Michael. 1988. *Talking Culture: Ethnography and Conversation Analysis*. Philadelphia: University of Pennsylvania Press.

———. 1996. "The Field of Analyzing Foreign Conversations." *Journal of Pragmatics* 26, 147–58.

Nagarjuna. 1995. *The Fundamental Wisdom of the Middle Way*. Translated by Jay Garfield, New York and Oxford: Oxford University Press.

Nandy, Ashis. 1983. *The Intimate Enemy: Loss and Recovery of Self Under Colonialism*. Delhi: Oxford University Press.

Odello, Luigi. 2002. *Espresso Italiano Tasting*. Brescia, Italy: Centro Studi Assaggiatori.

———. 2003. *Espresso Italiano Specialist*. Brescia, Italy: Centro Studi Assaggiatori.

Plato. 1961. *Euthedymus*. In *The Collected Dialogues of Plato*, Edith Hamilton and Huntington Cairns (eds.), Princeton, NJ: Princeton University Press.

Peitersma, Henry. 1977. "Husserl's Views on the Evident and the True." In Frederick A. Elliston and Peter McCormick, *Husserl: Expositions and Appraisals*. Notre Dame: University of Notre Dame Press.
Proust, Marcel. 2004. *In Search of Lost Time*, Vol. IV (*Sodom and Gomorrah*). New York: Viking.
Psathas, George. 1976. "The Structure of Directions." *Semiotica* 17, 111–130.
———. 1979. "Organizational Features of Direction Maps." In G. Psathas (ed.), *Everyday Language: Studies in Ethnomethodology*. New York: Irvington Publishers, 203–226.
———. 1980. "Approaches to the Study of the World of Everyday Life." *Human Studies* 3, 3–17.
———. 1986a. "Some Sequential Structures in Direction-Giving." *Human Studies* 9, 231–246.
———. 1986b. "The Organization of Directions in Interaction." *Word* 37, 83–91.
———. 1987. "Finding a Place by Following Directions: A Phenomenology of Pedestrian and Driver Wayfinding." *Man-Environment Systems* 17, 99–103.
———. 1988. "Extended Sequences in Interaction: The Study of Direction-Giving." Paper presented at the Conference on Linguistics, International Christian University, Tokyo.
———. 1991. "The Structure of Direction-giving in Interaction." In Deirdre Boden and Don Zimmerman, *Talk and Social Structure*. Oxford: Polity Press.
———. 1992. "The Study of Extended Sequences: The Case of the Garden Lesson." In Graham Watson and Robert Seiler (eds.), *Text in Context: Contributions to Ethnomethodology*. Newbury Park, CA: Sage Publications.
———. Ricoeur, Paul. 1974. "Creativity in Language: Word, Polysemy, Metaphor," in Erwin W. Straus (ed.), *Language and Language Disturbances*. Pittsburgh: Duquesne University Press, 49–71.
———. 1978. *The Rule of Metaphor*. London: Routledge.
Robillard Albert B. 1999. *Meaning of a Disability: The Lived Experience of Paralysis*. Philadelphia: Temple University Press.
Sartre, Jean-Paul. 1956. *Being and Nothingness*. New York: Philosophical Library.
Saussure, Ferdinand de [see de Saussure, Ferdinand].
Schrag, Calvin. 1992. *The Resources of Rationality*. Bloomington, IN: Indiana University Press.
Schutz, Alfred. 1970. *Reflections on the Problem of Relevance*. New Haven: Yale University Press.
———. 1971. *Collected Papers, Volume II: Studies in Social Theory*. The Hague: Martinus Nijhoff.
———. 1978. "Parsons' Theory of Social Action," in Richard Grathoff (ed.), 8–60.
Shantideva. 1981. *Byang chub sems dpa'i spyod pa la 'jug pa* [Entering the Path of Enlightened Action]. Dharamsala, India: Tibetan Cultural Printing Press.
Silverstein, Michael. 1992. "The Indeterminacy of Contextualization." In Peter Auer and Aldo Di Luzio (eds.), *The Contextualization of Language*. Philadelphia: John Benjamins, 55–76.
Spencer, W. B., and F. J. Gillen. 1899. *The Native Tribes of Central Australia*. Macmillan: London.

Stanner, W. E. H. 1966. *On Aboriginal Religion*. The Oceania Monograph No. 11, University of Sydney.
Sudnow, David. 1978. *Ways of the Hand: The Organization of Improvised Conduct*. New York: Bantam Books.
———. 2001. *Ways of the Hand: A Rewritten Account*. Cambridge, MA: The MIT Press.
Tsong Khapa (Tzong Kha pa). 1999. *Dbu ma dgongs pa rab gsal* (*Elucidation of the Thought of the Middle Way*). Bylakuppe, India: Sera Je Monastic University.
Thibault, Paul J. 1997. *Re-reading Saussure*. London and New York: Routledge.
Wieder, D. Lawrence. 1970. "On Meaning by Rule." In Jack Douglas (ed.), *Understanding Everyday Life*. Chicago: Aldine, 107–135.
———. 1974. "Telling the Code." In Roy Turner (ed.), *Ethnomethodology*. Baltimore: Penguin, 144–72.
———. 1984. "Toward a General Theory of the Communicative Situation." Address given to the Annual Meeting of the International Communication Association, San Francisco.
Wittgenstein, Ludwig. 1953. *Philosophical Investigations*. London: Macmillian.
———. 1978. *Remarks on Colour*. Berkeley: University of California Press.
Zahavi, Dan. 2003. *Husserl's Phenomenology*. Stanford: Stanford University Press.

# INDEX

accounting practices, accountability, 33–34, 85, 98, 101, 105–108, 115, 117, 123–124, 146, 150, 164, 192
Adorno, Theodor, 138, 223–224, 229, 231, 234, 249, 250, 251, 259, 271, 273, 276, 277
aporia, 59, 80, 105, 122, 208
authochthonous, 13, 21, 43, 117, 120, 283
authorization, 108, 117

Bar-Hillel, Yehoshua, 183, 195
Benjamin, Walter, 210
Benveniste, Emile, 135
Bohm, David, 119
Brown, B.A.T., 69, 72

Cabezòn, José, 185
Caputo, John, 277
Carbone, Mauro, 51
coherency, 43, 47, 48, 80, 81, 83, 126, 240, 246
collaborative work, & collective action, 6, 87, 92, 95ff. 104, 108, 113, 141, 146, 155, 194, 205, 213, 218, 219, 234, 235, 248, 274, 278, 279
communication, 47, 135ff., 141, 145, 151, 154, 192, 193, 195
compliance production account, 111
concerting a local order, 31, 194
confidence, 57, 63, 69, 82, 87, 100, 246
Coulter, Jeff, 114

Dahl, Gören, 239
Dastur, Francoise, 141
Derrida, Jacques, 4, 119, 136, 137, 141, 143, 150, 153, 164, 166, 250, 269, 277

displays (*see also* exhibits), 22, 23, 35, 121, 130, 143, 144, 146, 148, 156, 164, 176
documentary method of interpretation, 5, 74, 239–241, 243–245, 264–265, 284
Dodd, James, 273
Durkheim, Emile, 3, 6, 83, 99, 100, 113, 120, 149

Elkin, A.P., 113
et cetera, 140, 150, 176
embodied sense, 67, 68
emptiness, 139, 167, 175, 205–210, 287fn6
empirical, 69
ethnomethods, 26, 28, 31, 33, 37, 43, 165, 212
Evidenz, 221, 222, 228, 270
exhibits (*see also* displays), 22, 23, 33, 34, 96–98, 100, 112, 119, 121, 126, 188, 251

Fanchel, David, 191–192
Fele, Giolo, 233, 288
Fink, Eugen, 113, 268
formal analysis (limits & benefits), 49, 62, 64, 66, 69, 81–82, 91, 114, 117, 136, 149, 175, 183–184, 187–188, 191, 192, 195, 206, 221, 249, 280

Galileo, 274–275
Garfinkel, Harold, 1–8, 20, 33, 36, 42–51, 62–64, 68, 79, 81–82, 104, 109, 112, 117, 119, 124, 139, 140, 141, 152, 144, 147, 164, 166, 178, 180, 181, 183, 184, 185, 188,

Garfinkel, Harold (*continued*)
  240–241, 247, 251, 252, 256, 266, 280, 283, 285, 286
Gendlin, Eugene, 149
gestalt contexture, 20–21, 33, 42–43, 48, 117
Giuliano, Peter, 247
Goffman, Erving, 118
gratuitous concurrence, 59, 85, 93, 101, 123, 124, 157, 158, 165, 166, 172, 173, 174
Greimas, Aljirdas, 139
Gurwitsch, Aron, 5, 20, 21, 43, 48, 125, 276, 280

Halliday, Michael, 135
Hanks, William, 136, 139
Heidegger, Martin, 119, 140, 170, 183, 222, 240
Hegel, G.W.F., 138
Heritage, John, 33
hermeneutics, 55, 75, 88, 90, 93, 137, 167, 210, 246
horizon of meaning, 155, 195, 197, 265, 267
Husserl, Edmund, 1, 20, 50, 90, 113, 120, 122, 136, 139, 140, 149, 225, 231, 246
Hutchins Edwin, 68

immortal ordinary society, 138
in and as, 47, 81, 82, 94, 130, 231, 252, 292
*in vivo*, 8, 47–48, 51, 73, 85, 185, 276, 277, 278
indeterminacy, 85, 92ff. 108–109, 120, 122, 136, 139, 140, 149, 225, 231, 246
indexical meaning, 107, 144, 156
individualist social mythology, 115
Indology, 179–180
intercultural communication, 61, 68, 142, 144, 154ff., 169–170, 177–178, 278
intersubjectivity, critique of, 115, 192, 194, 247, 249, 272, 279

James, William, 7, 21
Jameson, Fredric, 224
judgmental dopes, 141
"just what," 47, 51, 62, 185, 195, 272, 277, 278

Khubchandani, L.M., 162

Labov, William, 191–192
Laurier, Eric, 69, 72
Lavinas, Emmanuel, 257
Lewis, David, 68
lifeworld, 7, 227, 272, 276, 279, 284
Livingston, Eric, 21, 115, 284, 285, 181, 192, 276, 283fn2, 285fn18
locally concerted practices, 1, 12, 16–18, 21, 26, 31, 33, 35, 36, 87, 112, 113, 145, 148, 191, 197, 203, 217, 274
locally contingent details & methods, 108, 111, 114, 142, 143, 145, 148, 165, 166, 167, 174, 176–178, 249, 251–252, 258, 261–262, 274, 276, 280
local methods, 41, 167, 247
looks of the world 8, 19, 20, 47, 49–50, 76, 124, 141, 155, 181, 188, 280
Lopez, Donald, 179
Lynch, Michael, 6, 146, 275, 276

Macbeth, Doug, 3
Mannheim, Karl, 5, 8, 48, 239–240
Merleau-Ponty, Maurice, 5, 42, 48, 53, 66, 67, 68, 69, 98, 119, 136, 137, 142, 145, 148, 150, 229–230, 269, 270, 276, 281
mimesis, 19
Moreman, Michael, 141
Mueller, Max, 180

Nagarjuna, 138–139, 208
Nandy, Ashis, 180
natural attitude, 113
negative dialectics, 211–213, 250

negotiation (critique of), 34–36, 111, 114–118, 123, 141, 145
non-conceptuality of occasions, 20, 42f., 45, 48–49, 67, 68, 119, 176, 189–190, 191, 250, 269, 272, 276
non-identity, 223
non-knowledge, 42, 119

objectivation, 45, 87ff., 105ff., 108, 112, 120, 121, 126, 189, 192, 194, 196–196, 198, 230, 272, 276, 284
objective & objectivity, 19, 23, 33, 51, 56, 72, 87, 99, 120, 126, 137, 144, 192, 194, 215–216, 221–224, 225, 226, 230, 232, 234, 237, 238, 239, 243–245, 247, 248–249, 252, 254–256, 259, 271, 273–274, 277, 278
observability, 22, 33
Odello, Luigi, 232–233, 257
openness, 48, 51, 56, 60, 75, 79, 107, 138, 142, 170, 250, 270, 278
orderliness and local organization, 22, 33, 41, 42, 43, 49, 50, 57, 64, 86, 93, 101, 103, 104, 108–109, 124, 144, 147, 155, 183, 187, 191, 192, 194, 230, 251
Parsons, Talcott, 141
perspicuous setting, 43, 273, 288
phenomenal field, 20–21, 24, 36, 41, 66, 67, 68
phenomenology, 4, 5, 8, 45, 49, 50, 119, 120, 121, 136, 164, 167, 176, 224–230, 239–240, 257, 264, 267–276, 279
Piertersma, Henry, 50
Plato, 201
Pound, Ezra, 45, 68
practical reasoning, 47–48, 74
projection, 225–226, 278
Proust, Marcel, 124–125
protean character of understanding, 77, 80, 105
public character of thinking, 63–66, 71, 72, 75, 76, 121, 145, 146

Psathas, George, 9, 46, 51

queues, 30–31

radical self-understanding, 246, 268, 270
ratification, 108
rational choice theory, 115, 117, 120
reflexivity, 50–53, 56, 86, 109, 121, 124, 143, 221, 238, 257, 259, 289
reification, 184–185, 270
repetition, 37, 196, 198, 206
Ricoeur, Paul, 139, 145
rules, 12, 16, 83ff., 108, 111–112, 117, 130, 134, 140, 148

Sacks, Harvey, 38, 148, 283
saliences 20–21, 40, 43
Sartre, Jean-Paul, 172
Saussure, Ferdinand de, 52, 53, 136ff., 142–143, 149, 163
Scheler, Max, 276
Schrag, Calvin, 183
Schutz, Alfred, 43, 49, 57, 98, 113, 115, 141, 189, 279
self-organizing, 21, 43
sense-making, 98, 137, 148, 234, 239, 268, 270, 272–275, 267, 278, 279, 281, 288
serendipitous resolution 43, 67, 141
shared agreement, 115–116, 118, 125
Silverstein, Michael, 146
slippage (of meaning), 105, 135, 166, 171, 235, 278
social facts, 108
social phenomenology, 1, 6, 43, 73, 125, 146, 185, 189, 269, 279–281
Spencer and Gillen, 113
Stanner, W.E.H., 113
subjectivity's relation to objectivity, 216, 218, 222–224, 228–230, 259, 268, 270, 273
substitution of objective expressions for indexical expressions, 112

Sudnow, David, 123

Thibault, Paul, 136, 137, 140, 141, 143, 144, 146
things, 3, 52, 247, 264, 272
thinking as a public activity, 20, 21, 33, 45, 59, 88, 95, 97–98, 107, 131, 188, 193
Tibetans, 4, 182, 191
Tibetology, 179ff.
truth, 49
Tsong Khapa, 284

unities of sense, 86, 227, 252, 271, 275, 278

White, Geoffrey, 68
Wieder, D. Lawrence, 88, 109, 117, 118, 119, 178, 233
Wittgenstein, Ludwig, 117, 215, 249, 275
worldly inquiries, 51

Zahavi, Dan, 50